CW00429388

Mutants

Mutants

Selected Essays

TOBY LITT

LONDON NEW YORK CALCUTTA

Seagull Books, 2016

© Toby Litt, 2016

This compilation © Seagull Books, 2016

ISBN 978 0 8574 2 333 7

British Library Cataloguing-in-Publication Data

A catalogue record for this book is available from the British Library.

Typeset in Dante MT Regular by Seagull Books, Calcutta, India

Printed and bound by Maple Press, York, Pennsylvania, USA

Contents

What I Think

What I Think

Tolstoy and Gogol via Ricardo Lísias

Adventures in Capitalism (1996), my first book, came out and was reviewed in the *Catholic Herald*. They called it 'A "Diary of a Madman" for the Shopping Channel Generation.'

Yes, I was flattered; flattered to be reviewed and not condemned.

It took me years, though, to realize that—apart from being a lot more than merely flattering—the Gogol comparison was as right as it could be.

I admire other writers more than Gogol—Austen, James, Kafka, Mandelstam, Beckett—but there are none I feel so like.

This isn't self-flattery. Gogol isn't Tolstoy. And the Gogols of this world will always lose out to the Tolstoys.

Gogols are in love with the grotesquery of paradoxical revelation, more than with truth. Gogols find themselves cat-mesmerized by contradictory effects, by shimmers, undertones and fluorescences, rather than by the pure matte tones. If Gogols can do something bass ackwards, even build a temple, they will. Gogols, as they themselves will admit, will insist upon, are not to be trusted as Tolstoys are. (Gogols mistrust trustworthiness.)

Readers like writers they can plainly trust.

It is safer for civic folk to erect a statue to Tolstoy in the forum, for Tolstoy stands for something, erectly, statuesquely.

A Gogol statue would have to show him posed in a parody of how figures on statues stand, or cowering behind the plinth in order not to be seen as shamefully statue-worthy, or frankly pissing.

When I read Ricardo Lísias' story 'Evo Morales' (2012, translated by Nick Caistor), I saw straight off that it was Gogolian— his narrator is great-great-great-grandson to the Madman in 'Diary of a Madman' (1835).

But I saw more than that—in the beautiful polyphony of referents (comedians call them 'callbacks'), in the grotesquely fractured form (switching to epistolary two-thirds of the way through *because it just does*), and in the gorgeous political slyness of the whole thing (Evo Morales may or may not be amused)— in every word I saw a true untrue Gogol; and I felt joy.

Headfuck Fiction via Carlos Labbé

I like fiction that seems to reinvent itself as it goes along—to change not only its rules but also the premises on which those rules are based. This is a fiction that goes beyond metamorphosis and becomes, instead, a kind of seething, perpetual mutation. It doesn't start from a state of generic-genetic purity; it was hybrid to begin with. Each stage of its development is one of mutation from mutation, outgrowth from outgrowth. And yet, when it reaches an end, dies or slides off out of sight towards further incarnations, it is possible to discern that this creature-of-literature had a consistent form—and an indwelling set of premises that weren't discernible before. One of these premises may have been, for example, *Consistent identity is boring*. This would lead to the rule *Never repeat a gesture*. Another, more extreme extrapolation would be *Follow the line of development that promises the greatest instability of identity*. This is all extremely unsettling for some readers. But I like it. You could call it *headfuck fiction*.

Carlos Labbé's *Navidad y Matanza* (2007) (at least in my reading) begins to fuck with your head from its very first word—moving through journalese, financial reporting, whodunnit,

Joseph Conrad, Raymond Chandler, Vladimir Nabokov to David Lynch.

The character Boris Real is Francisco Virditti is Boris Real Yáñez, or maybe not—maybe his name is a taunt: he's a king, he's cash money, he's Keyser Söze.

I'm reminded of Jim Thompson's great quote, 'There are thirty-two ways to write a story, and I've used every one, but there is only one plot—things are not as they seem.'

Navidad y Matanza is a novel, and I've only read what's printed here; I have no idea where it goes—although I'd be prepared to bet things get extremely, get gorgeously fucked up.

B. S. Johnson

There's a shock coming up. A big, glorious, true shock. It's at the bottom of page 163.

Do not look at page 163—at least, not until you've read the following paragraph:

If you want to receive *Albert Angelo* (1964) as B. S. Johnson would have wanted you to receive it, and as I would prefer you to receive it, then start with the Beckett epigraph and let page 163 happen to you when it does.

To those of you who have already skipped ahead to page 163 and returned here: *Welcome back to the present. Welcome back to your usual condition of avoiding big, glorious, true shock by checking, in advance, to see—click—what that shock might consist of, if it were ever truly to be experienced. Welcome back to knowingness.*

To those of you who have not skipped ahead, but are still reading this rather than the Beckett epigraph: *Well done. Now, go away and come back later, when you've been entertained, lectured, touched, shocked.*

To those of you who have returned after reading *Albert Angelo*, and are wondering whether I didn't perhaps diminish the shock by mentioning it in advance: *I apologize. That was the best I could do. Because that is the best we can do—resist the temptation to preserve ourselves from shocks, even though we often know quite a lot about them already. Avoid spoilers. Avoid creating spoilers. But I couldn't write about* Albert Angelo *without mentioning the shock. Because* Albert Angelo *turns on the shock of self-accusation.*

I have many problems with my contemporaries, but most of all with their willingness to believe they've learnt from the mistakes of others—and that, as a result, they'll never make those mistakes. This, however, is knowingness rather than knowledge. Knowingness brings a suspicion of idealism. Because we have never made the mistake of having unreasonable ideals, we are comforted by knowingly calling all ideals naive. Because this or that radicalism is said to have failed, we knowingly take it that radicalism always leads to failure.

Taking knowingness for knowledge is the worst mistake of all.

Albert Angelo is a very easy book for a certain kind of contemporary to sneer at. It is a crudely experimental novel. It is an example of a rudimentary, struggling, English postmodernism. It is, bless it, not quite clear what it wants to be.

To which I want to reply: *There is no experiment without crudity.*

Think of all modern art, from Cezanne's faulty visions of faulty vision, to the outrageous unevenness of *Les Demoiselles d'Avignon*, to Francis Bacon's inexplicably orange *Three Figures at the Base of a Crucifixion*; from the head-banging momentum of *Boléro*, to the cut-and-pasted sound-blocks of *The Rite of Spring*, to the gnarly lurches of Steve Reich's *It's Gonna Rain*; from D. H. Lawrence's bodged-together anti-psychologies, to

Donald Barthelme's choreographies of elegant incoherence, to the deliberate longeurs of David Foster Wallace's *The Pale King*; from Emily Dickinson's wonky hymns to perhaps-God, to 'The Waste Land', to Sylvia Plath's brutal 'Daddy'.

These were not classical masters who had calculated the balanced effects of what they were putting in accustomed place. These were desperate strugglers with blocks and bloops of slimy, coming-alive-and-dying-and-coming-alive-again stuff.

To which, escalating, I want to reply: *There is no experiment without uncertainty.*

The worst knowingness of any contemporary version of history is that it itself idealizes the way things happen. It makes masters out of strugglers. It loses a sense of events as—in their flux, in their happening—entirely unclassical moments of snafu. It suggests a form of supreme judgement exists, if one can recognize the patterns. It has no praxis.

When B. S. Johnson wrote *Albert Angelo*, it was an experiment in these important and easily forgotten senses: B. S. Johnson did not know that *Albert Angelo* would not be a novel that became overwhelmingly popular—a bestseller. B. S. Johnson did not know that his shocking outburst of 'OH, FUCK ALL THIS LYING!' would not become a rallying cry for all fiction. B. S. Johnson did not know that he was not fundamentally changing English writing. B. S. Johnson did not know that he was not fundamentally changing English society.

Yet which contemporary writer would think it worth writing an experimental novel in the hope of drawing attention to the government's failing education policy?

On the final page of the 'Disintegration' of *Albert Angelo*, B. S. Johnson's out-from-behind-the-curtain narrator writes that the book is 'Didactic, too, social comment on teaching, to draw attention, too, to improve: but with less hope, for if the government wanted better education it could be provided easily enough, so I must conclude, again, that they specifically want the majority of children to be only partially-educated.'[1]

B. S. Johnson has 'less hope' of this possible improvement, but he still has hope. Which contemporary writer would have any?

And, finally, this makes me to want to reply: *There is no experiment without hope.*

Because, *this time*, the experiment might succeed. The slimy stuff might become beautifully and permanently alive. The idealism might be fulfilled. The radicalism might generally convert. Things might change for the good, because of something written.

It would be very easy to make *Albert Angelo* seem a repository of traditional fictional pleasures. One might stoop so low as to mention Dickens. There are some fine descriptive passages, etc. There is even Albert's gratifyingly reactionary confessional: 'Of course, I would really like to be designing a Gothic cathedral, all crockets and finials and flying buttresses . . . .'[2] Which can be translated into: 'Of course, I would really like to be writing *Bleak House*, all digressions and eccentric minor characters and implied Ten Commandments . . . .' This reaction, however, is retracted—and the continuation applies to both Gothic cathedrals and *Bleak House*: '[B]ut I must be of my time, ahead of my time, rather, using the materials of my time, the unacknowledged legislators, and so on, in accord with, of, my age, my time, my generation, my life.'[3]

The greatest thing about *Albert Angelo* is its wholehearted uncertainty. Uncertainty is the substance of each passionately blocked-out sentence; uncertainty is the book's underlying oomph, push, spasm, yearn—uncertainty of its main character, an architect who does not make buildings forced to become a schoolteacher who does not want to teach and does not want to do anything but teach—uncertainty of Albert Angelo, misogynistically mourning his true love, Jenny, and their idyllic hours-among-rocks—uncertainty of B. S. Johnson speaking of himself and his art/life-struggles through Albert Angelo until he can't bear the falsity of that any longer, and then isn't sure if the attempted-truth isn't worse—uncertainty of the reader who is confronted by an anguish that mocks itself, and a laughter that wants to crawl further into the black, and a love for truth that is shockingly pure.

Notes

1 B. S. Johnson, *Albert Angelo* (London: Picador, 2013), p. 176.
2 Ibid, p. 107.
3 Ibid.

Kafka

I have avoided writing about Kafka. A few years ago, Lawrence
Norfolk invited me to contribute to a website. Writers were
offering reactions to Kafka's long aphorism or short story about
never getting to the next village.[1] I'm afraid I ignored Norfolk's
invitation. Footnotes to Shakespeare are fine and very often
dandy. We riff off *The Tempest* endlessly. And because no one
expects something significant to occur, there is no humiliation
in adding nothing. A footnote to *The Tempest* may be worth
writing, and will join an established society of footnotes. All
that has barnacled onto Kafka could be scraped away, without
loss. This isn't to say I am not grateful for what Benjamin
wrote. Or that Auden didn't have insights. Or that I learnt
nothing from Deleuze and Guattari. But Kafka is not sociable,
like Shakespeare. His illuminators are a crowd of solipsists. And
so I have avoided writing about Kafka. Because—put as simply
as I can—Kakfa writes to make writing about Kafka impossible.
This is absolutely not his main aim; that, I think, stays within
the reader and their possibility-of-a-soul. Kafka's main thrust is
towards inscrutability. He wants to open out possibilities so infinite that the original wanting is entirely moot, and the opening
eternally backgrounded. He makes statements the end of

which we can never hope to reach. For example: 'Before the Law'.[2] I would quote 'Before the Law' in its entirety. Quote it twice. Instead, I will assume you have dutifully reread it in-between the previous sentence and this one. Or, at least, you have recalled some of the abysmal horror of it. Kafka makes statements the end of which we can never reach. In this, he is comparable to Emily Dickinson, and who else? William Blake in 'The Proverbs of Hell'? Zeno? Heraclitus? Sappho? A few other absolutists. Yet Kafka is social. He came from alleys, not the sun. And I am sure a third-hand acquaintance with the Jewish theatres of Praha, in Kafka's enthusiastic time, would not be meaningless. And a close textual reading through nothing but the Torah might be more pointlessly correct than any other. And Robert Walser, Bruno Schulz, Isaac Babel are in worthwhile correspondence. But my experience of reading Kafka is that he places me far. Not *far from*. He places me within a far relating only to itself.

This is not quite the far of the story within a story within a story we reach in 'Description of a Struggle'—the universe within a universe within a universe. At this early stage (1904–05), Kafka's far still has some tenuous connection to our near. But unities of time and space have become moot, ridiculous. If you wanted to be straightforward, you could say 'Description of a Struggle' is a great fantasy story, a piggyback *Alice's Adventures in Wonderland*. At points it reads, very strangely, as a parody of Chekhov. The tragic timidity of Chekhov's characters ('Live!' we beseech the page, like Henry James's Strether, 'Live all you can; it's a mistake not to.'[3]) becomes, through Kafka, the tragic timidity of Chekhov the creator. If only his young men had been able to levitate! If only they could have touched the lamp posts beside the horizon! If only they had dream-visited other worlds, not shabby Moscow! How much further into their predicaments they would have gone—and we would have gone with them! This is, on Kafka's part, creative misprision. It's a mutant Chekhov he presents—distended, involuted, irresponsible, cute. But this is almost certainly completely wrong.

I do not know. This introduction could come down to that. I have avoided writing about Kafka because *I do not know*—*I do not know* where he is; *I do not know* what to say; *I do not know* what I do not know about Kafka. My suspicion is *I do not know* because Kafka did not want me or any reader to know. At my most pissed off with him, I look at his stories and novels as clock-work contraptions for making mystification. This is the allegorical reading of 'In the Penal Colony'—and in this tale the mystification is figured as excruciation. As a quick aside, I don't find Kafka a hoot. Some readers think this is the true test of whether you 'get it'. Does *The Trial* (1914–15) make you laugh out loud? With me, no. Is 'Metamorphosis' (1915) funny? For me, no. Kakfa makes me more profoundly anxious than any other writer. I am pretending to take a stroll, across a void, because the *far* is all around me in every direction—compass points, up and down. As another quick aside, I only read Kafka in English. How can I know if I could even tolerate Kafka's German prose? I know Willa and Edwin Muir. I know Tania and James Stern. I know Malcolm Pasley. (And I give them all my truest thanks.) At my most pissed off with my English-rendered Kafka, I think of Auden's definition of a poem as a 'verbal contraption'.

The word contains both con and trap. At my most pissed off—
and Kafka pisses me off more than any other writer—I view
each sentence as both a con and a trap. Involutions of a certain
sort imply the infinite. Here is false scripture, pimping off the
Biblical and the Toraic. Here is pseudo-profundity, confusing
Confucius and dumbing down the Dao. Here is profound shock,
but only of a routine short circuit: 'The crows maintain that a
single crow could destroy the heavens. There is no doubt of that,
but it proves nothing against the heavens, for heaven simply
means: the impossibility of crows.'4

He pulls the carpet, and the floor, and the earth out from
under our feet; they are still there, draped, behind his back:
'Leopards break into the temple and drink the sacrificial vessels
dry; this is repeated over and over again; finally it can be calculated in advance and it becomes a part of the ceremony.'5

But the aphorism I think about most often halts me in my
annoyance. Restores me to loyalty and awe. Here is a sternness
that doesn't seek publicity. Here, the con is internalized as con-
science. Here, the trap is experienced from within. Kafka does,
I sense, laugh at himself: 'There are two cardinal human sins
from which all others derive: impatience and indolence.
Because of impatience they were expelled from Paradise,
because of indolence they do not return. But perhaps there is
only one cardinal sin: impatience. Because of impatience, they
were expelled, because of impatience, they do not return.'6

I have avoided writing about Kafka, but I have tried to write
through him, off him. I have written stories I could not have
written without the stories referred to in this essay: 'Investigations of a Dog' (1922), 'The Burrow' (pub. 1931), 'The Problem

of Our Laws' (pub. 1931). In my stories, I was trying to write Literature. (What a shaming confession.)

Kafka's contraptions seem, when I have ceased to be pissed off, worthwhile. They are Literature in a very high form.

Two examples will do: 'Investigations of a Dog' and 'The Burrow'. Here, unlike most writers, Kafka does not seem to be writing towards something. In both stories, the opening sentence is a foreclosure. 'How much my life has changed, and yet how unchanged it has remained at bottom!' and 'I have completed the construction of my burrow, and it seems to be successful.' These remind me of Jane Austen's perversely absolute negation, at the beginning of *Persuasion* (1817), of one character's possibility of any development or change: 'Vanity was the beginning and the end of Sir Walter Elliot's character . . . .' Where to go from there? Nothing so crass as an arc or a journey or a redemption. And Kafka's investigating dog and burrowing creature get nothing of that sort. By this point in his writing (1922–24), Kafka is only interested, on the page, in exploring *states*—almost, in exploring *stasis*. What happens within the reader, though, the vast shifts and splinterings and abandonments of hope, is something entirely different. These stories are often referred to as failures—worse, as boring or incompetent failures. They have nothing like the economy and elegance of 'In the Penal Colony' (1919) or 'Metamorphosis' (1912). Traditional values like this have been departed from. We are in the middle of a far with no edge. These stories read, critics say, as first drafts. Their effects are insufficiently calculated. They go on for too long. But, for my Kafka, calculable effects are negligible as compared to incalculable ones. 'In the Penal Colony' and 'Metamorphosis' are agonies we witness; 'Investigations of a Dog' and 'The Burrow' engulf us in our own passions. That is Literature.

Today, I was trying to write a definition of that old-fashioned value, Literature with a capital L.

Literature is not Literary Fiction. That is not my definition, but it's a place to start because it's the place we have to start. The marketplace, etc.

Literary Fiction is read as the attempt to write Literature, and Literature is recapitulated as the Literary Fiction of the past.

I propose Three Ways to Tell Literature from Literary Fiction.

1. Literature requires rereading.

2. Literature reinvents reading.

3. Literature reconfigures the reader.

At a later point, I am going to reconfigure the word 'reconfigures'; for now, I am going to unpick each proposition.

Literature Requires Rereading

A book that requires rereading is, in some ways, radically unsatisfying. It will not please the market. It will not please the majority of readers.

Most Genre Fiction is written expressly for a single reading; most Literary Fiction is written implicitly not to be read at all.

If Literary Fiction is not read, then it can, without difficulty, be pointed to as Contemporary Literature. And then, because we can point to Contemporary Literature and next year more

Contemporary Literature again, we need have no anxiety about the idea that we are not producing any Literature for those who follow us.

'Literature is writing that has the capacity to fascinate the future.' That was my old definition of Literature with a capital *L*.

Because you cannot hope to know what will fascinate the future, you cannot hope self-consciously to set out to write Literature.

To attempt to write Literature is to accept one's own bewilderment as one's start point.

Literary Fiction is Pin the Tail on the Donkey without being spun round and round, and without the blindfold.

Literature Reinvents Reading

One of the reasons you need to return to a book that is Literature is because, on the first reading, most of what it is doing is teaching you how to read it.

Your bewilderment on first reading Literature is one proof it is Literature.

There are lots of different ways of being bewildered; each writer of Literature will bewilder you uniquely.

First readers help later generations to be less bewildered. 'Kafka is this kind of writer,' they say. 'Kafka was a modernist.' 'Kakfa was a proto-absurdist.' 'Kafka was an existentialist.' 'Kafka was a very funny guy.' But, despite this, Kafka will never be anything less than a total mindfuck.

Literature Reconfigures the Reader

By temporarily or hopefully permanently changing how you read, Literature subtly changes how you are.

How you read affects how you read the world; but this is far too utilitarian. Kafka is not self-help. Kafka is anti-self-help.

You are an established fact. Literature makes you realize that you are not an established fact.

Perhaps I should not have said, *Literature reconfigures the reader*.

Perhaps I should have said, *Literature rediscovers the reader*.

No, perhaps I should have said, *Literature resurrects the reader*.

Of course, Literature, in attempting-to-be-post-Judeo-Christian, needs to rival the promises of the Old Testament and the fulfilments (or not) of Christ.

Without being heretical, Literature loses a major part of its reason for being.

(Kakfa wants to relate to Saint Paul; Kafka desires heresy.)

Some Definitions of Literature with a Capital L

Literature is a refusal to accept a generalized view of what is.

(Too unspecific, this. Philosophy might be covered. Or contrarianism.)

Literature is the written record of unprecedented souls.

(Too elevated.)

Literature is a form of perfectly accomplished bewilderment.

Or, Literature is a perfectly accomplished form of bewilderment.

This is why: The pleasures of Literary Fiction are the pleasures of orientation; the pleasures of Literature are the pleasures of bewilderment.

What do you say, while you are being bewildered? What do you say afterwards? *I do not know. I do not know.*

The stories I have chosen to mention below are the ones that make me say *I do not know* most powerfully. Because, with several of them, *I do not know* if they are good or bad, or whether that even matters. *I suspect* they are unreasonably great.

I would like to say something about what *I suspect* can be learnt from Kafka. And, as a preface to this, you need to read Kafka's description of his ideal, from a letter to Felice Bauer, 14–15 January 1913:

> I have often thought that the best mode of life for me would be to sit in the innermost room of a locked cellar with my writing things and a lamp. Food would be brought and always put far away from my room, outside the cellar's outermost door. The walk to my food, in my dressing gown, through the vaulted cellars, would be my only exercise. I would then return to my table, eat slowly and with deliberation, and then start writing again at once. And how I would write! From what depths I would drag it up![7]

This is a young man trying to impress a young woman. It is also a writer wishing to be simultaneously unconvincingly imprisoned ('outside the cellar's *outermost* door') and to be kept as a pet (Kafka's food materializes as mysteriously as that of the dogs' in 'Investigations of a Dog').

The writings of Kafka from which (*I suspect*) we have most to learn are his rhapsodies of perpetual clarification: 'Investigations of a Dog', 'The Problem of Our Laws' (1920), 'A Report to an Academy' (1917), 'A Hunger Artist' (1922), 'The Burrow'. In them, we do not behold the sentences of Flaubert—aspiring to be carved in marble, academized. Instead, we witness the as-live struggles of a meaningful animal—exhausted, hungry, short of breath—to express something of both imminent and immanent value.

The greatest writers, like the greatest athletes, are capable of great precision at great speed. It's their velocity of thought that makes this possible. A writer can think far faster than Charlie Parker could play—yet Charlie Parker is the best depiction I know of speed-of-thought. With great writing we travel farther, in each sentence, than seems possible. Words are doing more than words can do—without some kind of influx of the miraculous; not *miracle*, because that suggests tableaux and adoration. This is pure flow, which we—lucky—follow. The model is 'To be or not to be . . . .'

Reading this kind of writing, our breathing comes more in sync with the writer's. The breath in a Flaubert sentence is many-times breathed; in Kafka, there seems to an unnatural amount of chill oxygen—because we are in the giddy, gainful, terrifying phase of hyperventilation. The throat is scoured. All Kafka's stories read as if written by a guest of the Ice Queen. The air stabs us with lung-clarity. The heart vomits thick blood.

I think Kafka goes headlong into his writing. He bends forward and his head fully enters the paper of the page and he lifts up into a perfect handstand on the desk. Then his legs start to sprint through the empty air as he feels himself beginning to drown.

Everything he wrote was a transcription of this experience. He was not a palimpsest-maker. He attempted to do an absolute draft, not a first or a second. He performed himself, or his persona, directly into the page. His technique (as such) was developed to keep up with this. Not a follower of a dutiful routine; shamefully more like an inspired poet. Which leaves the wannabe writer little of use from which to learn. This method is irresponsible. 'When it arrives, go with it.' And this method is more likely than any other to produce stream-of-pompousness shit; sub-Beat extemporizing on the tedious self; whatever's echoing in your unvoid head. This method depends on preparation. The real work must go into revising the possibility-of-a-soul. Unfortunately, you'd have to call this spiritual discipline.

Kafka finds his world populated by intolerable things. It is through the absoluteness of his avoidances that we most know him. He sprints and dodges, dead-ends and doubles back—ridiculous upside-down legs, kicking the shit out of the icy air. What would be default for us is anathema for him. And, in conclusion, he does not write what other writers write.

Kafka created subject areas where other writers saw only frustration. He, so far as I know, lived through the Great War without allowing it to nudge his hierarchy of what is fictionally important. If inscrutability was his thrust, he went further out into it than anyone but Shakespeare. How did he achieve this eminence? You already know that *I do not know*.

However, *I suspect* it was partly because he believed *everything* depended on what he wrote; and not a reasonable *everything*.

Notes

1 Franz Kafka, 'The Next Village' in *The Collected Short Stories of Franz Kafka* (Willa and Edwin Muir trans) (London: Penguin, 1988), p. 404.

2 Franz Kafka, 'Before the Law' in *The Collected Stories of Franz Kafka* (Willa and Edwin Muir trans) (London: Penguin, 1988), p. 3.

3 Henry James, *The Ambassadors* (London: Penguin, 1982), p. 140.

4 Franz Kafka, *The Great Wall of China and Other Short Works* (London: Penguin, 2002), p. 84.

5 Ibid., p. 82.

6 Ibid., p. 79.

7 Franz Kafka, *Letters to Felice* (London: Secker & Warburg, 1974), p. 156.

Ballard

I'd like to propose another thought experiment: We have got
J. G. Ballard wrong. The whole lot of us. One hundred per cent
wrong. J. G. Ballard isn't, truth be told, a writer at all—not in
the sense we might commonly understand it. He writes, yes,
that has to be admitted, hundreds of thousands of remarkable
words, words worthy of close academic scrutiny, but that isn't
the focus of his life, and never has been. Here is the secret. All
J. G. Ballard's literary activity is a monumental diversion, an
autobiographical smokescreen, in the creation of which he has
only a passing interest. He can write as he does without ever
giving his whole self to it; perhaps he gives 10 to 15 per cent of
his attention, sometimes. He puts the words down extremely
fast, his mind often elsewhere; he is impatient to get back to his
true vocation. Because James Graham Ballard (born 15 November 1930 in Shanghai) is not a novelist and short-story writer.
Not essentially. He is a tunnel-builder, a colleague of ants,
moles, rabbits and badgers, and of the narrator of Kafka's 'The
Burrow'. Beneath the gloriously shabby house in Shepperton
there exists a vast network of steel-lined passages, taking the
form of a pyramid. Through this three-dimensional maze, for
that is what it is, only Ballard knows his way. Only Ballard
knows his way because, extravagant as it may seem, Ballard is

the only human being ever to have entered these tunnels. The great pyramid-maze has been excavated single-handedly over the course of the past 47 years. Entered through a small pad-locked trapdoor, located immediately beneath Ballard's desk, it is the reason Ballard moved to Shepperton in the first place; it is the reason—of course, there must be a reason—why he has never moved. Here is where the Spielberg wealth went. Here is the reason for the widening gaps between books. Here is the masterpiece. The first tunnel Ballard built reached from beneath his house to a secret location yards from the Thames riverbank. This was necessary; so that he would have some-where inconspicuously to dispose of all the excavated soil and rock—without having to resort to *The Great Escape* trouser-leg tactics. Also, he could set up a small warehouse here, to which deliveries of equipment might be made. Since that initial earth-work was completed, around 1964, Ballard has been tunnelling obsessively. Work on the deepest floor of the pyramid only reached completion in early May of 2007. And still no one knows about it, still Ballard remains silent on the subject of his greatest achievement. That his literary career has drawn so much attention to him is, almost, an embarrassment to Ballard—especially since what he wanted most of all from writing was a small income and plenty of free time. Because of his growing notoriety, Ballard-the-tunneller has had to build up a convincing cover story, psychologically convincing. To this end he has meticulously faked a lifelong obsession with all things aerial: pilots, flight, spacecraft, etc. Whereas, as now becomes clear, his concerns have always been chthonic. If he could, picking one of the Verne-journeys, he would travel not to the moon but to the centre of the earth. He has no real interest in the overhead world nor, when it comes to it, in the surface-level world. At all costs, though, the pyramid-maze must be protected. So Ballard has had to fake a curiosity about what goes on in the overhead and surface-level worlds. Often, he has merely taken that which was closest to hand. He could not be bothered to put in the research that traditional literary writing would require—research, that is, into traditional literary writing. And so, he has used what was in front of his face. The places he could not help but go. The buildings illness and bureaucracy required him to enter. The roads which took him there and back. And, thus, the pyramid-maze has been protected. Between it and discovery stands Ballard-the-writer, Ballard-the-autobiographer, Ballard-the-bluffer. And what it contains, at the very centre, a point reached after two hours of intricate descents, traverses and climbs, in a steel-lined room standing over three stories high, is . . .

This, I'd suggest, is just about how wrong we may have got J. G. Ballard. And, perhaps, also, how wrong he's got himself. We think he's a writer when, in fact, he is a tunneller; he thinks he's a tunneller when, in fact, he's a writer. For me, the least interesting Ballard of all is Ballard's Ballard—a reduced, explicated, psychologically prompted character: a technological writer with no interest in technology; a profound psychopathologist with little knowledge of psychopathology; a humanist who couldn't care less about humanity; an Englishman who, in his own country, remains abroad. What is he, then, if not these things? I don't know. I do know, with absolute certainty, that I am likely to be as wrong about Ballard as anyone else.

Spark

I will begin with straightforward affection: *I love Muriel Spark's books*.

I also, incidentally, think that some of them are great books, but I will leave that for later.

I love Muriel Spark's books for their straightforwardness and their perversity, for their acuity and their inscrutability, for their gossip and their metaphysics and, most of all, for their primly devastating prose.

They are not particularly cosy books. To love them is not, as a reader, to feel all that close to or accepted by them. They maintain a proper distance. Perhaps it would be more accurate, though unfortunately more affected-sounding, to say that I *adore* Muriel Spark's books. To a great extent, they insist upon elevation. If I want to reach their level, it may be necessary for me to learn to fly—or at least, to borrow a stepladder.

It would be presumptuous of me to say that I also loved Muriel Spark as a person. I met her only on a very few formal occasions. It is probably enough to say she did not disappoint, and almost everyone does. Everyone who's anyone, especially.

I interviewed Dame Muriel Spark—as she was quite keen on being called—by phone, around the time her penultimate novel, *Aiding and Abetting* (2000), was published. I didn't tape-record the conversation. But, in preparing this essay, I have looked back at my notes. The first thing I wrote down, underneath Spark's phone number in Tuscany, is the sentence, 'I always write briefly.'

And it is here that I would like to begin to explain Muriel Spark's greatness. Because one of the commonly recognized attributes of greatness is magnitude. And one of the reasons, I think, that people are reluctant to speak of Muriel Spark as a great writer is simply that many of her books are short. Or, to put this another way—when asked to name great writers, either living or very recently dead, the usual list would be dominated by male Americans who have self-consciously attempted to write the Great American Novel. In fact one of them, Philip Roth, even wrote a novel called *The Great American Novel*. Unsurprisingly, it wasn't. The others, Saul Bellow, John Updike, Don DeLillo, David Foster Wallace, are all known for writing *big* books. Any women added to this list are likely to match this gigantic profile: the hyper-prolific Joyce Carol Oates, or the historically ambitious Toni Morrison.

Recently, the *Observer* asked a number of British writers, including myself, to nominate what they believed was the best novel of the past 25 years.

When faced with this sort of question, most people's response is to try to remember novels which *did a lot*. A kind of giganticist mentality takes over. Which novel has fitted in the most, has land-grabbed and colonized the largest area of the contemporary world? This is why books like Salman

Rushdie's *Midnight's Children* (1981) or Zadie Smith's *White Teeth* (2000) end up getting mentioned.

There's also, in making one's selection, a feeling of worthiness. Very few people, for example, would consider mentioning an absolutely perfect comic novel. Books which are funny tend to suffer in a general context of greatness-hunting, as do books which have no element of grind to them. Because if we work hard to read something, beginning to end, then it's a good idea to persuade ourselves that time was well spent.

In the final *Observer* list, Muriel Spark was cited once, for *A Far Cry from Kensington* (1988). The most-selected novel was *Disgrace* (1999) by J. M.Coetzee, followed by Martin Amis' *Money* (1984) and Anthony Burgess' *Earthly Powers* (1980).

In an article announcing this result, Robert McCrum wrote, 'As readers, we want our "great novels" to include as much as possible of experience and to address the great issues of our time.'[1] This is, fairly clearly, a plea for novelistic magnitude— of ambition if not explicitly of page-length. Very few of Muriel Spark's novels are inclusive in this way. Most delineate their micro-worlds quite clearly: a school, a convent, a New York apartment, a finishing school. Also, with perhaps the exception of *The Mandelbaum Gate* (1965), they do not attempt the kind of higher reportage McCrum is describing. If anything, Spark's novels address the great issues not of 'our time' but of time itself.

(Incidentally, although it may seem highly disloyal in this context, the novel whose name I gave the *Observer* was not by Muriel Spark. [Please forgive me.] It was Samuel Beckett's *Ill*

Seen, Ill Said (1981)—a work far shorter and more circumscribed even than Spark's shortest.)

Earlier this year, Hermione Lee, chair of judges for the 2006 Man Booker Prize, gave her own explanation for the rationale behind their shortlist: 'Each of these novels has what we as judges were most looking for, a distinctive original voice, an audacious imagination that takes readers to undiscovered countries of the mind, a strong power of story-telling and a historical truthfulness.'[2]

I would like to pause here for a moment, just to ask what 'historical truthfulness' has ever had to do with works of fiction?

Lee continues: 'Each of these novels creates a world you inhabit without question or distrust while you are reading, and a mood, an atmosphere, which lasts long after the reading is over.'[3]

The first half of this sentence, I would say, is an almost perfect description of everything Muriel Spark's fiction *does not do*. It is exactly 'question' and 'distrust' which I feel while reading, say, *Not to Disturb* (1971) or *The Hothouse by the East River* (1973). And this intense dubiousness is a high aesthetic pleasure. What Lee describes, by contrast, seems the equivalent of wanting to believe that—in some way—what you're reading about is true, really happened, can be relied upon. This is exactly the 'reality effect' described by Roland Barthes: 'the "real" [detail or *notation*] is assumed not to need any independent justification, that it is powerful enough to negate any notion of "function", that it can be expressed without there being any need for it to be integrated into a structure, and that the *having-been-there* of things is a sufficient reason for speaking of them.'[4] W. H. Auden said that, 'The truest poetry is the most feigning'; Lee, and other lovers of 'historical truthfulness', insist that 'the greatest novel is the least fictional.' I would call this taste infantile: Realism may con you into believing it completely, and you may find that comforting, but the real Real World is not trustworthy or truth-speaking.

But, whether or not I like it, this is the way in which many contemporary readers judge novels. The non-fictional element is their value-added. Read *Captain Corelli's Mandolin* (1994) and you get not only a *story*, you also get to learn about life on a Greek island in wartime.

It is against this background that I'd like to write a little about what I feel literary greatness is, and why it might be worth our maintaining it as a value—a value that, in itself, corroborates or agglomerates other values.

Academic literary critics are reluctant to discuss greatness. It smacks too much of F. R. Leavis and his followers—particularly of *The Great Tradition* (1948), and Leavis' search, ending with D. H. Lawrence, for a contemporary writer who ticked enough of the pre-existing boxes to qualify.

For the most part, academic literary critics avoid making explicit value judgements. If you historicize aesthetic judgements to any extent at all, then the only reason to venture them ends up being a wish to make a fool of yourself in the eyes of the future. Think of those poor eighteenth-century fools who thought Dryden superior to Shakespeare.

But I don't believe that historicism entirely explains what I perceive as the difference in quality between Shakespeare and Dryden. This may go back to the level upon which I write: word by word, sentence by sentence. I believe that when I change a particular phrasing, I am—quite objectively—improving it; improving it if not in the context of all eternity then, in an only slightly more modest way, as a step up a ladder positioned within infinite space. This is the way in which artists work. If they did not make thousands of minute and instantaneous aesthetic value judgements, novels, paintings, music could not come into existence. Of course, some of these judgements may be wrong. You only have to watch Henri-George Clouzot's film *Le Mystère Picasso* (1956) to realize this. But also, in watching this film, you realize that it was Picasso's willingness to question or even pervert his own aesthetic taste which made him, ultimately, a great artist. He plays with his playing.

And so, in attempting to define what I mean by 'greatness', I am going to have to find some available ground between an assertion of eternal aesthetic values and an entirely subjective choice of *what appeals at the moment*. It will not be a middle ground, because it is closer to the eternal than to the momentary. Embarrassingly so. I am enough of an academic myself to know the arguments against these kind of assertions.

Greatness, then, is the expression of a relationship between perishable words and human-perceived time.

Greatness does not exist, or not to any extent worth mentioning, in geological or non-human-perceived time. As far as the mountains are concerned, we are a winking in and out of vision—the equivalent of lichen on a rock.

Thomas Hardy approaches this question in his poem 'At Castle Boterel' (1913), creating a scene that exists at once in human and non-human time, but in which human time is seen to be momentarily triumphant:

> Primaeval rocks form the road's steep border,
>> And much have they faced here, first and last,
> Of the transitory in Earth's long order;
>> But what they record in colour and cast
>>> Is—that we two passed.[5]

Greatness, seen in this way, is part of the structure of secular human time; the time of lifetimes, ours and our predecessors'. If we are Hardy, and the rocks are the earth, then we are right to believe we have left our emotional mark upon them, even when we know that, seen inhumanly, we are untraceable in what remains, and will remain. Because we can never *see* inhumanly, we live within inflected time—time inflected by human presences; those presences which, through artworks, have outlasted their own time; those ones we call great.

I would go further than this, though. Not so far as to argue that the great are immortal, but that, for all human purposes, they might as well be.

To be great, in these terms, is to approximate closely to supra-temporal values. Values that transcend not time per se but human time. The great are immortal, but only in the sense that one human being's works may eventually come to outlast all human lives. Shakespeare will be around longer than the human race, although that will mean nothing to the illiterate matter of the universe. The values expressed in works of greatness, paradoxically, continue to maintain their worth even beyond the destruction of the object in which they were contained.

This is an argument harder to put forward with writing than with, say, music or mathematics. Pythagoras inscribed certain formulae upon the universe, and even if proof of his existence were entirely erased, they would still hold true as *something which had been done, and done beautifully*. Similarly, it would continue to mean something that Bach had existed, even though every note he composed had somehow been lost—and even though the criteria of human meaning had also been destroyed.

The question this raises is, what about the unknown great—those whose works remained in a drawer, were found and burnt unread? I would say that they cannot be counted great because they never came to exist within human-time. Hopkins or Emily Dickinson were not great at the moment of their deaths. They had to be born into human-perceived time. The true difficulty here is: How many readers are necessary? You could argue just one. I would not. Enough to affect the discourse of a literature. Enough to become literature. If philosophers of vagueness cannot agree how many grains of sand it takes to make a pile, I am unlikely to be able to give you a number of readers to make up a literature. But, if that reader is themselves a great writer, it may take only one. For Whitman to become great it took only one reader—Emerson. Emerson was aware of this, and expressed it in his famous letter back to Whitman, after reading an early version of *Leaves of Grass*. 'I greet you at the beginning of a great career . . . .' In other words, by greeting you, and by being who I am, I initiate the period of greatness.

I doubt these are questions to which Muriel Spark gave very much thought. Greatness does not exist in relation to theological time. To the Christian God, temporal greatness is an irrelevance; salvation or damnation, that is the only abiding question. All artists, in one way or another, are Doctor Faustus, and have become so after requesting an interview with Mephistopheles. This is true even of those who create an art which shows itself subservient to religion. Spark's theology is a whole other subject—one I do not want to go into here. It is enough to say, her novels are not based upon quibbles, as are Graham Greene's *Brighton Rock* (1938) and *The Power and the Glory* (1940), nor upon a snobbishness of the soul, as with Evelyn Waugh's *Brideshead Revisited* (1945)—where Catholicism is the literary equivalent of syrupy strings on a film soundtrack.

As a generalization, I would say that Spark's theology generates or germinates her novels at a structural level. In many of them, it is that idea that, as perceived by God, temporality does not exist—that He perceives the universe from beginning to end as in a single instant, and that therefore events which are yet to occur are in no way metaphysically different, essentially, to those which have already occurred. In such a God-perceived world, cause and effect became a matter of ironic comedy rather than anything else. (Perhaps, in this downgrading of causality, Spark has something in common with David Hume, another child of Edinburgh.)

Spark's masterpiece is usually taken to be *The Prime of Miss Jean Brodie* (1961)—and I agree with that judgement. But because it is the most read, and most discussed, of Spark's works, I don't intend to focus on it now. It is worth mentioning, however, in the context of causality, that the novel's most striking feature is its use of anachronism: 'And many times throughout her life

Sandy knew with a shock, when speaking to people whose childhood had been in Edinburgh, that there were other people's Edinburghs quite different from hers, and with which she held only the names of districts and streets and monuments in common.'[6]

These moments, as I said just now, are structurally essential to the novel—they are not realist details or *notations* of the sort Barthes describes. They place the girls' lives in relation to theological or God-perceived time.

Once *The Prime of Miss Jean Brodie* is accepted as Spark's masterpiece, though, things begin to get interesting. The search is on for her *other* masterpieces—and among these, I believe, *Not to Disturb* is chief. It, too, depends upon a violent distortion of causality. The servants in a Swiss chateau impassively await the violent death of their master and mistress, absolutely sure of what will occur—sure to the extent that they have already sold the film rights to their memoirs of the supposedly future event. They, like many of Spark's characters, exist in a kind of moving stasis. The question arises of whether they can be said ever really to *do* anything—*do* rather than enact or carry out. And this is the point at which the 'question' and 'distrust' so disliked by Hermione Lee are at their maximum.

The novels to which I would like to pay most attention, from now on, are those which form what you might call the middle period: *The Public Image* (1968), *The Driver's Seat* (1970), *Not to Disturb* (1971), *The Hothouse by the East River* (1973) and *The Abbess of Crewe* (1974).

In looking around for a way to express the qualities for which I feel Muriel Spark should be accounted great, I thought almost immediately of Italo Calvino's *Six Memos for the Next Millenium* (1988). These Charles Eliot Norton lectures, of which only five were completed before Calvino's death, lay out the literary values which Calvino saw as most worthwhile. They offer an alternative to the commonplace, prize-giving, giganticist idea of greatness. Calvino's values are 'Lightness', 'Quickness', 'Exactitude', 'Visibility' and 'Multiplicity'. The final, unwritten lecture, was to have been called 'Consistency'.

I think already you will be able to see how apt these qualities are to Muriel Spark's work—and how, in relation to them, a heavyweight novelist like Saul Bellow is immediately diminished. Not because he has nothing to do with any of the values; merely that only half of Bellow's values are shared with Calvino, the other half being direct oppositions. And so, for Lightness read Heft, for Quickness read Expansiveness and for Exactitude read Inclusiveness, or Missing Very Little Out and Taking as Many Pains as Necessary to Ensure This. Visibility, Multiplicity and Consistency are, I would say, values upon which Calvino and Bellow are largely agreed—although their definitions of all vary considerably.

Muriel Spark and her writings, however, are quite in accord with all Calvino's terms. It would be difficult to find six words which better described her qualities—particularly if Quickness is allowed to include quickness of wit.

Lightness is most readers' first impression of Spark's writing, on all levels, from sentence to chapter to novel. And those more familiar with Spark can see that, even on the level of Complete Works, lightness abides. Because of this, it seems almost unnecessary to quote an example. Take any sentence at random and it will show itself to be deeply light. Here is the final paragraph of *Not to Disturb*. Listen, as I read it, to the internal rhymes, *hall*, *all* and *walls*, *night* and *sunlight*:

> The plain-clothes man in the hall is dozing on a chair, waiting for the relief man to come, as is also the plain-clothes man on the upstairs landing. The household is straggling up the back stairs to their beds. By noon they will be covered in the profound sleep of those who have kept faithful vigil all night, while outside the house the sunlight is laughing on the walls.[7]

And here is Lise, the protagonist of *The Driver's Seat*, checking in at the airport for what she knows will be her final flight:

> 'And hand-luggage?' The busy young official looks at her as much as to say, 'What's the matter with *you*?' And Lise answers in a voice different from the voice in which she yesterday spoke to the shop assistant when buying her lurid outfit, and has used on the telephone, and in which early this morning she spoke to the woman at the porter's desk; she now speaks in a little-girl tone which presumably is taken by those within hearing to be her normal voice even if a nasty one. Lise says, 'I only have my hand-bag with me. I believe in travelling light because I travel a lot and I know how terrible it is for one's neighbours on the plane when you have great huge pieces of hand-luggage taking up everybody's foot-room.'[8]

A common criticism of Spark's novels, particularly the later ones, is that they are too light. But that is because many readers are expecting heft of a sort that Spark jettisoned before she even started. Her novels are miraculously airborne—they begin by leaving the ground, and never once afterwards touch down. Her seriousness is not of a sort that feels it worthwhile to insist upon appearing serious: if readers miss it, they miss it. The job of the Sparkish writer is to insist upon nothing—to avoid entirely being a burden upon the reader. Each reader's burden is their own self, their own soul.

As a value Lightness is intimately related to Quickness—so much so that, at times, they appear to be the same thing. But it is quite possible to have incredibly massive objects moving with great speed. They are, however, difficult to divert—and Spark's writing is also notable for its instantaneous changes of direction. This can only be achieved with objects, or subjects, approaching weightlessness. Perhaps this is one explanation for the insubstantial nature of the characters in *The Hothouse on the East River*. Lise, in *The Driver's Seat*, wishes to become what used to be known as 'a light woman'—and moves quickly to achieve her wish.

What Calvino himself has to say about lightness is worth quoting:

> After forty years of writing fiction, after exploring various roads and making diverse experiments, the time has come for me to look for an overall definition of my work. I would suggest this: my working method has more often than not involved the subtraction of weight. I have tried to remove weight, sometimes from people, sometimes from heavenly bodies, sometimes from

cities; above all I have tried to remove weight from the structure of stories and from language.[9]

Spark had, I think, a similar desire. But it is another aspect of Spark's Quickness that I'd like to explore now; specifically, its relation to the idea of how great writing should occur, and how great writers should speak of it. At this point, I'd like to return to Barthes. In *Writing Degree Zero* (1953) he describes the moment that Literature became, by definition, laborious:

> [A]round 1850, Literature begins to face a problem of self-justification; it is now on the point of seeking alibis for itself; and precisely because the shadow of a doubt begins to be cast on its usage, a whole class of writers anxious to assume to the full responsibility of their tradition is about to put the work-value of writing in place of its usage-value. Writing is now to be saved not by virtue of what it exists for, but thanks to the work it has cost . . . . Labour replaces genius as a value, so to speak; there is a kind of ostentation in claiming to labour long and lovingly over the form of one's work. There even arises, sometimes, a precocity of conciseness (for labouring at one's material usually means reducing it), in contrast to the great precocity of the baroque era (that of Corneille, for instance).[10]

Here, in our interview, is Spark arguing herself out of greatness.

LITT. How much revision do you do?

SPARK. Very little . . . I think of the book first, and then I strike. If I do [any revision], it's as I go along. I go through the typescript for commas. [The finished book] is virtually the first draft. I go through the proofs, usually adding.

LITT. Do you do much revision on a sentence-by-sentence basis?

SPARK. No. I really don't. I think in the style that I write, and have a way of manipulating sentences in my mind. It pours out very quickly. I've been doing it for a long time, so it comes quite naturally to me.[11]

Here, Spark is violating the Flaubertian taboo, as described by Barthes: great writing must never be spoken of as easy.

Exactitude is another quality of Spark's writing that any randomly chosen quotation could illustrate. What is perhaps more distinctive are the moments where a particularly exact inexactitude is employed. Here is a wonderful example from *Not to Disturb*: 'Hadrian has prepared a tray on which he has placed a dish of scrambled eggs, a plate of thin toasted buttered bread, a large cup and saucer and a silver thermos-container of some beverage.'[12]

'Some beverage'—this seems an almost direct assault upon the kind of self-serving realist details Barthes analyses in 'The Reality Effect': 'notations which no function (not even the most indirect) will allow us to justify: these details are scandalous (from the point of view of structure), or, even more disturbingly, they seem to be allied with a kind of narrative *luxury*, profligate to the extent of throwing up "useless" details and increasing the cost of narrative information.'[13] One of the examples Barthes gives, from 'Un Coeur Simple', is a description of the room occupied by Madame Aubain, Félicité's mistress, where 'on an old piano, under a barometer, there was a pyramid of boxes and cartons'.[14] This is excessive information. With Spark's description of the tray, the excess seems even greater, until we come to the 'some beverage'. For if the narrator *knows* what is on the dish, why don't they know what is in the thermos? Is it merely because the thermos is closed whereas the dish is open to plain view? Such a blurring is exquisitely mischievous— and gives an example of the games Spark plays with the next of Calvino's values, Visibility.

Almost every paragraph of Spark's writing makes use of sudden appearances, gentle dematerializations, inscrutable veilings and abrupt extinctions. Her middle works are particularly concerned with the visibility that is fame, or notoriety. I have already mentioned the prescient media interest in the events of *Not to Disturb*. In *The Abbess of Crewe*, a closed order of nuns similarly becomes the object of international press scrutiny. In *The Driver's Seat*, every mundane detail has, in advance, an afterimage of publicity. '[Lise's] nose is short and wider than it will look in the likeness constructed partly by the method of identikit, partly by actual photography, soon to be published in the newspapers of four languages'.[15] *The Public Image*, as its title suggests, is almost entirely founded on the relationship between the seen and the unseen, and also, this being Spark, the foreseen and the unforeseen.

> In those early days when she [Annabel] was working in small parts her stupidity started to melt; she had not in the least attempted to overcome her stupidity, but she now saw, with the confidence of practice in her film

roles, that she had somehow circumvented it. She did not need to be clever, she only had to exist; she did not need to perform, she only had to be there in front of the cameras. She said so to Frederick, as if amazed that she had not thought of it before. He was exasperated, seeing shallowness everywhere . . . [16]

For Annabel, as Bishop Berkeley had it, 'Esse est percipi'— 'To be is to be perceived.'

Spark's relationship to Multiplicity is yet more complex. I would call this, along with Simultaneity, one of the central technical problems of prose fiction. Spark's characters are generally not multiple in and of themselves, as are James Joyce's in *Finnegans Wake* or Proust's in *In Search of Lost Time*. A definition, for example, 'Rose Stanley was famous for sex', tends to encapsulate them. In this context, I usually think of Austen, who was—when she needed to be—merciless in delineating and delimiting her characters. On the second page of *Persuasion*, she writes, 'Vanity was the beginning and the end of Sir Walter Elliot's character; vanity of person and situation.'[17] From which verdict, Sir Walter Elliot has no hope of escape. This is the obverse of subjective multiplicity. Sir Walter Elliot is less a consciousness than a morality play personification—like Shakespeare's 'Rumour, Painted full of Tongues'. Whether or not Muriel Sparks' characters are *entirely* imprisoned by their definition is debatable. It is usually in their attempt to escape it that they more fully become it. *The Abbess of Crewe* is a novel about whether or not the woman who becomes the Abbess of Crewe will become the Abbess of Crewe. The fascination of the book is that we flit back and forth between the woman who *is* the Abbess of Crewe and the woman who fears that the impossible will somehow occur, and she will fail to become the Abbess of Crewe. (Because Christianity is founded upon impossibility, she is right to fear this.)

As this shows, Spark's characters are multiple in *time* rather than in *being*. They are burdened, as are we, by singular souls, and their deterministic fates are upon them even as we watch them attempt to exercise free will.

All of Spark's qualities come into play in a passage such as this from *The Prime of Miss Jean Brodie*:

Mary Macgregor, although she lived into her twenty-fourth year, never quite realized that Jean Brodie's confidences were not shared with the rest of the staff and that her love-story was given out only to her pupils. She had not thought much about Jean Brodie, certainly never disliked her, when, a year after the outbreak of the Second World War, she joined the Wrens, and was clumsy and incompetent, and was much blamed. On one occasion of real misery—when her first and last boy-friend, a corporal whom she had known for two weeks, deserted her by failing to turn up at an appointed place and failing to come near her again— she thought back to see if she had ever really been happy in her life; it occurred to her then that the first years with Miss Brodie, sitting listening to all those stories and opinions which had nothing to do with the ordinary world, had been the happiest time of her life. She thought this briefly, and never again referred her mind to Miss Brodie, but had got over her misery, and had relapsed into her habitual slow bewilderment, before she died while on leave in Cumberland in a fire in the hotel. Back and forth along the corridors ran Mary Macgregor, through the thickening smoke. She ran one way; then, turning, the other way; and at either end the blast furnace of the fire met her. She heard no screams, for the roar of the fire drowned the screams; she gave no scream, for the smoke was choking her. She ran into somebody on her third turn, stumbled and died. But at the beginning of the nineteen-thirties, when Mary Macgregor was ten, there she was sitting blankly among Miss Brodie's pupils. 'Who has spilled the ink on the floor—was it you, Mary?'[18]

Which brings me to the last and most difficult of Calvino's six values—Consistency. Because he did not live to write this lecture, it is hard to know what Consistency meant to Calvino—and which writers he would have chosen as illustrations. But the five other lectures perhaps give a hint, returning, as they do, time and again to the same central authors: Leopardi, Boccaccio, Ovid and, above all, Dante. It is hard to believe Calvino would have concluded without a final acknowledgement of them.

In some ways, Ovid and Dante could be seen as opposites: the poet of unceasing metamorphosis and the poet of decisive eternity. But they meet at their extremes: an eternity of metamorphosis is a fate as final as any other; constant change is absolute consistency, of a sort.

It is exactly at this crux, I think, that Muriel Spark's novels begin and end. *Her* consistency is, above all, her constant return to this intersection of time and eternity. That she doesn't write directly about eternity only makes it all the more her subject.

In his final lecture, 'Multiplicity', completed only a short time before his death, Calvino wrote, 'Overambitious projects may be objectionable in many fields, but not in literature. Literature remains alive only if we set ourselves immeasurable goals, far beyond all hope of achievement. Only if poets and writers set themselves tasks that no-one else dares imagine will literature continue to have a function.'[19]

I agree. I think Muriel Spark would have, too.

Notes

1 Robert McCrum, 'What's the Best Novel in the Past 25 Years', *Observor*, 8 October 2006; available at: http://goo.gl/R18Y6G (last accessed on 27 November 2015).

2 Hermione Lee, quoted in Sarah Crown, 'Sarah Waters Heads Booker Shortlist', *Guardian*, 14 September 2006; available at: http://goo.gl/X9WrKB (last accessed on 27 November 2015).

3 Ibid.

4 Roland Barthes, *The Rustle of Language* (Richard Howard trans.) (Oakland: University of California Press, 1986), p. 147.

5 Thomas Hardy, 'At Castle Boterel' in *The Collected Poems* (London: Macmillan, 1972), p. 331.

6 Muriel Spark, *The Prime of Miss Jean Brodie* (London: Penguin, 1961), p. 33.

7 Muriel Spark, *Not to Disturb* (London: Penguin, 1971), p. 96.

8 Muriel Spark, *The Driver's Seat* (London: Macmillan, 1970), p. 27.

9 Italo Calvino, *Six Memos for the Next Millennium* (Patrick Creagh trans.) (Cambridge, MA: Harvard University Press, 1988), p. 3.

10 Roland Barthes, *Writing Degree Zero* (Annette Lavers and Colin Smith trans) (New York: Hill and Wang, 1968) pp. 62–3.

11 Muriel Spark, interview with the author.

12 Spark, *Not to Disturb*, p. 17.

13 Barthes, *The Rustle of Language*, p. 141.

14 Ibid.

15 Spark, *The Driver's Seat*, p. 26.

16 Muriel Spark, *The Public Image* (London: Penguin, 1970), p. 11.

17 Jane Austen, *Persuasion* (Oxford: Oxford University Press, 1923), p. 4.

18 Spark, *The Prime of Miss Jean Brodie*, p. 15.

19 Calvino, *Six Memos for the Next Millennium*, p. 112.

Literature and Technology

I have found this talk very difficult to write. As soon as I approach the subject, my thoughts turn spiral. I try to write about literature in a technological world and I find myself writing about altered human subjectivity within a technological world. So, I turn to writing about altered human subjectivity and find myself writing about how readers read (or don't read) in a technological world. So, I turn to writing about readers and find myself writing about science fiction and inhuman subjectivities. And so on.

Some obvious points: Literature isn't alien to technology, literature is technological to begin with.

Literature depends on technology—a society needs to be able to do more than subsist before it produces a literature. An oral culture, yes, that is possible—but I am talking specifically about words on the page, words on the screen.

By literature and technology I mean literature and contemporary technology: we can begin to understand this by unbundling an iPhone—we have a wireless computer capable of wireless emailing, social networking, tweeting; we have a digital camera capable of taking still and moving images, capable of recording sound files; we have a games console.

My Futuristic Past

I would like to begin by talking about how I became a writer—
I would like to talk about my futuristic past.

When I began writing, it was out of desperate boredom,
and because I had no alternative. I cannot be certain, of course,
but I think that if I had had an alternative, any alternative, I
would not have begun writing.

I was born on 20 August 1968—11 months to the day before
the first Apollo moon landing.

For several years, between approximately 1976 and 1979, I
wasn't interested in anything earthbound. The two most
important films of my boyhood were *Star Wars*, which showed
me where I wanted to be, and *Close Encounters of the Third Kind*,
which showed me a possible means of getting there.

I've written about my desire to leave Planet Earth in a story
called 'Of the Third Kind'. This ends with a scene between an
11-year-old boy, based on myself, and his mother, not based on
my mother:

'Try me,' she said. 'Try and explain.'

If I could go back now and sit opposite her, inside
the boy that I was, I'm still not sure I'd be able to say
anything. At that age, I didn't have the words—and the
ones I did have, I wasn't allowed to use. There was no
way I could tell her how much I loved her or how far
away from her I wanted to be. It would have killed her.

For the first time in my life, my mother was
prepared to listen to me as if I were an adult. But I was
trying so hard to think of the best lie that, for several

minutes, I completely forgot she was there. Finding the best lie was all that mattered. But the best lie wouldn't come. There was something in the way—something new.

Then, suddenly, I wanted to try and tell her the truth. But I didn't know where to start, because there was no start. There was only the all-around yearning, the background radiation of my universe. There was only the UFO, now plunging away from me and Robert, out into the infinity of faraway space, leaving us behind, leaving us stranded on this terrible, incomprehensible planet.[1]

I wasn't personally promised the 1950s future, as were the baby boomers. (I am an echo of the baby boom.) But I came across vestiges of the 1950s future in outdated children's books. These contained images of jetpacks, robots, etc.

Many of the first books I read for pleasure were science fiction—Arthur C. Clarke, Isaac Asimov, A. E. van Vogt. But I didn't *read* a great deal; I much preferred watching television. Even though television, at this time, wasn't very interesting for someone of my age. And very few good science fiction films had been made. I did not watch *2001: A Space Odyssey* in full until much later.

I wanted a future I have, as yet, received only piecemeal. I wanted the technologies of the future.

In preference to Ampthill, Bedfordshire, in 1979, I would have taken any dystopia. There was no armed rebellion against Margaret Thatcher, and certainly not one involving laser guns.

If the video games which exist now had existed back in 1979, I would have spent all my free time playing them. I would not have read any books, I think—I would not have seen writing as an adequate entertainment; I would not have seen going outdoors as sufficiently interesting.

Similarly, I find it difficult to understand why any 11-year-old of today would be sufficiently bored to turn inward for entertainment.

Last year, I spent three months playing World of Warcraft—partly as research for a short story I was hoping to write, mostly because I became life-avoidingly addicted to it.

The question arises: How are writers to come about, without 'silence, exile and cunning'[2]—without the need for these things?

I was formed, myself, by the boredom of the place in which I lived. Philip Larkin said it was 'not the place's fault'[3]—in my case, I think it was. And then, the being taken out of the place into another place (boarding school) where I was unable to have any privacy. This developed an appetite for privacy in me. Which began to come out as poetry, as a diary. It's not that I didn't do these things before—they just became essentials, for self-preservation. That's how I read myself, anyway.

> When I think about the experiences that formed me as a person they involved mystery, discovery, solitude, and the kind of fear that you only feel when you think you're truly alone in the world. And I don't know how anyone feels those things any more?[4]

Some of the first things I ever remember writing were collaborations with my friends. We had a rock group called

Senator, although, between us, for instruments, we only had a
Bontempi organ, a Spanish guitar and a snare drum. We wrote
songs that were based on science-fiction scenarios; we would
never have written a love song. We wrote about an invasion by
aliens, causing apocalyptic destruction.

Another project was to design planets. We got out our pro-
tractors, drew circles on paper, coloured them in—blue for
water planets, brown for desert planets. We gave them names.

This planet-creation may only have been the game of one
or two afternoons, but I remember it clearly. I have often
referred to it when asked how I started writing—that I started
by co-designing planets. Or rather, I designed planets which I
felt were inferior to those designed by my best friend Luke. His
planets looked better, had better names. Everything he did
seemed to be better than everything I did.

Why were we designing planets? Because we were bored.
Because there was nothing better to do.

One point I would like to make is that our designs began
with a blank page. We did not have templates to help us. We
were not being creative with the options offered us by a dropdown menu. But almost always we gave up on our designs
because they dissatisfied us so much—they didn't look very
good. If we could have produced something of the sort today's
boys are capable of, we would have been much happier. Similarly, we would have been happier playing a computer game that
allowed us to visit planets designed by professional designers.

We were excited by the possibilities of technologies that
did not yet exist—spaceships, lasers, communicators.

Because we did not have access to the originals, we made copies; because of the limitations in our technology, our copies were very different from the originals; our copies therefore turned out to be creative rather than derivative.

This is how the Beatles started. Senator were not the Beatles.

The Writer and Technology:
The Desktop World

I am writing this on an Apple iMac8,1 desktop computer.

Jonathan Franzen contributed 'Ten Rules for Writing Fiction' to the *Guardian* on 20 February 2010, in response to Elmore Leonard's 'Ten Rules'. Franzen's eighth rule, or statement, was:

'8. It's doubtful that anyone with an internet connection at his workplace is writing good fiction.'[5]

My iMac has an Internet connection. I am trying to write better fiction than Jonathan Franzen writes. (So, I guess, is Jonathan Franzen.)

Here is another thought-spiral I have tried to avoid: The writer has to write about subjects (people) who live through technology and for people (readers) who live through technology and who will read what the writer has written through technology and as a positive choice rather than engaging in the other technologies available to them. The writer is one of the people who reads what technology-inhabiting writers write. The writer then writes using technological means. The writer writes about subjects (people) who live through technology, etc. . . .

The writer is only marginally less distracted than her subjects.

The Internet connection offers all of us the constant temptation of snippets, of trivia. We don't live, as writers in the past did, without these particular temptations. They had their own temptations—clearly. Byron wasn't undistracted. Yet there were greater acres of emptiness, surely. Travel took weeks, not hours. Winters isolated. Boredom was there as a resource for daydreaming, trancing out.

Aside: I am not panicking here. I think writers will continue to occur, as they have. But technology and its trivia will cause us to lose something, just as we lost something when we lost the classical education. We write worse because we cannot write classical prose. Yet classical prose is useless for describing the world of Almeria in 2010, the world that is there—ready to buzz—in your pockets and purses.

Our perceptions outrun the sedentary sentence by much too much; just as we listen to MP3s to hear what an album *would* sound like were we actually to sit down and listen to it, so we skim-read the classic books to get a sense of what they would be like were we to sit down and dwell with them.

The Means of Writing and Technology

I'm going to limit what I say here to a single topic: The Sentence. I could just as well talk about the novel as a whole or the page as an entity, but The Sentence will allow me to deal with the issue of word-processed prose, and to reveal what I call the Curse of the Cursor.

I teach the MA in creative writing at Birkbeck College in London. Many of my students aspire to write literary fiction. Almost all of my students work exclusively on computers, laptop or desktop. When I print out their stories to read before a class, it may be the first time it has existed in a physical rather than an electronic form.

And I believe I can tell, with some accuracy, how any text has been created. Whether it has always existed on a computer or whether the writer did a draft by hand or whether they work mainly with pen and paper, only typing up towards the ultimate draft. There are sentences which, to me, stand out very clearly as word-processed.

When writers first started using typewriters, it was thought that it would alter the prose produced. And I think, in some subtle ways, it did. There is a different rhythm to flowing ink than there is to clattering metal. But what is consistent between handwritten prose and typewritten prose is that, for each new draft that is required, each sentence of each draft has to be physically redone—re-inscribed, re-typed.

In other words, the sentences pass again and again through the writer's mind, their inner ear, and through the writer's body, their fingers. Word-processing obviates the need for this. A sentence may be altered many times without ever being physically redone, start to finish, as a whole. And this is where The Curse of the Cursor comes in. Because the way these word-processed sentences are altered is by the writer reading them through on screen, then deciding they want to change something, then moving the cursor to the area of the screen on which they want to focus. At its worst, this leads to sentences that accumulate material through the now-over-here, now-over-there opening points the cursor creates—sentences that lose all propulsion of sense and all sense of rhythm, if they ever had any to begin with.

Superadded to this is the clicky, semi-silence in which they are created. The Curse of the Cursor would be mitigated slightly were these writers to read aloud what they had just written every time they made an alteration—read it aloud, and the sentences immediately before and after. Without this, sentences come into existence that have no sense of rhythmic or musical or conceptual cohesion. These word-processed sentences are, instead, a generalized flow of meaning—as long as what the writer wants to say is in the paragraph *somewhere*, that'll do.

In a very old-fashioned analogy, I think good sentences by any prose writer can be tested like wineglasses: tap them with your fingernail and the cracked ones go tink!, the uncracked ones go ting!—and they go ting! because they have start-to-finish integrity. They have a sense of themselves as sentences, and a take on what a sentence can achieve. They aren't made of bits badly inserted into unheard streams of this-is-vaguely-what-I-mean-to-say.

This is entirely an issue of technology—without computers, it would not arise.

How do I deal with it, practically, as a teacher? I advise my students to physically go through their work, repeatedly physically go through their sentences. If their prose suffers particularly badly from The Curse of the Cursor, I tell them they should do all their first drafts by hand.

I tell my students, *There are no shortcuts*, and I hope they listen.

But I think there is most likely a fundamental problem of disengagement here. If contemporary writers produce their texts glibly, their texts will be glib.

I'm going to quote myself from something I'm going to say later: 'There are no shortcuts to the sublime; the sublime is the thing that is reached without shortcuts.'

To finish off talking about the means of writing and technology, I would say there are similar issues to do with the ease with which a writer can access information, can do research, via Google and Wikipedia. In fiction, information is far less useful, and far more likely to stick out and look plasticky, than knowledge. And facts work less well in prose than feel.

The Technological Text

At the heart of this talk is a missing section, The Technological Text—necessarily missing.

If I were Robert Coover, The Technological Text would be the whole of my subject, and the whole of my recent career.

In fact, I saw Coover—some of whose writing I admire greatly—talk on this subject in Barcelona a couple of years ago. It was at a conference dedicated to the work of J. G. Ballard, whom I'll return to later.

Also at the talk was the novelist Hari Kunzru, author of *The Impressionist* (2002). We both listened to Coover enthuse about the technological possibilities for future fiction, and give a demonstration of a piece of software called The Cave.

Frankly, the whole thing was pathetic and embarrassing. The Cave, with its clunky redbrick castle in 3-D, looked like the first-person shooter classic Doom—but without the shooting or the gore or the fun. Any 20-year-old interested in writing for a similar medium would be nowhere near an English department. They would be working for Blizzard, the company that creates the astonishingly complex and exquisitely rendered World of Warcraft.

So, in this empty place, where The Technological Text might have been, I'd like us to place the totemic figure of Robert Coover, standing in his Cave. I'd like us to imagine him reading on the virtual walls around him a deeply sincere Lament for Hypertext by whoever is his star student this semester. Inspired by the possibilities opened up by this exciting new medium, Robert is moved to tears—which cause his virtual-vision goggles to short-circuit.

The Means of Reading and Technology

Kindle. iPad. Apps. The death of the book. Blah blah blah.

I'm not all that interested in analysing the specifics of this.

Books with fixed parameters of text size, page numbering, etc.—already these are looking old-fashioned. They don't give consumers the pathetic notion they are being creative (by choosing the textual equivalent of a ringtone or a screensaver) or being collaborative (by reading only parts of a text that was meant to be read slowly and as a whole). I'm sorry but selecting one of 10 options from a dropdown menu is not being creative—not even if you do it repeatedly. This is fake customization, not creation; true customization, which can be creative, involves using technology in a way its designers never intended.

Readers more accustomed to screens—web pages on computer screens, iPhone displays—will scan a page of text for its contents, rather than experience it in a gradual linear top-left to bottom-right way. This will make for increased speed and decreased specificity. These readers will be half-distracted even as they read; their visual field will include things other than the text, because they won't feel happy unless those things are there. A writer of long, doubling-back sentences such as Henry James will be incomprehensible to them. They won't be grammatically equipped to deal with him. They won't be neurologically capable of reading him. Their eyes will photograph fields rather than, as ours do, or did, follow tracks.

Apply this scanning approach to the sentence. For these readers, the fact they are reading word-processed sentences won't matter. As long as the content is there somewhere on the page, the job of writing is done.

Perhaps future writers will, therefore, to satisfy this readership, create vague fields of possible meaning; more Charles Olson than Ezra Pound. The exact sequence of sounds, the precise inflexion of grammar—these things will seem prissy. We will be back to the eighteenth century, pre-Flaubert.

Isaac Babel's famous sentence from his story 'Guy de Maupassant' (1932): 'No iron spike can pierce a human heart as icily as a period in the right place.'[6] Prissy.

Our books are already becoming less accurate. Many academic textbooks, as you will know, are not professionally proofread or indexed. The academics do it themselves, but their work is not double-checked. How will this affect, say, philosophy, which depends on absolute accuracy of statement?

If the truth of your statement depends upon the exact placement of a comma, retire.

The Reader and Technology

Not that 'The Novel Is Dead' but that the people novels have conventionally been written about are gradually ceasing to exist.

Here I am afraid I might overstate (as if I haven't already). Novels have always belonged to aristocrats of time; not, I say, merely to aristocrats, although they have been disproportionately represented, but to those subjects who have a freedom of choice about how to act within time. The Fordist factory-line workers, performing a repetitive task all day, cannot interest the novel for more than a few moments while they are at work. It is only when the machine stops that the story begins.

Perhaps novels will continue, but instead of the machine it will be the connectivity that stops, or becomes secondary.

The time-relation which created the novel has ceased to exist; that compact with boredom has been (again) broken.

The human race is no longer sufficiently bored with life to be distracted by an art form as boring as the novel.

What did people do before television came along? They sat and waited for television to be invented and were terribly, terribly bored. Some of them knitted.

Life used to be very boring; Life is no more exciting than it was: both these statements are true.

I am so beastly tired of mankind and the world that nothing can interest me unless it contains a couple of murders on each page or deals with the horrors unnameable and unaccountable that leer down from the external universes.[7]

Some of these arguments about the boredom of contemporary readers are bricolaged in David Shields' *Reality Hunger: A Manifesto* (2010). My original review of this, which was rejected by the *Financial Times*, tried to express my feelings about his argument in aphoristic form:

Reality Hunger is an excessively provoking book, for both positive and negative reasons. Mainly negative.

Look, here is a photograph of a leopard on the summit of Mount Everest.

'Living as we perforce do in a manufactured world, we yearn for the "real". We want to pose something nonfictional against all the fabrication—autobiographical frissons or framed or filmed moments that, in their seeming unrehearsedness, possess at least the possibility of breaking through the clutter. I doubt very much that I'm the only person who's finding it more and more difficult to want to read or write novels.' David Shields.

Evidence for the prosecution: *America's Next Top Model* and all Reality TV, YouTube, Twitter, Wikipedia and all Web 2.0, the iPod, David Eggers, Kanye West, James Frey . . .

'So wrong, it's right.' But it's still wrong. But it's still right.

The form of *Reality Hunger* is aphoristic, fragmentary, like some of the great works of twentieth- (but not so much twenty-first-) century argument: Wittgenstein's *Tractatus*, Benjamin's *Arcades Project*. David Shields—'an American writer and professor of English'—constructs his argument from quotes, but sometimes interjects his own mini-essays. The quotes are almost always slightly rewritten.

I have too many disagreements with *Reality Hunger* to compress them into 700 words. But I am thinking of Mount Everest.

DJ culture and hip hop, sampling and mixing—Shields' argument centres on these. All culture, even the supposedly highest, is now (he says) dependent upon these models. Models which themselves derive from collage. *Reality Hunger* itself is sampled and mixed. But hip hop requires dope beats, and Shields' sense of rhythm is wack. As a cultural DJ, his mixing is inept. He *never* drops a quote that just kills.

Reality Hunger is both diagnosis and symptom. As symptom, it is acute; as diagnosis, can I get a second opinion?

Collections of aphorisms homogenize the radically differing worldviews of the aphorists. Read *The Oxford Book of Aphorisms* cover to cover, most of it will seem to have been written by the same jaded patrician polisher of fine words. (Jaded patricians use fine words like 'perforce' and 'yearn' and 'afterward' and 'sublime'.) Even a sensibility as unique as Kafka's can be made to fit:

Leopards break into the temple and drink the sacrificial vessels dry; this is repeated over and over again; finally it can be calculated in advance and it becomes part of the ceremony.

The first time Kafka's leopards broke in, however, they scared the crap out of *everyone*. David Shields may partly be bewailing while simultaneously justifying his own failure to be a leopard.

Why do the songs of the late seventies and afterward hold very little appeal to me? Somewhere along the way, as recording technology got better and better each year, the music lost something; it became too perfect, too complete. In this rush of technological innovation, we've lost something along the way and are going back to try and find it, but we don't know what the thing is.

Wrong. It's surely the *musicians* who have lost something, because the technology has made music-making too facile. Music seems to have been made when it hasn't. Kanye West can cut together a record sampling James Brown's beats, but Kanye West is never going to bring such sublime beats into existence. Why not? Because he's not the Hardest Working Man in Show Business. He's not even funky enough to be one of James Brown's drummers.

There are no shortcuts to the sublime; the sublime is the thing that is reached without shortcuts.

'Paid the cost to be the boss.' James Brown.

Look, here is a photograph of David Shields on the summit of Mount Everest holding up a large photograph of Sir Edmund Hillary and Tenzing Norgay on the summit of Mount Everest. David Shields has travelled to the summit of Mount Everest by helicopter. He will be back home in time for his tea. 'How is the view?' the photographer asks. 'Sublime,' says David Shields, 'but I still can't see any leopards and I'm getting hungry.'

'Dedication's what you need—if you wanna be a record breaker, yeah!' Roy Castle.

DJ Leopard, remix this book immediately. Please.

The Technological World

We live in the Age of Impatience.

We are present in simultaneous otherworlds of distant and virtual communication.

'Impatience is a Virtue,' as a recent advertising slogan informed me—no less propagandically than 'The Central Committee of the Party and the Workers, United in Developing Socialism'.

We have gone from charm to chat-up lines to Craig's List.

Would it be going too far to explain the explicit return of international governments to torture as an expression of state impatience?

This—the Age of Impatience—is a pre-quantum age. The quantum age will be the Age of Already—as in, 'I have already worked out the answer to the question you are just about to realize that you need to ask.'

Writing that Retreats from Technology
(Saul Bellow, or the Soul Man under Technologism)

I've just had my first student in creative writing (at Birkbeck College) tell me that she was writing a novel set in the 1990s *entirely* because she didn't want any of the characters to have access to the Internet or to mobile phones.

What we're going to see more and more of is the pseudo-contemporary novel—in which characters are, for some reason, cut off from one another, technologically cut off.

Already, many contemporary novels avoid the truly contemporary.

It's not that things won't continue to occupy the cultural space created by the idea of the novel. People are still creating ballets. There is a cultural space called 'ballet', although it has no cultural force whatsoever—no social impact whatsoever.

The basic plots of Western literature depend on separation by distance—Odysseus separated from Penelope; the *Odyssey* doesn't exist if Odysseus can catch an Easyjet flight home, or text Penelope's Blackberry. Joyce's *Ulysses* doesn't exist if Bloom can do his day's business from a laptop in a Dublin artisanal coffee shop.

I don't want to overemphasize this. You could imagine a similar anxiety over how the telephone would undermine fiction. Perhaps it is just a matter of acceleration.

But I don't think I am alone in being already weary of characters who make their great discoveries while sitting in front of a computer screen. If, for example, a character, by diligent online research and persistent emailing, finds out one day—after a ping in their inbox—who their father really is, isn't that a story hardly worth telling? Watching someone at a computer is dull.

Saul Bellow was awarded the 1976 Nobel Prize in Literature. The citation read: 'Saul Bellow for the *human understanding* and subtle analysis of contemporary culture that are combined in his work.'

I'd like to go back to Saul Bellow's Nobel Lecture, as published in *It All Adds Up: From the Dim Past to the Uncertain Future* (1994). The subtitle is, I think, very suggestive. Uncertain.

Here, Bellow speaks of dehumanization—it is seen to be in line with 'collective powers'. By which, I think, Bellow meant communist totalitarianism more than capitalist hegemony.

What is at the center now? At the moment, neither art nor science but mankind determining, in confusion and obscurity, whether it will endure or go under [. . .] Out of the struggle at the center has come an immense, painful longing for a broader, more flexible, fuller, more coherent, more comprehensive account of what we human beings are, who we are, and what this life is for. At the center, humankind struggles with collective powers for its freedom, the individual struggles with dehumanization for the possession of his soul. If writers do not come again into the center, it will not be because the center is preempted. It is not. They are free to enter. If they so wish.[8]

I'd call Bellow's argument Wilful Humanism, although perhaps Wishful Humanism would be as accurate. If one adopts it, it saves one the trouble of engaging with—of having to inhabit—another kind of selfhood; a clearly impoverished selfhood, exiled from cathedrals, symphonies and Proust.

The technological subjectivities of contemporary human beings—their trivial existence from status update to tweet to cute YouTube clip to text—these would not be of interest to Bellow.

Believe in the human soul, for the simple sake of enriching one's fiction; this is the core message of Saul Bellow.

Or because the effort of disbelief, the integration and reinvention of soulless selfhood for fiction, is simply too much; soul-nostalgia, in other words, is preferable and should therefore be defended. Awards are given for this.

Writing which does not presume—with Bellow—which does not *presume the soul* is bound to be worse, because the structure of Western culture is against it. Discuss.

Writing which is fundamentally intellectually dishonest is trash. Discuss.

But Saul Bellow's novels are clearly not trash.

Aside: I realize these arguments aren't new. In the Nobel Lecture, Bellow has a go at the logic of Alain Robbe-Grillet: 'The message of Robbe-Grillet is not new. It tells us that we must purge ourselves of bourgeois anthropocentrism and do the classy things that our advanced culture requires.'[9] This is some properly streetwise sarcasm. Those Europeans, so classy. But, right now, Bellow's fiction is looking a good deal less dog-eared than Robbe-Grillet's.

Perhaps I have caricatured Bellow's argument. Perhaps it runs more like this: *If it takes place within the sphere of human perception, then its reality is utterly human.*

Put it another way, *If this is what people believe themselves to be—troubled tremulous souls—then I will allow that recourse to my characters; let them continue in ignorance of the true state of affairs.*

Reduce this even further: *If the box is the body and the body is us, is where we live, how can we think outside it? And even if we could, what would be the point?*

Writing That Accepts Technology as a Given

Introduce a technologized subject at the centre of your novel and immediately lose 99 per cent of your human-biased readers or viewers.

Introduce a technologized subject and you will not win the Nobel Prize in Literature.

Writing that is about the inhuman will inevitably begin to aspire to the condition of maths.

Higher mathematics has a popular audience of approximately zero.

Only entirely anthropomorphized robots can star in movies: *Bicentennial Man; I, Robot; A.I.; Wall-E.*

We—as consumers—are unable to focus on anything that is not involved in a Quest for Love.

All mainstream science fiction wants to force Spock to fall in love with Kirk.

Meaningfulness is bestowed by the human touch, or out-flows from the beating heart within the initially inhuman.

We can play a video game as a robot avatar, but we would not enjoy watching two equally matched robots fight (not if they weren't controlled by humans). Formula One racing is tedious enough, and this still does involve a minor human factor.

Relations between true othernesses are of as little interest to the majority of humans as listening to two speakers in an entirely foreign language.

But, personally, I'm interested in the future *as* future, not in visions of the present cloaked in Bacofoil.

J. G. Ballard's 'The only truly alien planet is Earth'—often misquoted as 'Earth is the alien planet'—is a statement we've hardly reached the beginning of.[10]

Ballard has a greater honesty than Bellow. Bellow is a greater writer than Ballard. Discuss.

The characters of *Vermilion Sands* (1971) or *Crash* (1973) or, even more, of *The Atrocity Exhibition* (1970) exist almost without subjectivity. Their exterior world is their only dreamscape, they don't need a psychology because, instead, they have a psycho-geography. We view them moving through the architectures of their collective psychosis; all desire to enter their heads is negated. We are already in their minds and their minds contain nothing beyond visions of their surroundings. All their names do is label an area of focus within the space of the text. If you could call out to them, crying their name, they wouldn't turn around.

Do we want to read about this kind of person, but this kind of person additionally using information technology every minute of the day, technology to which Ballard was always personally allergic?[11] Or do we want to read about Herzog, Humboldt and Henderson? Richer, deeper, more bogus selfhoods.

Conclusion

I'd like to finish by referring to Henry James' idea of operative irony, as he put it in the 'Preface to Volume 15 of the New York Edition'.

(Operative irony, not the humans who exist, but the humans who *should* exist.)

I have already mentioned the particular rebuke once addressed me on all this ground, the question of where on earth, where roundabout us at this hour, I had 'found' my Neil Paradays, my Ralph Limberts, my Hugh Verekers and other such supersubtle fry. I was reminded then, as I have said, that these represented eminent cases fell to the ground, as by their foolish weight, unless I could give chapter and verse for the eminence. I was reduced to confessing I couldn't, and yet must repeat again here how little I was so abashed. On going over these things I see, to our critical edification, exactly why—which was because I was able to plead that my postulates, my animating presences, were all, to their great enrichment, their intensification of value, ironic; the strength of applied irony being surely in the sincerities, the lucidities, the utilities that stand behind it. When it's not a campaign, of a sort, on behalf of the something better (better than the obnoxious, the provoking object) that blessedly, as is assumed, *might* be, it's not worth speaking of. But this is exactly what we mean by operative irony. It implies and projects the possible other case, the case rich and edifying where the actuality is pretentious and vain. So it plays its lamp; so, essentially, it carries that smokeless flame, which makes clear, with all the rest, the good cause that guides it. My application of which remarks is that the studies here collected have their justification in the ironic spirit, the spirit expressed by my being able to reply promptly enough to my friend: 'If the life about us for the last thirty years refuses warrant for these examples, then so much the worse for that life. The constatation would be so deplorable that instead of making it we must dodge it: there are decencies that in the name of the general self-respect we must take for granted, there's a kind of rudimentary intellectual honour to which we must, in the interest of civilisation, at least pretend.' But I must really reproduce the whole passion of my retort.[12]

In the future, *all* novels will (will have to) invoke a kind of operative irony; post-Twitter, post-whatever-comes-after-what-comes-after-Twitter. Who are these 'supersubtle fry', your characters, who have all this time in which to become rich, deep selfhoods? Where do you find these interesting subjects of yours?

Or, as Henry James appears to us, so we will appear to the readers of the near-future: existing in a differently, slow-flowing time which they will need to make an extreme effort of deceleration to access.

I think there will be great nostalgia for the pre-trivial age, not to mention the pre-genetic-manipulation age.

Literature can accommodate nostalgia, but only as a house guest; if nostalgia becomes the landlord, architect and psychoanalyst, Literature will have to evict itself.

Notes

1 Toby Litt, *Exhibitionism* (London: Penguin, 2003), pp. 116–17.

2 James Joyce, *A Portrait of the Artist as a Young Man* (London: Viking, 1956), p. 247.

3 Philip Larkin, 'I Remember, I Remember' in *Collected Poems* (London: Faber & Faber, 1988), p. 82.

4 Jennifer Egan, interview with author, 7 October 2010.

5 Jonathan Franzen, 'Ten Rules for Writing Fiction', *Guardian*, 20 February 2010. Available at: http://goo.gl/bw3i1d (last accessed on 24 September 2015).

6 Isaac Babel, *The Complete Stories of Isaac Babel* (Nathalie Babel ed., Peter Constantine trans.) (New York: W. W. Norton, 2002), p. 445.

7 H. P. Lovecraft, quoted in Michel Houellebecq, *H. P. Lovecraft: Against the World, Against Life* (Dorna Khazeni trans.) (New York: Gollancz, 2008), p. 29.

8 Saul Bellow, 'Nobel Lecture', 12 December 1976. Available at: http://goo.gl/nRlDpK (last accessed on 24 September 2015).

9 Ibid.

10 This statement appears in J. G. Ballard, 'Which Way to Inner Space?', *New Worlds* (May 1962), reprinted in *A User's Guide to the Millennium: Essays and Reviews* (London: Flamingo, 1996), pp. 195–8.

11 There was a typewriter on his work table, not a wordprocessor. However, I do have an email his partner, Claire Walsh, wrote in order to pass on a message from Jim.

12 Henry James, 'Preface to Volume 15 of the New York Edition' (1909) in *The Art of the Novel: Critical Prefaces* (New York: Scribner, 1947), pp. 221–2.

Sensibility

This, and the following pieces, 'Souls' and 'Swing', were first delivered as lectures to the creative writing MA students at Birkbeck. I have kept them in their original form, rather than convert them into essays, because I speak too directly—right from the start—to the students in front of me. By 'you', I mean 'writers who think you might have something to learn from me'. So, imagine yourself seated at a table in Room 101, 30 Russell Square, at 6 p.m. on an early summer evening. It's a high, narrow, wood-panelled space, and traffic noise comes through the tall windows. I am in front of you, wearing a black V-neck jumper, white T-shirt, dark trousers. I am about to start speaking.

I don't think you're going to like this. It's probably going to hurt. If it doesn't hurt, there's a problem.

As part of your coursework, you'll have read Flannery O'Connor's essay 'Writing Short Stories' (1957).

She begins by saying this:

I have heard people say that the short story was one of the most difficult literary forms, and I've always tried to decide why people feel this way about what seems to me one of the most natural and fundamental ways of human expression. After all, you begin to hear and tell stories when you're a child, and there doesn't seem to be anything very complicated about it. I suspect that most of you have been telling stories all your lives, and yet here you sit—come to find out how to do it.[1]

As do you, here today.

Then last week, after I had written down some of these serene thoughts to use here today, my calm was shattered when I was sent seven of your manuscripts to read.

After this experience, I found myself ready to admit, if not that the short story is one of the most difficult literary forms, at least that it is more difficult for some than for others.

I still suspect that most people start out with some kind of ability to tell a story but that it gets lost along the way. Of course, the ability to create life with words is essentially a gift. If you have it in the first place, you can develop it; if you don't have it, you might as well forget it.[2]

When, last term, I asked my students what they thought of the essay—a good, teacherly question—the first of them to speak up said, 'Well, I think she's a bit of a git.'

Although Flannery O'Connor had—of course—read none of this particular student's writing, and this student was not at all being told to 'forget it', still this student felt compelled to take the comment personally; which, I think, is exactly how Flannery O'Connor intended it to be taken.

'Forget it . . . '—This is not the way we're used to being spoken to, particularly nowadays. We are accustomed to being given the party line on the American Dream: 'If you believe, you can achieve.'

Flannery O'Connor is advising some of us, some of you, to stop dreaming and forget it.

Forget it because you do not have the gift of creating life with words.

I'm going to return to forgetting it a bit later, but not in Flannery O'Connor's way.

I should start by saying, that for much of this talk you're probably going to think I'm a git, too.

Maybe even a bigger git than Flannery O'Connor because I *don't* believe that 'most people start out with some kind of ability to tell a story'.

I'm going to take that away from you.

I do believe that most people start out with some kind of ability to paint a wonderful, free, energetic picture in primary colours.

If you compare the paintings of three-year-olds to the paintings of thirteen-year-olds, there's no doubt that—during the intervening years—some element of uninhibited genius has disappeared.

Adolescent art is always the worst art.

I will go along with Flannery O'Connor so far as to say that you were all gifted, at an early stage, with the ability to speak charmingly, innovatively. You will have said things, in trying to speak the world clearly, which came at it sideways and got it more right than clichéd adult speech almost ever does.

But this haphazard charm of accuracy is something quite different to being able to tell a story.

And most of the time, you were probably running around shouting poo-bum-willy-fart poo-bum-willy-fart as all children do; all children who are allowed to get away with it, anyway.

Even though I've grown up to be a writer, I don't feel that, as a boy, I ever had a great, free, natural ability to tell stories. But Flannery O'Connor is quite stringent, quite determinedly gittish. All she's granting any of us is '*some kind* of ability'.

I'm going to make a number of statements to you—about writing, about good writing, about bad writing. I don't expect you to agree with all or any of them, but I'd like you to listen to them as carefully as possible; because I am saying them on the basis of a belief that there are potentially good writers who nevertheless write badly—potentially good writers who have always written badly.

As an aside, I can imagine someone objecting: 'You can't just say some writing is good and some bad.'

To which I'd reply, 'Yes, you can.'

Bad writing is mainly *boring* writing. It can be boring from any number of different causes. It can be boring because it's too confused or too logical, or boring because hysterical or lethargic, or boring because nothing truly happens.

If I give you a 400-page manuscript of an unpublished novel—something that I consider is made up of bad writing—you may read it to the end, but you will suffer as you do.

It's possible that you've never, in fact, had to read 80,000 words of bad writing.

The friend of a friend's novel.

I have.

On numerous occasions.

If you ask around, I'm sure you'll be able to find a really bad novel easily enough.

I don't mean by someone who is in this room, who has taken our classes.

I mean someone who has spent isolated years writing a book they are convinced is a great work of literature.

And when you're reading it, this novel, you'll know it's bad and you'll know what bad is.

The friend of a friend's novel may have some redeeming features—the odd nicely shaped sentence, the stray brilliant image. But it is still an agony to force oneself to keep going. It is still telling you nothing you didn't already know.

As an adjunct to this, I'd like to say one more thing:

Our tastes as readers may differ considerably, but it's very rare that when Russell (Celyn Jones), Julia (Bell) and I mark your dissertations, we disagree by more than two or three marks. And it's almost unheard of for us to end up disagreeing as to what mark a piece should receive.

We are by no means objective judges; I'm not asserting that. But we find consensus on bad writing 100 per cent of the time.

So, here are my propositions about bad writing—which you may still not believe exists.

Bad writers continue to write badly because they have many reasons—from their point of view, very *good* reasons—for wanting to continue writing in the way they do.

Writers are bad because they cleave to the causes of writing badly.

Bad writing is almost always a love poem addressed by the self to the self—even, or especially, when its overt topic is self-disgust.

Bad writing accepts that the person who will admire it first and most and last is the writer herself.

While bad writers may read a great many diverse works of fiction, they are unable, because unwilling, to perceive the things these works do which their own writing fails to do.

The most dangerous kind of writers for bad writers to read are what I call *Excuse Writers*—writers of the sort who seem to grant permission to others to borrow or imitate their failings.

I'll give you some concrete examples of Excuse Writers— Jack Kerouac, John Updike, David Foster Wallace, Virginia Woolf, Margaret Atwood, Maya Angelou.

Bad writers bulwark themselves against a confrontation with their own badness by reference to other writers of the past and present with whom they feel they share certain defence-worthy characteristics.

In order to protect their badness, bad writers form defensive admirations: 'If Updike can get away with these kind of half-page descriptions of women's breasts, I can too . . . ' or 'If Virginia Woolf is a bit woozy on spatiality, on putting things down concretely, I'll just let things float free . . . '

If another writer's work survives on charm, you will never be able to steal it, only imitate it in an embarrassingly obvious way. This writing will be adolescent, and adolescents lack charm—adolescents don't value charm.

Bad writing is written defensively; good writing is a making vulnerable—a making of the self as vulnerable as possible. The psychic risk of a novel such as Virginia Woolf's *The Waves* (1931) is vast—particularly for someone for whom psychic risk was so potentially debilitating and ultimately dangerous. When John Updike began writing *Rabbit, Run* (1960) all in the present tense, it was either going to be a great technical feat or a humiliating aesthetic misjudgement. (Excuse Writers aren't, in themselves, bad writers; not at all.)

Good writing is a hymn of praise to everything the self feels itself incapable of perceiving.

Good writing is of necessity a betrayal of the known self, of the version of the self we believe we know, and through that a betrayal of the known world—a betrayal into truth.

What are some of the direct causes of bad writing? What are some of the good reasons people have for continuing to write badly?

I'm going to suggest four mains ones—there are others, I'm sure.

1. Often, the bad writer will feel that they have a *particular* story they want to tell. It may be a story passed on to them by their grandmother or it maybe something that happened to them when they were younger. Until they've told this particular story (which may be what

has drawn them to taking writing seriously), they feel they can't move on. But because the material is so close to them, so precious to them, they can't mess around with it enough to learn how writing works. And, ultimately, they lack the will to sufficiently betray the material to make it true.

Bad writers think: 'I want to write this.'

2. Bad writers often want to rewrite a book by another writer that was written in a different time period, under completely different social conditions. Because it's a good book, they see no reason why they can't simply do the same kind of thing again—with the characters wearing different clothes, eating different food. They don't understand that even historical novels or science-fiction novels are a response to a particular historical moment. And pretending that the world isn't as it is— or, perhaps more accurately, that the world should still be as it once was—pretending this is disastrous for any serious fiction.

Bad writers think: 'I want to write this.'

3. Conversely, bad writers often write in order to forward a cause or enlarge other people's understanding of a contemporary social issue. Any attempt at all to write in order to make the world a better, fairer place—to write *stories*, I mean, not essays or polemics—any attempt to write world-improving fiction is almost certain to fail. Holding any value as more important than learning to be a good writer is dangerous. Put very

simply, your characters must be alive before they seek justice; justice will never be achieved by cardboard cutouts or mannequins; cardboard cutouts and mannequins don't need justice.

Bad writers think: 'I want to write this.'

4. Bad writers often believe they have very little left to learn, and that it is the literary world's fault that they have not yet been recognized, published, lauded and laurelled. It is a very destructive thing to believe that you are very close to being a good writer, and that all you need to do is keep going as you are, rather than completely reinvent what you are doing.

Bad writers think: 'I want to write this.'

Good writers think . . .

What do you think good writers think?—I think good writers think: 'This is being written.'

I'd like to sidestep. You've probably heard the words *good* and *bad* enough for one day. Although I'm afraid—git that I am—that they'll be recurring later.

What I'm now going to do is quote another essay by O'Connor. This one called 'The Nature and Aim of Fiction': 'In fact,' Flannery O'Connor says, 'so many people can now write competent stories that the short story as a medium is in danger of dying of competence. We want competence, but competence by itself is deadly. What is needed is the vision to go with it, and you do not get this from a writing class.'[3]

Competence, obviously, lies in between bad and good writing. But the territory isn't as simply mapped as that.

Competent can be a lot further from great than awful is.

To go from being a competent writer to being a great writer I think you have to risk being—or risk being seen as—a bad writer.

Here are a few propositions about competence:

Competence is deadly because it prevents the writer risking the humiliation that they will need to risk before they pass beyond competence.

Competence will never climb the trapeze, take a pie in the face, put its head in the lion's mouth, transfix a raging audience through wit and will and voice. Competence will never truly entertain because it will never run away to join the circus.

To write competently is to do a few magic tricks for friends and family; to write well is to run away to join the circus.

Your friends and family will love your tricks, because they love you. But try busking those tricks on the street. Try busking them alongside a magician who has been busking for 10 years, and earns their living busking.

When they are watching a magician, people don't want to go, 'Well done.' They want to go, 'Wow.'

Competence never makes people go wow.

At worst, on this course, we will have shown you how to do some magic tricks; at best, we will have taught you how to be a good magician; beyond that, though, is doing magic—and that you will have to learn for yourself. For what we can't show you is *how to do things you shouldn't be able to do.*

By this point in your Birkbeck creative writing MA, you are all far more likely to be competent writers than bad writers.

You're probably at the high point of thinking I'm a git, now.

You didn't take a creative writing MA in order to be told to run away with the circus.

The situation isn't that extreme, is it?

What's the point of saying all this if it isn't going to help; if I'm not going to give you some way of improving, as a writer?

But that's exactly what I'm going to do.

First, though, I'd like to take another sidestep—from the circus to high-level physics.

One of the questions that teachers of creative writing get asked most frequently, apart from 'How do I get an agent?' is 'Can creative writing be taught?'

For a long time, I didn't have a satisfactory answer to this. I would say that I believed creative writing couldn't be *taught*, but that it could be *learnt*. In other words, the process of going through a creative writing course could radically improve a student's stories, even though it perhaps wouldn't be the taught element which caused this improvement. I would say that the most useful thing for me, when I studied creative writing at the University of East Anglia, was to feel that I had a small audience who weren't (unlike my friends and family) emotionally committed to me as a person. I could hand in a piece of work to the class in the knowledge that they would respond without thinking they had to spend the rest of their week, or maybe even the rest of their lives, dealing with the consequences of being negative. It's a completely different feeling, knowing that you are writing for a small group of committed readers, rather than for the judges of open competitions, for skim-reading agents or work-experience people in publishers' offices. This, I used to say—the provision of an audience of peers—was how creative writing was learnt.

But a while ago I came up with what I thought was a better answer. *Yes, creative writing can be taught* but only in this sense: what we teach you on the creative writing MA is equivalent to Newtonian physics. In other words, it's a pretty good way to do the basic jobs of dealing with matter. If you want to predict where the moon will be at a certain time in the future, Newtonian physics will enable you to do this—at least to the extent that your telescope won't be pointing in completely the wrong direction. Newtonian physics, for most things you're going to come across, gets the job done.

However, as we've discovered since Newton, the universe— including both the moon and the telescope and also your eye— the universe doesn't operate according to Newtonian physics. The universe exists on a quantum level, and the rules of quantum physics are often in direct contradiction of Newtonian physics. In the quantum world, things can simultaneously exist and not exist. In the quantum world, things can travel backwards in time. Quantum physics means matter can do things it shouldn't be able to do.

Now, transferring this over to creative writing: what we do on the MA is, I'd say, to teach you the equivalent of Newtonian physics. The technical stuff that we go through—point of view, use of time, narrative tone—all of this will let you find the moon, observe it, predict it. But if you want to do good or great writing—what I think of as good or great writing—you are going to have to step up to Quantum physics. And this is where the analogy between creative writing and physics starts to break down. Because while you *can* teach quantum physics to very bright students, it's almost impossible to teach creative writing on the quantum-equivalent level.

Why?

Because on that level it's ceased to be creative writing and has become just really good or great writing. And to say anything useful about that, your tutor would have to be in your head, commenting on your vague plans and your specific choices within sentences. But commentary, at this point, is probably the last thing you need. You may not even, strictly, be conscious of what you're doing. You'll just be following your developed instincts as to what seems right.

Good writers think: 'This is being written.'

To tie this in with the running away to join the circus: Newtonian physics makes the crowd say, 'Well done'; quantum physics makes the crowd say, 'Wow'.

I'd like to turn now to the subject of this talk, which I've done a remarkable job of not mentioning before: Sensibility.

The reason for this is that Sensibility belongs very much to the quantum world of writing. And, in order to reach it, I needed to pass through bad and competent writing.

And, yes, for those that are worried, I'm soon going to come to that quintessentially quantum writer, Fernando Pessoa (1888–1935), whose *The Book of Disquiet* (published in 1984) I asked you to look at in advance of today.

The best thing I've heard said about Sensibility came in an interview between the poets John Betjeman and Philip Larkin in a documentary (*Down Cemetery Road*) made in 1964 for the BBC programme *Monitor*.

John Betjeman asks Philip Larkin: 'What sort of attitude do you take to adverse criticism?' And Philip Larkin replies:

> Well, I don't know [if] you feel this, but I feel it very strongly—I read that, you know, I'm a miserable sort of fellow, writing a sort of Welfare State sub-poetry; doing it well, perhaps, but it isn't really what poetry is and it isn't really the sort of poetry we want; but I wonder whether it ever occurs to the writer of criticism like that that really one *agrees* with them but what one writes is based so much on the kind of person one is, and the kind of environment one's had, and has now, that one doesn't really choose the poetry one writes, one writes the kind of poetry one has to write or can write.[4]

Here, although he doesn't say it, Larkin is describing Sensibility. His own disappointing Sensibility.

What do I mean by Sensibility? Is it the same thing as in the title of *Sense and Sensibility* (1811) by Jane Austen?

In a way yes, and in a way no.

It was in the mid-eighteenth century that the idea of Sensibility came to prominence—as much as something to be mocked as something to be proud of. Novels were full of what my father would call 'sensitive little flowers'.

Slightly later, the Romantic poets adapted the idea of a distinctive hyper-sensitivity to the things of the world; if one had Sensibility, one would be able to react appropriately or even originally to (here's a very common example) the sight of the snow-covered heights of Mont Blanc. One might even feel moved to write a sonnet on the feelings stirred in one by the vision.

The understanding of Sensibility I'm talking about has developed from this proud Romantic notion. It's the particularity of someone's response to Mont Blanc that displays their particular Sensibility. And, because we're no longer Romantics, or we try to kid ourselves we're not, this sensibility doesn't necessarily have to express itself as appreciation of the sublimity of the natural world.

W. H. Auden, for example, said: 'Apart from nature, geometry's all there *is* [. . .]. Geometry belongs to man. Man's got to assert himself against Nature all the *time* [. . .]. I hate sunsets and flowers. And I loathe the *sea*. The sea is formless . . . '.[5] Here, Auden is defining himself as an anti-Romantic Sensibility, by aesthetically attacking the things the Romantics held dearest. Where they valued mountains, he would value disused Victorian industrial machinery.

And he would do this, he asserted, even before he became a poet: 'From the age of four to thirteen I had a series of passionate affairs with pictures of, to me, particularly attractive water-turbines, winding-engines, roller-crushers, etc., and I was never so emotionally happy as when I was underground.'[6]

Auden was unusual in having a Sensibility that revealed itself, to him and to others, even in adolescence. People like Auden end up being called geniuses. But I think it's more likely that they are people who begin working on their Sensibility very hard and at a very early age—even if they are not aware that that's what they are doing.

Which brings me, at last, to Fernando Pessoa and to *The Book of Disquiet*.

Although to call it a book is to make it appear more planned and finished than it ever was.

If you've researched Pessoa a little, you will have found out the unimportant facts:

— that he lived a quiet life, working as a translator in Lisbon

— that he was known in his life as a poet; in fact, as *more than one poet*, because be wrote in completely different styles under a series of what he called 'heteronyms'

— that *The Book of Disquiet* was left unfinished by Pessoa, and that each printed *Book of Disquiet* we have is a version created after Pessoa's death by editors who have tried to put his fragmented manuscripts into readable order

— that whichever edition of *The Book of Disquiet*[7] you have looked at, you won't have read all of it—and unless you learn Portuguese and become a Pessoa scholar you probably never will

So, why did I choose Pessoa as the required reading?

Well, I hope you will remember my earlier reference to the bad novel you might borrow, and the bad writer who had written it—the friend of a friend: 'I mean someone who has spent isolated years writing a book they are convinced is a great work of literature.'

This was Pessoa:

Today's dreamers are perhaps the great precursors of the ultimate science of the future, not that I believe in any such ultimate science [. . .]. Sometimes I invent a metaphysics like this with all the respectful scrupulousness of attention of someone engaged in real scientific work. As I've said before, it reaches the point where I may really be doing just that.[8]

This was Pessoa, and he was not deluded—he *was* writing a great work of literature.

But *The Book of Disquiet*—in creative writing MA terms, in Newtonian physics terms, in some of my own terms—looks very like bad writing. It has many of the faults that the worst writing has. It centres on one isolated autobiographical character who believes, against all evidence, that they are worthy of universal attention. It hardly ever engages this character with another character. There is almost no dialogue. There are very few scenes. The character is depressed and, probably to some readers, depressing. There appears to be no chance of change within his life. There is no story as such. The writing is disorganized, repetitious, seemingly directionless. The world described is limited, drab, boring.

And yet—and this is where we flip to the quantum world, and go beyond creative writing—and yet this is a great, endlessly readable, endlessly fascinating work of fiction.

Why?

Sensibility.

The Book of Disquiet is a book that works consistently to remove anything from itself which is neither an examination of Sensibility nor an expression of Sensibility.

Take any random page and it will almost certainly contain a statement of the sort: 'I see things like this' or 'I have always seen things like this' or 'I wish I hadn't always seen things like this . . .'

I took a random page and found:

When I first came to Lisbon the sound of someone playing scales on a piano used to drift down from the flat above, the monotonous piano practice of a little girl I never saw. Today, through processes of assimilation I fail to comprehend, I discover that if I open the door to the cellars of my soul, those repetitive scales are still audible, played by a girl who is now Mrs Someone-or-other, or else dead and shut up in a white place over-grown by black cypresses.[9]

Imagine how this would be workshopped—'Look, this is just an inert description. How about if another girl moves in above the narrator and starts playing scales, and how about if he meets and falls in love with her mother, or with her, or with the idea of playing piano himself? Make something happen.'

Pessoa is about the removal of making-something-happen in order to allow Sensibility to take the happening's place.

In this, and in other things, he is a more extreme version of other modern writers of a similar period—Franz Kafka, Robert Walser, Bruno Schulz, Marcel Proust, Virginia Woolf—all of whom I would recommend you investigate with Sensibility in mind.

Pessoa's writing is great because, and only because, he has a fascinating Sensibility. It is a Sensibility he has cultivated but it is also a Sensibility that oppresses and poisons him.

The Book of Disquiet is constantly summing itself up, but here is one definition of Pessoa's project: 'Abdicate from life so as not to abdicate from oneself.'[10]

This is quantum writing—writing that has risked total humiliation in order to pass beyond competence. It is great or it is worthless. It is doing something that it shouldn't be able to do.

So, why don't we teach Sensibility as part of the MA?

Perhaps if we had an exclusively tutorial system and 10 years with each student, we could.

I doubt it, though.

Because Sensibility is partly about rejecting those things which can be taught—rejecting those things which others believe worth teaching.

Sensibility is the difference between creative writing and writing—meaning good writing and especially great writing.

This is why I chose Sensibility as something worth talking about at this stage of this term. If you'd heard it mentioned in Week One, it would have become just another thing to angst over: 'Oh God, not only is my use of point of view wobbly but I don't have an original and fascinating Sensibility. Maybe I should forget it?'

Forget it.

Which brings us back to where we started, that old git Flannery O'Connor. Perhaps now she seems less of a git than she did; now that I've become the über-git. But I hope I've supplied an explanation of her words on telling stories and on competent writing.

My definition would be: 'Competent writing is writing that lacks an interesting Sensibility.'

However, Flannery O'Connor was clearly aware of Sensibility, she just called it something else: 'We want competence, but competence by itself is deadly. What is needed is the vision to go with it . . . '[11]

I think Sensibility is a better word than Vision because it not only suggests that you need to see a different world, it also suggests that you need to *inhabit* and *create* a different world.

And I've already said that Sensibility is unteachable.

Does that mean that the talk is going to end right now?

Bummer.

No.

Because I think that, without teaching you, I can give you some suggestions which might help you develop as a writer and, through this, develop your Sensibility.

First, you do need to forget it. Forget it and give up completely and for ever.

Then, immediately, you need to start again, but *not* from where you finished before. Do try to forget where that was—for the moment at least.

Cease to attempt to be what you will never succeed in being. If you are Larkin, there's no point in you trying to be (as he did) D. H. Lawrence or W. B. Yeats. A great deal of the business of developing a unique Sensibility is to do with the failure to be X or Y, the failure to be other than one is.

I repeat, slightly altered, cease attempting to become what you stand no chance of ever convincingly being.

93

To develop as a writer, and so as a Sensibility, there are four basic things you can do: writing, rewriting, reading, rereading.

I wouldn't put them in this order of usefulness, though. My ranking would go something like this, from least useful to most useful:

4. Writing

3. Reading

2. Rereading

1. Rewriting

Here, by rewriting, I also mean intensively and honestly rereading what you have written.

These four things should be obvious to you by this point in the course. Here are a few other, less usual suggestions:

Write a list of your obsessions. Allow it to be as short or as long as it wants to be. Add to it over the following week, whenever a forgotten thing occurs. At the end of the week, go over it once more. Take out any item you think is there to impress or in any way speak to other people. Now, who does this list remind you of? Read it. Read it again. Then destroy it. A week later, repeat the exercise. You can try to remember what was on the first list, if you like, but it's better to return to the question, 'What obsesses me?' This second list, you can—if you want—keep. Perhaps it will come in handy.

Take five good but not necessarily great novels quickly, randomly, from your bookshelves. Read the opening page (just that, not a word more)—the opening page of each of them. Then read just the opening page of your most recent piece of work. How do they announce themselves to you, these other writers?

And how do you find yourself announcing yourself? How, if you could choose, would you like to announce yourself?

Create a pseudonym you don't care for, and begin immediately to write as that person. Don't worry any longer about whether or not what you are writing is good. Just write as energetically as you can. After a week, compare what you wrote, spontaneously-as-another, with what you wrote the week before, consciously-as-yourself. How do the two periods compare? Is one truer to you than the other? If not, why not?

Choose a writer whose work you know really well. Now, write a parody of them—exaggerating every feature of their style but still applying it to the kind of subject matter they applied it to. A week later, reread what you've done. Where do you fail to be true to the parodied writer? Are there any gaps through which you can peak at your own Sensibility? Writers always used to learn by imitating. (The first thing we have by Keats is an imitation of Spenser.) Because when a writer puts a piece of work forward and says, 'This is an imitation of so-and-so,' the reader looks for the places where the imitation succeeds but more so for the places where it fails. And these failures are where the two Sensibilities fail to coincide. So they are places you can use to investigate your own Sensibility. If you were to do conscious imitations of a series of writers, you would learn a great deal about yourself as a writer.

After you have done the previous exercise, write another parody, this time trying to take the original writer's Sensibility but using it to write about something they never (to your knowledge) wrote about. If it's Hemingway, say, have your version of him write about the doings of a family of white mice or a women's institute coach trip to London to see *Priscilla, Queen of the Desert*. If it's Jane Austen, have your version of her write about a mafia killing or a speed-dating event or zombies.

Maybe not zombies.

Stop writing your first drafts on a computer. Even if you find your handwriting unusable (because illegible, because slow), a page of handwritten manuscript will reveal more to you of your own Sensibility than the neutrality of Microsoft Word ever will. The faults of your writing are covered over when not actually exacerbated by wordprocessing. The stage of typing up a handwritten draft—of seeing it transform from rough scribbly letters to respectable-looking text—is very clarifying. But if the words have never been rough and scribbly they will never gain those qualities that rough scribbly writing often has—intimacy, transience. In one way, the words will always have been public. And a feeling of privacy is one of the most attractive qualities in writing.

Also, the physical labour of writing is useful; increase rather than decrease this for yourself. By doing this (handwriting) you are inhabiting your sentences, allowing them to pass through your body in a less distanced way than if you simply type them out. Don't try to rush to the final draft; learn the difficult art of dwelling.

In all of these things, don't be concerned at all whether you are writing badly or well. Simply try to write as energetically, as committedly, as you possibly can.

I'm going to conclude with a third set of propositions. I began by trying to define good and bad writing. Then I went on to competent writing—with some side references to running away to join the circus, busking magicians and quantum physics. I'd like to finish by making some propositions about Sensibility. This is on the basis that great writing is writing that displays or reveals a fascinating and unique Sensibility.

A unique Sensibility begins to find things very important which the majority of others have always seen as trivial.

A unique Sensibility will find mountains which are not mountains.

A unique Sensibility refuses not to see as *still* important things which the majority of others believe were last year or last decade or last millennium's concern.

And original Sensibility is formed by encountering original obstacles. The great writer discovers a unique obstacle, just for herself. There are far fewer obstacles than styles or Sensibilities.

Proust's obstacle: to incorporate the time of a life into a book.

Joyce's: to refer to everything all the time without a moment's cease.

Beckett's: to remove human referents as totally as possible without removing human referents totally.

Woolf's: to depict idiosyncratic minds which are yet still porous to other idiosyncratic minds.

Pessoa's: to write about no subject other than writing about Sensibility.

Where do differences in individual Sensibility stem from? This is perhaps the trickiest question.

I would say that it has something to do with time.

A person's Sensibility stems from a person's unique relation to time, of which we have very few maps.

There are conventional relations to time, as expressed in fiction. Genre fiction depends on conventional relations to time. Literary fiction is a kind of genre fiction.

There are also dominant relations to time, in any given literary period.

I'd say that a writer like Raymond Carver has a limiting, standardizing relation to fictional time—if you imitate him too closely. The simplification of tenses, avoiding even the past perfect, and allowing the past historic to overtake all, reduces the chances for writers to display their unique relation to time.

In other words, 'She had . . . ' predominates over 'She had had . . . ' or 'She had been having . . . ' or 'She hadn't been having . . . ' or 'She might perhaps have been having . . . ' or 'She will have been having . . . ' or 'She would have been, perhaps, having . . . '

I'm not trying to encourage you to write like Henry James or Proust. Just to realize that Carver's obstacle isn't your obstacle. His time isn't your time.

Examine your unique relation to time and examine how you express it in words.

I have used enough of your time.

Good luck.

It's time for questions.

Notes

1 Flannery O'Connor, 'Writing Short Stories' in *Mystery and Manners: Occasional Prose* (Sally and Robert Fitzgerald eds) (New York: Farrar, Straus and Giroux, 1957), p. 87.

2 Ibid., pp. 87–8.

3 Flannery O'Connor, 'The Nature and Aim of Fiction' in *Mystery and Manners: Occasional Prose* (Sally and Robert Fitzgerald eds) (New York: Farrar, Straus and Giroux, 1957), p. 86.

4 Philip Larkin, Interview with John Betjeman, *Monitor* (BBC Television), 1964. Available at: https://goo.gl/VxQC9W (last accessed on 1 December 2015).

5 W. H. Auden, quoted as 'Weston' in Christopher Isherwood, *Lions and Shadows* (London: Vintage, 2013), p. 142.

6 W. H. Auden, *The English Auden: Poems, Essays and Dramatic Writings, 1927–1939* (Edward Mendelson ed.) (London: Faber and Faber, 1977), pp. 397–8.

7 The two most easily available editions in English are: *The Book of Disquiet* (Margaret Jull Costa trans.) (London: Serpent's Tail, 1991); *The Book of Disquiet* (Richard Zenith trans.) (London: Penguin, 2001).

8 Pessoa, *The Book of Disquiet* (Margaret Jull Costa trans.), p. 172.

9 Ibid., p. 57.

10 Ibid., p. 156.

11 O'Connor, 'The Nature and Aim of Fiction', p. 86.

Souls

Why Souls?

What could be more irrelevant?

What's Souls got to do with anything, Toby?

You're not going to go all Archbishop of Canterbury on us, are you?

I do this summer lecture every year. When deciding what its subject is to be, I think about two things:

What will be useful for you to hear,

and

what will be useful for me to learn to say.

I try to choose the thing that has been bugging me the most, because it's been on the point of expressing itself.

And I try to speak very directly to you about questions beyond the conventionally technical—point of view, dialogue, etc. However, this year, in a very immediate way, it seems to me that Souls—and the attitude you as a writer take towards them—*are* a matter of what might be called *deep technique*. Not style—Souls don't seem to have a lot to do with that. Not style, but the *matter* of what you are doing in your writing, and what it is within that writing that will make it matter to another person. I think this addresses the ways most readers judge writing: *Do I believe in this character? Do I care about what's going on? Is this piece of writing alive—alive enough for me to forget that it's just a piece of writing?* And, if I'm not wrong, what I will give you today is a deeply practical way of addressing the technical problems of unconvincing characters, inert situations and dead or deathly writing.

A couple of years ago, my summer lecture was about Sensibility; last year, it was Sentences. Sensibility is the *what*—the *what* of your writing; Sentences are the *where*. Souls, the easy answer says, are the *who*. But I think that's not exact. Souls are also what (or who) you write with, what (or who) you write about and what (or who) you write for.

I'm going to call this set of relationships *the triangle*: on one point is you, on the next is your human or human-like subject, on the last is the reader. Existing between all three points are the English language in its current state, fiction in its current state and the world in its current state. When I say *the triangle*, this is what I mean.

But immediately I am going to complicate the triangle by drawing in a line to show there is a difference between, a distance between, you, the author, and him or her or it, the narrator.

This is already a philosophical question—whether, in writing, one can speak through or out of another person. It may be that one of the deep technical solutions we end up with is that, beyond the issues of who authors the words, the reader may be allowed to feel that their Soul is in communication or even communion with another Soul—not direct, but as close to direct as such communication ever can be. The narrator, if this is true, becomes irrelevant—and the reading becomes intensely, embarrassingly Romantic.

I am going too far too fast. But I hope I've now dealt with the opening questions-in-the-room: *Why Souls? What could be more irrelevant? What's Souls got to do with anything?*

These challenges, though, are likely to be reinforced by an even tougher set: *Why Lawrence? Who could be more irrelevant? What's* Women in Love *(1920) got to do with anything?*

Lawrence is, in a very deliberate way, a *catastrophic* writer; after him, the deluge—*with* him, the deluge. But the deluge never really came—or those flood waters that *did* come have now receded completely.

Some of you, I am sure, don't particularly like Lawrence. In fact, you hate him—hate him most of all for his irrelevance. One person here came up to me and said, 'You're making us read D. H. Lawrence. I had to read him at school and now, 20 years later, you're making me read him again.' Then, even without my saying anything, he said, 'I suppose once every 20 years isn't too bad.' And I back this up. Lawrence is someone you should read at least once every 20 years. But I know these are still questions-in-the-room: *Why should I have read this? I didn't get anything from it.*

And that's my first answer to *Why Lawrence?* Exactly *because* he is so hateful, so irrelevant; because, partly, he seems so gloriously ignorant of our technologies of self—the technologies with which we have replaced not Souls but (and I will come back to this soon) the very question of Souls.

A culture reveals itself nowhere more clearly than in those specific things it regards as useless. And, like it or not, you exist within this culture at this moment—and your writing will have to deal with it somehow, even if only by choosing in which direction and how fast you're going to run away.

At the start I said I chose to lecture on *the thing that's been bugging me the most*: so, Sensibility, Sentences, Souls.

In order to go forward, I need to give you an idea of why Souls have been bugging me, and why I've ended up forcing you to read *Women in Love*. I am going to travel quite a long way, partly into Toby Litt's autobiography, partly into literary history—this is necessary, not just as background but also as an exploration of the stuff that is going on all immediately outside of the triangle: the states of the English language, fiction, the world.

The beginning, for me, was a poem I wrote in 2005. It's an imaginary dialogue between me and another person, a sceptic. This is it:

Grant me the Soul—what then?
Speak as essence, badly; speak,
predictably, as putrescence. *No.*
So you refuse? Then grant me anything
essential at all. I'll take, I'll take
beauty, and an improvement towards
it, line by line. Even philosophy
might admit the seventh draft to be
better than the first. *No*, you say, *not
better—and certainly not more
beautiful.* Then at least leave me perception;

each eye to have its hole, seeing
outwardly. Or less even than that,
direction, not place, point or origin.
Grant me the length of the line,
sideways.

Then *No* again.
No repeatedly and without anger.

I understand—I hold your
refusal to be absolute. And that
I will take; there I will start; this I will say.

At the time, I wasn't sure why I was writing the poem; I'm still not sure. Maybe just as a way of getting the word *Soul* onto the page for the first time, in a reasonably unironic form.

Jump to another inexplicable act, much more recent. At the end of last year I was going down the stairs into SKOOB books (in the Brunswick Centre), and I saw a water-damaged blue Pelican edition of F. R. Leavis' *The Great Tradition* (1948). It wasn't on sale. It was being given away for free. No one wants F. R. Leavis these days, water-damaged or pristine. But I picked the copy up, and later began reading it—and I found *The Great Tradition*, surprisingly, quite sympathetic; not repulsive; a bit simple- minded; very averse to any kind of paradox; ideological in an apparently non-ideological way; ultimately, and sympathetically, vitalist—on the side of vivid life. F. R. Leavis was the buried credo of my English teachers. And it's impossible to read *The Great Tradition* without observing Leavis constructing his lineage of greats—his generation-forming canon of what we should read, because it is what most reads us. 'What I think and judge,' he writes, 'I have stated as responsibly and clearly as I can. Jane Austen, George Eliot, Henry James, Conrad, and D. H. Lawrence: the great tradition of the English novel is *there*.'[1]

But Leavis leaves Lawrence out of the book itself, devoting a whole separate volume to him in *D. H. Lawrence: Novelist* (1955).

I found a copy of this in a charity shop in Bedford; and immediately switched my reading from the bits on George Eliot and Henry James in *The Great Tradition* to the volume on Lawrence. What was it about Lawrence that Leavis and, later, so many writers of the 1950s and 60s—mainly Larkin— found so exciting, so necessary? And why has Lawrence become so completely occluded, so shameful a light?

In my reading, I like to confront myself with oppositions— things I don't get. What's wrong with them? What's wrong with me?

As I began *D. H. Lawrence: Novelist*, and read alongside the short stories Leavis focuses on—'Daughters of the Vicar' (1914), 'The Captain's Doll' (1923) and 'St Mawr' (1925)—I found a wonderful, flexible writer—very much to my changing taste. But I also found difficulties.

These difficulties connected with another piece of confronta- tional reading I had recently done: Saul Bellow's *Herzog* (1964).

(If you are annoyed at me for forcing you to read *Women in Love*, be thankful I didn't add *Herzog*, too. Although, if you want any follow-up reading to this lecture, that's where you should head.)

Why did the difficulties I found in Lawrence connect with those I found in Bellow? What were my objections? This takes us back to what I said about the *matter* of your writing, and why your writing might matter to another person. I found that both Lawrence and Bellow *do* matter to me—in a way that Raymond Carver or Amy Hempel or J. G. Ballard or Jennifer Egan do not.

Both Lawrence and Bellow seem, to many critics, to have got the human subject completely wrong; to have engaged with a nostalgic or wishful version of what we essentially are. We are not Souls, we are the current technologies of the self. Both Lawrence and Bellow have, in their fiction and in their critical writings, made Souls more material than they can possibly be.

That's certainly what I would have thought, back at the time my first book was published, and even as late as 2010, when I lectured on 'Literature and Technology'. I am, in speaking about this, partly speaking against my earlier self; that's what I think is necessary, at this point; that's the thing I am learning how to say.

And so I chose Souls to talk about because it is a subject that has been profoundly bugging me—less spiritually than aesthetically; though the aesthetic is often where the spiritual manifests, when it's embarrassed.

There will be some embarrassment in this lecture, and some in this room; I hope so—unless the cheeks are glowing, the blood is making some display of itself, you're not really reading Lawrence; unless the gorge rises, and you force yourself not to swallow, you're not taking your Bellow neat.

This is the question of Souls, the one I've now arrived back at. (The autobiographical excursion is over; the literary historical one is just ahead.) Why do I now find that Lawrence and Bellow matter to me more than the other writers I named, and many others I didn't? More pressingly, why do I think they should matter equally to other people—to you?

The answer to this isn't an argument, it's a niggle—a niggling feeling—a niggling feeling to do with the triangle.

This is what Saul Bellow said in a talk he gave in 1975 called 'A Matter of the Soul': 'What novelists, composers, singers have in common is the soul to which their appeal is made, whether it is barren or fertile, empty or full, whether the soul knows something, feels something, loves something.'[2]

Here and elsewhere Bellow's assumption is of Souls at all points of the triangle: Souls as artists, Souls as subjects and Souls as audience.

That niggling feeling, arriving in me gradually, over the course of years, is this—that certain writers (chiefly Lawrence and Bellow) have something that other writers I admire (say Ballard and Egan) ostentatiously lack; something that I myself have lacked.

The something Lawrence and Bellow have is something at all three points of the triangle: in believing they might be possessed of Souls, in believing their human subjects might appear to be Soul-owning, and in believing their readers might be Soul-encumbered beings.

This is the niggle, put as clearly as I can put it:

What if—looking back over the art of the twentieth century—I have started to suspect that the most enduring of it (so far, and not much time has passed)—all right, try again: the most vivid art is art produced *on the basis of the question of Souls*. Not, I'd say, on the definite assumption of Souls; but around a negotiation with the question of what it means not to have a Soul, and to work towards a Soul, and to do so amid the doubt that anyone could ever attain such a thing.

I am going to have to define Souls, aren't I? I'm not going to be able to escape this room without doing so.

By Souls, I do not mean immortal Christian Souls, that—depending on the level of misbehaviour of their owners—can be dropkicked to heaven or doubled-parked in purgatory or trapdoored down to hell.

By Souls, I do not mean positive, singular entities but indistinguishable excesses to the merely physical, merely social.

By Souls, I mean what creates the possibility of seamless transition between different and otherwise incommensurate modes of being.

By Souls, I mean the assumption that what I write has access to meaning beyond the merely social.

In other words, that what I or you write is about something—and not about nothing.

I hope these definitions advance us a bit. They should become clearer, as we go along. For now, they are probably too wordy and therefore unsatisfactory.

As far as writing goes, let's leave it that Souls are characters who move in the direction of trying to create a Soul, even if they would explicitly disbelieve in such a thing. Characters are shown acting in the hope that their acts will be meaningful.

If I haven't satisfied you with a decent definition, at least grant that I have attempted—perhaps embarrassingly—to say what I mean. I'm going on niggles here, not notions. Professor Catherine Brown in the first of her Oxford lectures on Lawrence, which you can find on iTunes University, said that, 'Lawrence himself says that he can't define Soul, "but nor could a bike define its rider. Our mistake is to pretend that there's no-one in the saddle."'[3]

It's time for the historical excursion—back beyond the birth of the European novel, Cervantes' *Don Quixote* (1605).

This that follows is Jack Goody, surveying the change from religious to secular storytelling, in a two-volume, world-spanning book *The Novel*, edited by Franco Moretti.

> The early narratives of Christian Europe were legitimized as being accounts of heavenly miracles (the New Testament) or of the lives of saints, in the same way that painting and drawing became possible in the early Middle Ages if the subjects were drawn from religious sources. Even in the eighteenth century, it was this aspect of John Bunyan's *Pilgrim's Progress* that rendered it acceptable to many Nonconformist Puritans.
>
> The modern novel, after Daniel Defoe, was essentially a secular tale, a feature that is comprised within the meaning of 'realistic' . . . .[4]

But Defoe (*c.*1660–1731) isn't as crucial a break as Cervantes (1547–1616).

Don Quixote, the Man of La Mancha—wisely or profligately—spends his life in a delusory quest after the kind of glory gained by the knights-errant of his favourite reading matter. Don Quixote mistakes the banal objects of the world surrounding him for the enchanted objects of romance.

The American critic Harold Bloom writes this about *Don Quixote*, in his introduction to a new translation:

> Cervantes, like Shakespeare, gives us a secular transcendence [. . .]. However good a Catholic he may (or may not) have been, Cervantes is interested in heroism and not sainthood [. . .]. It is the transcendent element in Don Quixote that ultimately persuades us of his greatness, partly because it is set against the deliberately coarse, frequently sordid context of the panoramic book. And again it is important to note that this transcendence is secular and literary, and not Catholic.[5]

Going back again to the *Why Souls?* question, from the beginning: you, in your writing, are likely to be dealing with exactly this: 'transcendence [that] is secular and literary, not Catholic'. Harold Bloom, here, provides a pretty good definition of the epiphany story.

You may have gone along with asking, *What could be more irrelevant? What's Souls got to do with anything?* But if ever you decide to write an epiphany, I think you should at least be asking yourself, *Who or what is this experience happening to? Who or what is gaining knowledge in this chiming moment? Am I, in what I write, suggesting there is a meaning beyond the merely social?*

In your writing, I would suggest, you are all interested in 'heroism and not sainthood'.

Don Quixote is not principally a story about salvation, the only question for a good Catholic. *Don Quixote* is about asking the question of the Soul. What is this thing, this questing person, who may or may not be possessed of a Soul and whose actions may or may not affect or express the state of that Soul? What does or doesn't this person's quest mean?

To make a grand statement: the novel is not a form that orthodox Catholicism could ever have invented.

The Catholic establishment would have seen both the writing and reading of novels as, at best, a waste of time and, at worst, an encouragement to sin.

There *are*, belatedly, Catholic novelists—Graham Greene tries to be principally interested in salvation and damnation but he is, in fact, principally interested in theological quirks. To take the example of *The Power and the Glory* (1940), we are presented with a damned Soul (the whiskey priest) who is, despite this, the vessel of salvation (the mass); or *Brighton Rock* (1938), the Soul who seems inevitably damned, because evil (Pinkie), yet who achieves salvation through last-minute split-second but genuine repentance. But we as readers are not seeing every Soul at stake, within the novel; minor characters must take their own chances. Muriel Spark's *The Ballad of Peckham Rye* (1960)—displays the gaddings about of a maybe/maybe-not devil in a so-banal-as-to-hardly-seem-worth-redeeming world.

But the subject of Western art since the Renaissance has been the person—the mainly social being—the person who may or may not have a Soul that may or may not be immortal.

At the very cultural moment that the Soul became questionable, the novel came into being.

Here, the Soul is what's in doubt; and without something in doubt, there is no subject.

Without the question of the Soul, the human subject of fiction is (by definition) less meaningful. Because it was the Soul that was previously the element within a human being that gave their life meaning; because, now that the element of certainty had been taken away, we were and are left with the entirely rationally reduced physiological body, sociological presence, economic participant, mediated subject.

We are interested in all of these things, but to what extent?

One of my definitions of Souls was this:

By Souls, I mean what creates the possibility of seamless transition between different and otherwise incommensurate modes of being.

At the time, this was probably the most opaque definition. But what I mean is this: when writing about a character you can, within the same sentence, say what they think or remember, how they feel physically, how they are (in fact) physically despite them not even knowing it, or what they look like to another person. And, between these modes of being, there exist no transitions. You pass from one to the other quite without bump or friction. Because the thing experiencing them is the same being, even if—intellectually—you'd argue they aren't a unified whole of any sort. Fictional characters are unified subjects, existing under a name.

It seems to me that in this, in the fictional subject, there is—unless you spend a lot of time deliberately undoing it—an assumption of a Soul. Perhaps that Soul is merely the unity granted by referring to a character by a name. But I think it is also that the character is constantly being pushed (in action, in description) to expand beyond their name, and not being under-mined by being referred to as a completely physiological being.

Put very basically, people do not read Mills & Boon novels to read the chemical equations that might explain why *she* is attracted to *him*. Novels are expansive in meaning, not reductive.

This brings me to Saul Bellow's Nobel Lecture, which I asked you to read. After his social arguments, Bellow comes to a metaphysical climax:

> The essence of our real condition, the complexity, the confusion, the pain of it, is shown to us in glimpses, in what Proust and Tolstoy thought of as 'true impressions.' This essence reveals and then conceals itself. When it goes away it leaves us again in doubt. But we never seem to lose our connection with the depths from which these glimpses come. The sense of our real powers, powers we seem to derive from the universe itself, also comes and goes. We are reluctant to talk about this because there is nothing we can prove, because our language is inadequate and because few people are willing to risk talking about it. They would have to say, 'There is a spirit' and that is taboo. So almost everyone keeps quiet about it, although almost everyone is aware of it.[6]

This comes just after Bellow has said, 'At the center, humankind struggles with collective powers for its freedom, the individual struggles with dehumanization for the possession of his soul.'

What Bellow is saying here is very similar, I would say, to what Lawrence says in an essay, 'Why the Novel Matters' (1926). I don't want to quote that yet, but I do want to emphasize that 'Matters'—and start looking into it.

Let's turn to *Women in Love*. Lawrence's novels are about human encounters in all variations—male–male, female–female but mostly female–male / male–female—that *mean* something.

Even if you don't follow my argument far enough to reach the question of Souls, you would admit that for Lawrence the interrelation between, say, Birkin and Ursula *means* a lot more than the interrelation between any two characters in any J. G. Ballard or Jennifer Egan novel; in fact, means a lot more than between any two characters in any contemporary English-language novel.

(It is this striving to exist only in meaningfulness that is one of the things that makes people hate Lawrence.)

What goes on between the characters in *Women in Love*, moment by obsessed-observed moment, has an effect on what you might call the average level of cosmic rightness.

If there is disharmony, the entire universe is—overall—less harmonious; and less harmonious in a way that is greater than it would be, statistically, if Birkin and Ursula made up two billionths of the extant human material (in the universe).

Whether or not *these two humans* work something out between them *means* something, metaphysically, because upon it depends the question of whether *any* two humans can work it out.

This is what is at stake between Birkin and Ursula.

'I do think,' he said, 'that the world is held together by the mystical conjunction, the ultimate unison between people—a bond. And the ultimate bond is between man and woman.'[7]

Your object is already there on the page. Ursula says it: 'But it's such old hat . . . '

But I don't think this is old hat at all.

J. G. Ballard wrote a famous essay 'Which Way to Inner Space?' (1962) in which he said that science fiction should abandon journeys into outer space, and look into the human—well, he was J. G. Ballard, so he didn't call it a Soul. And also, as he was J. G. Ballard, he didn't look to Lawrence for an example of where an astonishing voyage into inner space might have already taken place.

'There is,' [Birkin] said, in a voice of pure abstraction, 'a final me which is stark and impersonal and beyond responsibility. So there is a final you. And it is there I would want to meet you—not in the emotional, loving plane—but there beyond, where there is no speech and no terms of agreement. There we are two stark, unknown beings, two utterly strange creatures, I would want to approach you, and you me. And there could be no obligation, because there is no standard for action there, because no understanding has been reaped from that plane. It is quite inhuman—so there can be no calling to book, in any form whatsoever—because one is outside the pale of all that is accepted, and nothing known applies . . . [8]

Ballard also said, in the same essay, 'The only truly alien planet is earth.' And that seems to be what Lawrence is getting at, not just in this passage but with the entire thrust of the novel. Birkin's speech describes creatures more alien than human.

This is what George Steiner meant when he called *Women in Love* one of the 'classics of imagined life'.⁹ The cowardly question does come up: *But would a person ever really say those words to another person?* This is irrelevant, and is much better asked backwards. *Isn't the person who says those words to another person far more worthy of our attention than the person who doesn't?*

We are at a societal high point here, in these meetings between Birkin and Ursula, Gerald and Gudrun, Birkin and Gerald—Lawrence is (to the infuriation of his critics) a believer in an aristocracy of the Soul.

(Does this mean that he himself is an aristocrat of the Soul? Well, yes, he would have to be—or else these questions would not be occurring to him.)

This is what Lawrence, objectionably, says about the non-aristocrats of the Soul in his essay 'The Education of the People' (1919):

> The slave, the serf, the vast populace, had no soul. It has been left to our era to put the populace in possession of its own soul. Left to itself, it will never do more than demand a pound a day, and so on. The populace finds its living soul-expression cumulatively through the rising up of the classes above it, towards pure utterance or expression or being. And the populace has its supreme satisfaction in the up-flowing of the sap of life, with its vast roots and trunk, up to the perfect blossom.¹⁰

'No, no, no!' you say. 'This is appalling.' But, without being facile, this sentence 'The populace finds its living soul-expression cumulatively through the rising up of the classes above it, towards pure utterance or expression or being' seems to me an extremely good explanation of celebrity culture.

And whether or not it's appalling, this is what Lawrence believed, and what we see being played out in *Women in Love*— particularly in the chapter 'The Industrial Magnate' where Gerald's reforms in his father's mines are described:

> [T]he miners were reduced to mere mechanical instruments. They had to work hard, much harder than before, the work was terrible and heart-breaking in its mechanicalness.
>
> But they submitted to it all [. . .] Gerald was their high priest, he represented the religion they really felt. His father was forgotten already. There was a new world, a new order, strict, terrible, inhuman, but satisfying in its very destructiveness. The men were satisfied to belong to the great and wonderful machine, even whilst it destroyed them. It was what they wanted. It was the highest that man had produced, the most wonderful and superhuman. They were exalted by belonging to this great and superhuman system which was beyond feeling or reason, something really godlike. Their hearts died within them, but their souls were satisfied.[11]

Their souls are satisfied exactly because they are not aristocratic Souls. And *Women in Love* is about Gerald (and Birkin, Ursula and Gudrun) because it is about dissatisfied, aristocratic Souls.

In this Lawrence is very close to Nietzsche, another believer in an aristocracy of the Soul; you see how anti-Christian (strictly) this is: Christianity being, above all, based on the equality (in the eyes of God) of all created Souls.

This belief in an aristocracy of Souls is a given of Lawrence's universe, on a metaphysical level, that takes it far beyond the merely anti-communist, anti-democratic.

Unless some Souls are more developed, or more capable of development, than others, there is no possibility for anything (any human action) to amount to anything.

Lenin, too, believed something similar—he had the idea of the party as the vanguard of the proletariat.

> By educating the workers' party, Marxism educates the vanguard of the proletariat, capable of assuming power and leading the whole people to socialism, of directing and organizing the new system, of being the teacher, the guide, the leader of all the working and exploited people in organizing their social life without the bourgeoisie and against the bourgeoisie.[12]

(As an aside, here is one of Lawrence's best jokes—one of the best jokes of the twentieth century. In the preface to 'The Grand Inquisitor' by Dostoievsky, Lawrence says, 'Lenin, surely a pure soul . . . '.)[13]

Again, *What's Souls got to do with anything?*

Well, most of you—I am pretty sure—are writing about one-off Geralds rather than about masses of miners. You are not writing about characters who are engaged in repetitive mechanistic labour. You are writing about subjects who have enough liberty of movement and thought to count among the traditional subjects of novels. You are writing about people who have enough agency within their lives to be able to change them, even to a very small degree. If behind this there isn't on your part a belief in an aristocracy of the Soul, there is instead a calculated hierarchy of interest. You are not writing to emphasize the meaninglessness of your characters lives, nor of human life in general.

Do events need the participation of Souls to become meaningful?

At this point, the argument risks becoming circular:

The novels which mean the most to us are those that—in the deepest of their techniques—allow themselves the opportunity to create the most meaning.

More is at stake for persons with Souls or the possibility of Souls than for persons without souls or the possibility of Souls.

Although you might not believe your characters or you are possessed of anything like a Soul, you would not take it as a statement of mere fact were your work to be described as either 'Soulless' or 'lacking Soul' or 'without Soul'.

It is possible to see all this as an attempt—rather adolescent, no?—an attempt by Lawrence and Bellow and other writers to invest the world with more meaning than it in fact possesses. (No meaning should be permitted, that is, beyond the physical, social, economic, mediated.)

Lawrence is ridiculous—he knows he is ridiculous; he believes, I am sure, that a lack of or a fearful avoidance of the ridiculous is inimical to 'vivid life'. This pleonasm (use of more words than necessary) is deliberate—and deliberately ridiculous: 'vivid life' is life within life, life upon life, life to the power of life.

But Lawrence is an essential countervoice to the assumptions of now.

Dismiss him completely, he still leaves behind a distinctive unease, the trace of burnt-hair smell that suggests both unburnt hair and hair burning.

Lawrence is so *not* of our technological now, and yet he was very much of another, post-industrial technological world—to which he speaks:

> Is it true that mankind demands, and will always demand, miracle, mystery, and authority? Surely it is true. Today, man gets his sense of the miraculous from science and machinery, radio, aeroplane, vast ships, zeppelins, poison gas, artificial silk: these things nourish man's sense of the miraculous as magic did in the past. But, now man is master of mystery, there are no occult powers.[14]

All you need to do with this sentence is replace the nouns: 'Internet' for 'radio', 'biological weapons' for 'poison gas'.

Again, why is this of importance to you? Why is this a technical question?

Because you need to address, in your fiction, what is happening and to whom it is happening. The distinctiveness and originality of what you write will issue from the freshness of your whats and your whos. You will have to decide what counts, for you, as an event. Generic events (murders, glances) or ungeneric events (of which, clearly, I can't give easy examples—you'll have to make them for yourselves).

I'm now going to quote from the Lawrence essay, 'Why the Novel Matters' (1936):

Let us learn from the novel. In the novel, the characters can do nothing but *live*. If they keep on being good, according to pattern, or bad, according to pattern, or even volatile, according to pattern, they cease to live, and the novel falls dead. A character in a novel has got to live, or it is nothing.

We, likewise, in life have got to live, or we are nothing.

What we mean by living is, of course, just as indescribable as what we mean by *being*. Men get ideas into their heads, of what they mean by Life, and they proceed to cut life out to pattern . . .

Turn truly, honourably to the novel, and see wherein you are truly alive, and you may be making love to a woman as sheer dead man in life. You may eat your dinner as man alive, or as a mere masticating corpse . . .

To be alive, to be man alive, to be whole man alive: that is the point. And at its best, the novel, and the novel supremely, can help you. It can help you not to be a dead man in life. So much of a man walks about dead and a carcass in the street and house, today: so much of woman is merely dead. Like a pianoforte with half the notes mute.

But in the novel you can see, plainly, when the man goes dead, the woman goes inert. You can develop an instinct for life, if you will, instead of a theory of right and wrong, good and bad.[15]

And here's where I'd like to return at last to the *triangle*.

What Lawrence is doing, and I think also what Bellow (self-consciously following on from Lawrence) also does, is try to grant every element here—you, subject, reader—as much vivid life as possible. And by this, I mean allowing each element to exist in a flux of becoming.

Lawrence assumes an alive-to-the-moment writer writing (in the moment) about imaginary but imagined as alive-to-the-moment human subjects for an alive-to-the-moment reader.

This, at the writer's point, is what F. R. Leavis describes as 'the free flow of his sympathetic consciousness'.

Here is where I think there may be a lesson of deep technique. It's not that I am asking you to start believing in the Soul. What I'm suggesting is that—in writing any sort of fiction—you are working within a form that was created out of the wreck of the Soul, and emerged in order address the question of the Soul.

It may be that when your characters are unconvincing, it's because you aren't allowing them to fight with this question—as Lawrence does—in their actions, through their relations.

It may be that when your situations are inert, it's because this question has been put entirely to one said—and your characters are existing in an world that is entirely and unproblematically physical, social, economic, mediated.

Finally, it may be that when your writing is dead or deathly, it's because it hasn't—out of embarrassment, or for some other very good reason—it hasn't made the attempt to be alive.

Show, Don't Tell is the great clanging cliché of creative writing courses. But here's Ursula, travelling towards Birkin, and is this *showing* or *telling*? And how else could a writer ever do this?

> She found herself sitting on the tram-car, mounting up the hill going out of the town, to the place where he had his lodging. She seemed to have passed into a kind of dream world, absolved from the conditions of actuality. She watched the sordid streets of the town go by beneath her, as if she were a spirit disconnected from the material universe. What had it all to do with her? She was palpitating and formless within the flux of the ghost life. She could not consider any more what anybody would say of her or think about her. People had passed out of her range, she was absolved. She had fallen strange and dim, out of the sheath of the material life, as a berry falls from the only world it has ever known, down out of the sheath on to the real unknown.[16]

Notes

1 F. R. Leavis, *The Great Tradition: George Eliot, Henry James, Joseph Conrad* (London: Pelican, 1972), p. 39.

2 Saul Bellow, 'A Matter of the Soul' in *It All Adds Up: From the Dim Past to the Uncertain Future* (London: Secker and Warburg, 1994), p. 77.

3 Catherine Brown, 'D. H. Lawrence, 1: Consciousness', lecture delivered at Oxford University, 15 February 2012. Available as podcast at: https://goo.gl/8dhhfC (last accessed on 5 October 2015).

4 Jack Goody, 'From Oral to Written: An Anthropological Breakthrough in Storytelling' in Franco Moretti (ed.), *The Novel, Volume 1: History, Geography and Culture* (Princeton, NJ: Princeton University Press, 2006), pp. 20–1. Available at: http://goo.gl/qOXIjT (last accessed on 5 October 2015).

5 Harold Bloom, 'Introduction: Don Quixote, Sancho Panza, and Miguel de Cervantes Saavedra' in Miguel de Cervantes, *Don Quixote* (Edith Grossman trans.) (New York: HarperCollins, 2003), pp. *xxiii–xxvii*.

6 Bellow, 'Nobel Lecture'.

7 D. H. Lawrence, *Women in Love* (London: Penguin, 2008), p. 169.

8 Ibid., pp. 162–3.

9 George Steiner, *Language of Silence: Essays on Language, Literature, and the Inhuman* (New York: Atheneum, 1967), p. 230.

10 D. H. Lawrence, 'The Education of the People' in *Phoenix: The Posthumous Papers of D. H. Lawrence* (London: Heinemann, 1936), p. 610.

11 Lawrence, *Women in Love*, pp. 259–60.

12 V. I. Lenin, *Essential Works of Lenin: 'What Is to Be Done?' and Other Writings* (London: Dover, 1987), p. 288.

13 D. H. Lawrence, 'The Grand Inquisitor' in *Phoenix: The Posthumous Papers of D. H. Lawrence* (London: Heinemann, 1936), p. 285.

14 Ibid.

15 D. H. Lawrence, 'Why the Novel Matters' in *Phoenix: The Posthumous Papers of D. H. Lawrence* (London: Heinemann, 1936), pp. 535–6.

16 Lawrence, *Women in Love*, p. 160.

Swing

(Well, here we are again . . .)

I am going to speak a lot about music this evening—specifically, about *jazz*, and even more specifically about that *Swing* without which it don't mean a thing.

Swing-focus was not my original plan; what I first thought I would do (in this lecture) was investigate four of the new aesthetic qualities that entered into or overtook the world during the twentieth century. (Aesthetic qualities—by which I mean: the new ways art had of being *good*, of *surprising* and *delighting*, of being *dug*.)

These four new aesthetic qualities were Swing, Funk, Soul and the quality that some contemporary music has but which doesn't seem to have a single noun that's also a verb: *Swing* music *Swings*, *Funk* music *is Funky* or *has the Funk*, *Soul* got *Soul*, but *Hip-hop* is *Hype* or is *Swag* or is lots of other things people can't quite agree on, yet.

Another new aesthetic or, perhaps in this case, *cultural* quality—another new thing that I could have talked about is *cool*. Cool has a fascinating and simultaneously very public and very obscure history. In some ways, it seems to me, the story of the twentieth century is the story of the rise and rise of

Cool. But although that's a story that will affect how what you write is read, or isn't read, it's not one that I can go into now.

I'm not going to speak about Cool, mainly because I think it's a fault in writing to have, as a major aim, being Cool. It can try to be hip, which is another thing altogether, because that can involve a quest for newness that's invigorating. But the quest for cool involves radically limiting your range of emotional expression.

On this, the defining words come from Cameron Crowe's film *Almost Famous* (2000), and are—I'm pretty sure—ones he wrote down in his notebook while on the midnight phone to Lester Bangs. That's how the scene plays out, with Philip Seymour Hoffman as the moral guardian of rock'n'roll, laying it down for ever.

'The only true currency in this bankrupt world is what you share with someone when you're uncool.'

So, I'm avoiding Cool, because it can be bad for you. And I'm not giving equal time to *Funk, Soul* and the unnamed quality—although I think they're all extremely important—because you can apply what I say about *Swing* to them as well.

All of these new aesthetic qualities emerged from music, popular music—and, as I said, I'm going to be talking quite a lot about *jazz*.

Now, I'm aware that the moment someone does this, talks about or even mentions jazz, there are a number of people who have to suppress the urge to flee the area.

Jazz is a music that, in the first half of its existence, was unprecedentedly good at making friends and that, in its latter half, has become uniquely gifted with the capacity to turn stomachs, turn off minds, lose arguments. If you don't like the sound of it, you just don't *like* it. All those brass instruments, doing different things at the same time. Chords that don't really seem to want to settle anywhere or commit to anything. Or, even worse, bloody George Benson smugly doo-doo-dooing along with the very same blue notes he's playing on his sweet smooth Gibson guitar. Single-handedly, I think, George Benson put jazz into a credibility coma. When you add in Kenny G, Candy Dulfer, Prince's jazz noodlings, very late Miles Davis, Radio 2's jazz programming, Jazz FM (. . . 'and smooth smooth jazz'), Jamie Cullum, Robbie Williams in a lounge suit—if you add these things together, it's clear that jazz has become a kind of cultural bile. And countering this by asserting the importance and allure it once had—the cultural honey it was in 1927 or 1961—doesn't work either. So, I'm going to ask you, if you're in the jazz-despising camp, to do some mental translation. When I say 'jazz', you're going to have to hear 'art' or 'writing' or 'stuff about art that applies to *your* writing directly and extremely intimately'.

When I am deciding what to talk about, in my summer lecture, I think most of all about *what we leave out of* our MA classes—the things we don't, usually because we can't, cover. Because it's too impractical, abstract, advanced, idiosyncratic. So, in the past, I've talked about *Sensibility* and *Souls*. Things beginning with *S*. And there is a deep continuity from one lecture to the next. I took a bit of a detour last year, speaking about *Sympathy* or *Sympathetic Central Characters*. But there's a lot in my thinking about *Swing* that comes from what I was trying to say about first *Sensibility* and then *Soul*.

To be exact, I ended the *Sensibility* lecture by saying, perhaps a little mystifyingly to most of the audience, 'Examine your unique relation to time and examine how you express it in words.'

If you want to develop your unique Sensibility—in other words, become a writer worth reading, then 'Examine your unique relation to time and how you express it in words.'

This refers back to a sentence a little earlier in the previous essay: 'A person's Sensibility stems from a person's unique relation to time, of which we have very few maps.'

I am partly taking jazz as my subject because—it seems to me—it is the best example there is of us being able to perceive the *unique relation to time* of dozens of geniuses—thanks to this relation having been made into sound and made into a gift. What's important is that this is a *live* relation to time. Most jazz recordings made prior to Miles Davis' *Bitches' Brew* (in 1970) don't involve much overdubbing or post-production. It's a one-take art form, even if the artists got 15 runs at that take. We hear, by and large, what we would have heard had we been in the room—at that time, in that ongoing moment. And the recordings we're lucky enough to possess give us a chance to re-enter those moments, again and again, alongside those geniuses. You can't rub elbows with Chekhov as he performs 'Lady with a Lapdog' onto the page but you can, second for second, get close to Charlie Parker as he nails 'Koko'.

I'm going to invoke a few of these time-presences here; this is The List: beginning, as it has to, with Louis Armstrong before doubling back to call up King Oliver, but also the unrecorded Buddy Bolden, and the many more what ifs, then stepping aside while acknowledging the mind-altering lyricisms of Scott Joplin and Jelly Roll Morton and Bix Beiderbecke, before moving on, always on, through the miraculous Django Rheinhart, to Duke Ellington, Fletcher Henderson, Count Basie, all the big names, and then the perpetual breaker-of-hearts that was Billie Holiday and the central-for-more-things-than-can-be-estimated Lester Young, next Coleman Hawkins, then into the period of my Art Saints with Charlie Parker, Dizzy Gillespie (who I wish I could love as much as he deserves), Charles Mingus (who I am scared to love), Thelonius Sphere Monk (who I love beyond expression), Miles Davis (who I admire but sort of hate), Chet Baker (who I know I shouldn't really admire) and—chief of all my Saints—John Coltrane. Glancing back, I realize the many I've missed: listing them would be wearying.

(And some of you are still hearing 'jazz'—hearing George Benson singing smugly along with his guitar, or hearing me insisting that bile really tastes of honey.)

But, after conjuring all those spirits, I need to take one moment to say to them, directly—Thank you—and to you, directly: I have learnt at least as much about art and how to make it from these presences than from any left-behind words of any writer. I have also learnt—from them—more about my writing and what it lacks, and writing as an art and what it lacks—than from any other teachers.

(Please do not go out of this lecture thinking it all it meant was, 'Toby likes jazz'; it meant, 'Jazz—whether or not I like it—changed what art does and is. If I want to have anything at all to do with art, I'm going to have to think about why Toby likes jazz.')

Mine isn't a controversial List. I'm not arguing that land-mark figures are unimportant, or that obscure ones are crucial. But I hope that what I hear in these artists, when I listen closely enough to them—what I perceive in their particular relations to time—I hope that what I hear is my own, and that it is my time's relation to theirs, my Sensibility's relation to theirs.

One thing to be said at this point, and expanded upon later, is that it's no accident that almost all of these artists were African Americans, were mixed-race or black. There is a cul-tural shift occurring here, a vast one, and it's to do with an Africanization of American culture and with a subsequent Americanization of world culture. American culture was Africanized through popular music, ragtime, jazz, blues, soul, funk, hip-hop. The 'jungle rhythms' that it's now embarrassing to admit that Ellington included in his repertoire at the Cotton Club, leading to the incessantly repetitive beats of rock'n'roll—this is quite a different thing to the many musics you'll find in Harry Smith's *Anthology of American Folk Music* or to the hor-rendous hoedowns of Aaron Copeland's 'Appalachian Spring'.

(Perhaps some of you don't like jazz because its time doesn't fit with yours. It may be that you feel more comfortable within regular, programmed beats; or within the broader flow of the symphonic; or within folk's disguised hurdygurdying.)

I don't need to make the cultural case for jazz here. I think it's unarguable, though you may disagree. I just need to point out, for the sake of my argument, that jazz is the clearest exam-ple of the relation of the sensibilities of genius to time because it is a one-take art form. If you listen to Glenn Gould playing

Bach's Goldberg Variations, either in 1955 or 1981, you will hear another genius–time relation, but it is a post-produced one.

Your own writing is post-produced; that is, you rewrite it. You go back in to the time of a particular sentence and try to make it a better time. You take the time of one sentence, over there, and cut'n'paste it in-between the different times of two other sentences, over here. And these small changes hopefully improve your writing overall, and improve you as a writer. Most of what we say in the MA is about this edited relation to edited time. But what I'm talking about this evening comes before and goes beyond that. At some point, there has to be a first draft and, to get back to my title, this is where the Swing comes in.

One of the things I say most often in class is that it's *impossible to retrofit excitement.*

If you want a takeaway idea, something to note down, it's that your first drafts need to Swing—however crudely— because you can't stitch together that kind of freedom and flow from bitty notes. You need to establish on the page a basic relation to time that gives you the opportunity, also, to be Funky, have Soul. If you lack these qualities, they will be missed.

So, here, I am really talking to the *you* that writes your first drafts. The *you* that performs your relationship to time onto the page. Writing courses, very much concerned with outcomes, are a little embarrassed about this live aspect of making literature. But given the limited length of a human life, you need to become better at writing things that can stand first time. It's possible to be a Flaubert, a god of post-production. Most novelists, however, have to make a compromise with mortality. The novel is, in my eyes, a form founded on compromise: *I have this amount of life left. I am not going to spend all of it writing one perfect novel, and possibly leaving it three-quarters complete. Instead, I am going to write it in adequate prose—that is, I am going to write it in a medium that often gestures towards the effects it wishes to achieve rather than achieving those effects by mimetic or invisible or seemingly magical means.*

What do I mean by this? I mean that prose will say, 'There was a vast crowd of people running down the street,' rather than, in some way, making you feel all of those people individually. If a painter wanted to achieve the same crowd effect, they would have to paint a hell of a lot of legs. Prose writers don't have to do legs; they generalize in a way that encourages the imaginations of their readers. You (the writer) say a crowd, they (the readers) do the legwork.

Novels are very often comprised of well-phrased gestures towards effects language is unable to arrive at, inhabit or mimic. Prose says, 'I will not attempt to solve all the problems of verbal art in this sentence—I will defer that, and in the deferring will come a story. The shape that my language leaves behind, of what it might have been, that will be the art.'

Some of the compromisers-with-language are amazing word-organizers: Henry James, Virginia Woolf, Samuel Beckett, Saul Bellow, Muriel Spark, David Foster Wallace. But they all, I think, realize that what they are doing isn't the pure attempt of poetry to be what it is. Prose points to a poetry that is elsewhere, in the embodied world. Prose is gestural, significant; poetry attempts to embody—leaving Yeats' dancer and dance inseparable.

It is almost impossible to get a sense of what a unique relation to time might be without experiencing that relation live.
And this is where jazz recordings, in the absence of being able
to be in a room where John Coltrane—with no tapes running—
is five feet away, preaching his particular truth; this is where
jazz can be a way of thinking writing.

There are infinite lessons to be learnt from an art form
that—before your ears—exists as both composition and performance; as idea, first draft and publication.

This is not to figure jazz as somehow instinctive or primitive. When you are translating, as I've asked you to, my saying
of 'jazz' into a saying of 'art' or 'writing', there is—I think—an
exact equivalent to those stages of development jazz musicians
used to call *woodshedding* or *getting your chops together* or *paying
your dues*.

If you are an experienced reader, it's possible to tell whether
a writer has properly woodshedded their prose, whether they
have got their verbal chops together, whether they have put in
the tens of thousands of words that add up to paying their dues.
Because—and this is where we really get to it—because their
prose will have started to *swing*.

Which brings me to James Baldwin's *The Fire Next Time*
(1963). I asked you to read this mainly so that you would read
a single section, the one on the difference between white music
and black music.

> This is the freedom that one hears in some gospel
> songs, for example, and in jazz. In all jazz, and especially
> in the blues, there is something tart and ironic, author-
> itative and double-edged. White Americans seem to feel

that happy songs are *happy* and sad songs are *sad*, and that, God help us, is exactly the way most white Americans sing them—sounding, in both cases, so helplessly, defencelessly fatuous that one dare not speculate on the temperature of the deep freeze from which issue their brave and sexless little voices. Only people who have been 'down the line', as the song puts it, know what this music is about. I think it was Big Bill Broonzy who used to sing 'I Feel So Good', a really joyful song about a man who is on his way to the railroad station to meet his girl. She's coming home. It is the singer's incredibly moving exuberance that makes one realize how leaden the time must have been while she was gone. There is no guarantee that she will stay this time, either, as the singer clearly knows, and, in fact, she has not yet actually arrived. Tonight, or tomorrow, or within the next five minutes, he may very well be singing 'Lonesome in My Bedroom', or insisting, 'Ain't we, ain't we, going to make it all right? Well, if we don't today, we will tomorrow night.' White Americans do not understand the depths out of which such an ironic tenacity comes, but they suspect that the force is sensual, and they are terrified of sensuality and do not any longer understand it. The word 'sensual' is not intended to bring to mind quivering dusky maidens or priapic black studs. I am referring to something much simpler and much less fanciful. To be sensual, I think, is to respect and rejoice in the force of life, of life itself, and to be *present* in all that one does, from the effort of loving to the breaking of bread.[1]

(And, I hope I don't need to add, to be present in the writing of sentences. To be present and to be Swinging, Funky, Soulful.)

I also gave you *The Fire Next Time* to read because it is political, full of rage, written by someone black about being black, and entirely relevant to this year as much as to the year it was written. But, for the immediate purposes of this lecture, I'm going to have to speak a little more about James Baldwin.

And, briefly, about myself. One of the main reasons I came to thinking about Swing is that I have been writing a novel whose first person narrator is black—a Ghanaian called Joseph Baidoo. Now, it's not at all that Joseph—because he is black—can instinctively Swing ('to be present in all that one does', to have a unique and satisfying relation to time); in fact, that's entirely his problem. Joseph does anything but Swing—in his body movements, in his sexuality, in his whole life.

In writing the novel, which is called *My Mother's Seven Spirits Demand Justice*, I have thought a lot about and through James Baldwin.

I first read *The Fire Next Time* probably 15 years ago.

For me, Baldwin's simple statement, 'White Americans seem to feel that happy songs are *happy* and sad songs are *sad*, and that, God help us, is exactly the way most white Americans sing them . . . ' was—the first time I read it—a revelation. He had managed to hit on exactly the reason why I liked the music I liked, and was the person I was.

Far more than *you can't retrofit excitement*, the thing I say most often in class is *Never do one thing at a time; always do two or three things at once*. Some of you will have heard this, repeatedly.

There is no such thing as 'a descriptive passage' or 'a section of dialogue'. If you describe a table, you are deepening our knowledge the characters associated with that table, and preparing a scene much later that takes place at the table, and using language rhythm-wise and sound-wise in ways which tells us about far more than the table, and probably doing many other things as well. But, more than this, what I have been trying to say, again and again, is what James Baldwin manages to say.

Don't write white.

Don't write happy sentences that are happy, or sad sentences that are sad.

Don't write happy stories that are happy, or sad stories that are sad.

Don't write happy novels that are happy, or sad novels that are sad.

Instead, write something 'tart and ironic, authoritative and double-edged'—or treble- or quadruple-edged.

Or find your own tone that is complex, alive, gripping, whatever.

In practical terms, I am trying to warn you off writing in a way that comes across—to agents and publishers, who are very sensitive to these nuances of authority—to readers, who wouldn't necessarily be able to express this but will be able to find something else to read or do—that comes across as devastatingly old-fashioned. Devastatingly, meaning you won't stand a hope of getting published.

You may disagree, and say there are still plenty of successful books written in an unswinging idiom. And you may be right, but I don't believe any truly significant prose has ever been written in imitation of an idealized previous version of what prose should be. Every great writer tries to push language to say things it hasn't quite been able to say before. This definition goes as much for P. G. Wodehouse as for James Joyce.

And now I'm coming to something like the heart of my argument, but several strands need to be brought together, and it's difficult to keep them all alive. So, say it like this: however much you might hate George Benson's smug singalong jazz, you have been fundamentally formed by new aesthetic qualities that entered the world via black music—Swing, Soul, Funk.

And, however much you might not like listening to jazz itself, you are definitely not listening to, say, German oompah music from 1910 or British parlour songs from 1888. We listen back to early recordings and find the whole thing laughably stiff, sexless, emotionally banal. Those voices that just sing the notes, exactly as they were written! Those instruments with frozen spines!

Which isn't to say that there isn't still a lot of triumphant whiteness in music. The banal *I've got to live my dream* sentiments of *Glee*, for example.

But generally, I think, we now demand art that has the qualities of Swing, Soul, Funk. If they are missing, they are missed.

Which *is* to say, in large, that Western Culture has become an attempt towards blackness—or, at least, towards the incorporation of virtues which (that horribly encapsulating phrase) Music of Black Origin brought to the table.

So, it isn't that you *like* Louis Armstrong's singing, it's that—beyond the classical world—Louis Armstrong's approach to time, time as expressed in words sung over music, has changed what we find bearable. Stick to the bar lines, come in purely on the notes (not sliding up or down to them), don't try to establish your own Swinging relationship to an implied melody behind the melody you are actually singing, and you will sound like the choristers at the start of The Rolling Stones' 'You Can't Always Get What You Want'. You will sound like an out-of-touch joke. Out-of-touch because out of touch with the moment in which you are living.

This is why, in the quotation I've been saving up for this point, 'It Don't Mean a Thing (If It Ain't Got That Swing)'.

The swing title of Ellington's song is, strictly speaking, wrong in lots of ways: it is grammatically incorrect—'don't' for 'doesn't', 'ain't' for 'hasn't'; it puts the conclusion before the statement; it presumes familiarity with rather than helpfully defining 'Swing'—*that* Swing. You know, *that*.

What it suggests is a radical shortcut to the truth.

At its most extreme, this form of address leads to speakers repeatedly throwing the question back on their listeners, rather than making any statement, 'You know what I'm sayin'?', 'You get me?', 'You know?', 'Innit?', 'Like . . . like . . . like.'

But at the level of this title, and in the way it influences contemporary writing and speech, it is about immediacy and connection. It's about being real.

As an experiment, why don't we take that title back through time, and turn it into what a BBC voice would have made of it in 1927. In other words, let's make that title completely grammatically correct, completely white?

'Unless it possesses the quality colloquially known as "Swing", it will be meaningless.'

Isn't that ridiculous? Didn't it lose your attention halfway through, because it was doing one thing at once?

'Unless it possesses the quality colloquially known as "Swing", it will be meaningless.'

There are still things to be achieved in this cast of prose, but it's essentially pastiche—as Kazuo Ishiguro's *Remains of the Day* (1989) was pastiche. It is what Cyril Connolly, in *The Enemies of Promise* (1938), called 'the Mandarin Style'. It used to be the way politicians spoke in the House of Commons, but no longer. Even they have abandoned this register.

I met a parliamentary reporter, one of those superfast stenographers who work for Hansard—taking down every word spoken in even the most obscure parliamentary committee. When I asked him whether there were still any great old-fashioned rhetoricians in the House of Commons—speakers who, whatever the content of their speech, employed Mandarin Style—he said there were only two, and both had recently gone off. One was Michael Gove who, he said, spoke entirely in classical Hansard Style, but whose speeches had declined catastrophically in quality since he entered the Cabinet and could no longer attack the Right Honourable Gentlemen from the Opposition benches; the other good speaker was Michael Berkow, now limited to barking 'Order! Order!' from the speaker's chair.

The Mandarin voice was the voice of the BBC, of government. The Mandarin voice spoke from position of disinterest, over and aboveness; it seemed to say *I am summing up the question, from outside time.*

This tone, we don't go along with any more (for better and worse). All speakers, we know, are embedded in time along with us. There are no grandees of existence, no magnificos beyond the moment. To convince, you need to be down with us, getting dirty in our milliseconds. We need to know you've lived. As Walt Whitman put it, with great Swing, 'I am the man; I suffered; I was there.'

Which, as the epigraph to James Baldwin's *Giovanni's Room* (1956), brings us right back to him.

In my favourite answer to any question, ever, Baldwin was once asked by a television interviewer: 'Now, when you were starting out as a writer, you were black, impoverished, homosexual—you must have said to yourself, "Gee, how disadvantaged can I get?"'

Baldwin's eyes go gleeful as he listens to the question, and then he replies, 'No, I thought I'd hit the jackpot.'

The audience laughs. The interviewer says, 'Oh great.'

Baldwin continues, 'Because it was so outrageous, you could not go any further—so, you had to find a way to use it.'

I would not use Baldwin as an instance of a totally successful, Swinging writer. *Giovanni's Room*, if you've read it, is an astoundingly stiff book; the sentences feel agonized into square shapes. More flowing, but still not as delightful as some of Baldwin's nonfictional prose, is *Another Country* (1962). His best-known short story, 'Sonny's Blues' (1957), gets closest to Swing—because it is trying to *be* what it is about; an apparent failure-in-life who, on the stand, can Swing. We'll come back to 'Sonny's Blues'.

Maybe it's time to be a little more formal in defining Swing. When I posted about this on Facebook, I got answers almost immediately from two professional musicians.

One, Oliver Coates, a wonderful cellist, said, 'It's interesting —the missive to a "classically" trained orchestra to "Swing" means simply converting straight quavers into triplets. It's simplified to a purely mathematical thing.'

The other, the multi-instrumentalist Martin White, said, 'For me, as a composer, "Swing" is a dry, technical, music-specific matter of triplets and syncopation, so I can't really relate to the synesthetic way of applying the concept to another medium, unless perhaps its in the rhythm of the prose.'

When I'm listening to jazz, I'm sure that I am often hearing straight quavers converted into triplets. But I'd like to bring in a couple of quotes that, directly or indirectly, will help me define *Swing* as I'm using it—in relation to writing.

The first is from Keith Richard's autobiography:

One of the first lessons I learned with guitar playing was that none of these guys were actually playing straight chords. There's a throw-in, a flick-back. Nothing's ever a straight major. It's an amalgamation, a mangling and a dangling and a tangling thing. There is no 'properly'. There's just how you feel about it. Feel your way around it. It's a dirty world down here. Mostly I've found, playing instruments, that I actually wanted to be playing something that should be played by another instrument. I find myself trying to play horn lines all the time on the guitar. When I was learning how to do these songs, I learned there is often one note doing something that makes the whole thing work. It's usually a suspended chord. It's not a full chord, it's a mixture of chords, which I love to use to this day. If you're playing a straight chord, whatever comes next should have something else in it. If it's an A chord, a hint of D. Or if it's a song with a different feeling, if it's an A chord, a hint of G should come in somewhere, which makes a 7th, which can then lead you on. Readers who wish to can skip Keef's Guitar Workshop, but I'm passing on the simple secrets anyway.[2]

The second quote leads directly on from this. It's from Meg Greene's *Billie Holiday: A Biography*. But the important quote is the one within this:

Although Holiday always denied that she was a blues singer, her style, strongly influenced by Bessie Smith, was grounded in the blues tradition. Horn players, such as trumpeter Louis Armstrong, also influenced Holiday's singing. Armstrong was among the first to develop improvisation and scat singing. According to jazz critic and historian Stanley Crouch, 'Armstrong, like Bessie Smith, was a master of inflection, capable of coming down on a note in almost endless ways, to the extent that one tone could jab, bite, simmer, dissolve, swell, yelp, sizzle, or grind.' Holiday always credited the development of her singing style to both Smith and

Armstrong, stating in one interview that 'I got my manner from Bessie Smith and Louis Armstrong, honey. I wanted [Bessie's] feeling and Louis' style.'[3]

I hope you can see the kinship here. Richards says the negative side, that 'There is *no* properly.' And Crouch says the positive, that Armstrong was 'capable of coming down on a note in almost *endless* ways.'

We are here, between nothing ('no') and infinity ('endless'). We exist in time, and express ourselves in arts that manipulate others' experience of time. Even paintings do this. We can do this with predictable regularity, which seems to me likely to become boring and say little, or we can surprise and delight by playing truant from the proper.

How do you achieve this in writing? I said earlier that I was really talking 'to the *you* that writes your first drafts. The *you* that performs your relationship to time onto the page.'

So, now I'd like to say some useful things to *that* you. I'm going to speak about being a jazz musician, which you can translate as you please.

In order to master an instrument, you first need to do it dutifully—you need to obey the rules and play the foursquare scales. You need to begin slowly; impatience will be punished by having to go back and unlearn bad habits. Often, you'll need to be stupider than you are, slower than you can be. Stories of Mozart sitting down at the keyboard and just being able to *play* won't help. You need to find a way of enduring being bad. Then, after a while, a certain fluidity will enter your playing. You'll make mistakes, but there'll be moments in-between the mistakes where it seemed to happen without you doing very much. Then, you'll have a basic mastery of your instrument: you'll be able, most of the time, when you're not pushing it too much, to get it to do the things it does for most other people. You will be a competent player. And this is an easy level to get stuck on, because becoming more and more competent can seem to go on for ever. Your playing can become smoother and smoother—the playing of a session musician (a bad session musician) who hits all the notes with technical correctness but doesn't need to emotionally connect. Eventually, you'll get to the point where the issue is not the instrument but the expression. What do you have to say, now that the technical means of saying it are within your compass? You've heard people saying similar stuff before. All this is very familiar. And the familiarity of it may be your downfall. You can't learn by other people's mistakes. You have to have the gumption to make them yourself; you have to have the ego, the lack of ego, the anger, the mischief, the sadness and the scrupulousness to be bad in a good way. Then, when the time comes, because all this has been *woodshedding*, you will have *the chops*, you will have *paid your dues*. The fingers will do, and out-do, what the mind and soul require of them. To get to this beyond-competence, you'll need to take the kind of risks with time that Louis Armstrong did when he started scat singing. You'll be able to dance along the edge of your own internal precipices; you won't freeze at the drop—you'll treat the narrow ledge as roof, the rope as floor. In other words, you'll *Swing*. You'll delight in your disobedience to how things formally should be done. Those looking on will see daredevilry, but you'll know the height is irrelevant. You'll wish you could go higher. All art is and has to be a high-wire act. And the risks have to be almost beyond the capacity of the performer to cope with, to bear. But by making your art in a Swinging way, you'll be doing the highest thing art can do—appearing to create energy from nothing, appearing unconstrained by time.

Most of what I try to teach is, in a very indirect way, the ability to cope with the arrival of the moment: people are listening, people are watching—what are you going to do with that? Are you going to delight them by playing with their relation to time, or are you going to entertain them momentarily (by failing) and then lose them entirely (by being predictable).

It Don't Mean a Thing (If It Ain't Got That Swing).

I'd like to end, because I haven't given any before, with some examples of Swing and non-Swing.

A lot of the influence of jazz happened in the 1950s. You had the publication of Jack Kerouac's *On the Road* (1956), originally written during the 1940s. One writer who took on the idea in his own particular way was Saul Bellow. This is the opening of his first novel *The Dangling Man* (1944):

> There was a time when people were in the habit of addressing themselves and felt no shame at making a record of their inward transactions. But to keep a journal nowadays is considered a kind of self-indulgence, a weakness, and in poor taste. For this is an era of hard-boiled-dom. Today, the code of the athlete, of the tough boy—an American inheritance, I believe, from the English gentleman—that curious mixture of striving,

asceticism, and rigor, the origins of which some trace back to Alexander the Great—is stronger than ever. Do you have feelings? There are correct and incorrect ways of indicating them. Do you have an inner life? It is nobody's business but your own. Do you have emotions? Strangle them. To a degree, everyone obeys this code. And it does admit of a limited kind of candor, a closemouthed straightforwardness. But on the truest candor, it has an inhibitory effect. Most serious matters are closed to the hard-boiled. They are unpracticed in introspection, and therefore badly equipped to deal with opponents whom they cannot shoot like big game or outdo in daring.[4]

In his *Paris Review* interview, Bellow addressed the turn in his writing.

INTERVIEWER. You mentioned before the interview that you would prefer not to talk about your early novels, that you feel you are a different person now from what you were then. I wonder if this is all you want to say, or if you can say something about how you have changed.

BELLOW. I think that when I wrote those early books I was timid. I still felt the incredibly effrontery of announcing myself to the world (in part I mean the WASP world) as a writer and an artist. I had to touch a great many bases, demonstrate my abilities, pay my respects to formal requirements. In short, I was afraid to let myself go.

INTERVIEWER. When did you find a significant change occurring?

BELLOW. When I began to write *Augie March*. I took off many of these restraints. I think I took off too many, and went too far, but I was feeling the excitement of discovery.[5]

And here's the famous opening to Saul Bellow's *The Adventures of Augie March* (1953)—restraints removed:

I am an American, Chicago born—Chicago, that sombre city—and go at things as I have taught myself, freestyle, and will make the record in my own way: first to knock, first admitted; sometimes an innocent knock, sometimes a not so innocent. But a man's character is his fate, says Heraclitus, and in the end there isn't any way to disguise the nature of the knocks by acoustical work on the door or gloving the knuckles.[6]

If you were to ask me who are the contemporary writers who, in their own way, Swing, I would say—Junot Díaz, Ali Smith, Niall Griffiths, ZZ Packer.

But I would like to end with James Baldwin, and most of all with the end of Baldwin's 'Sonny's Blues', beginning with the words 'We went to the only nightclub . . . ' and ending with 'that he would never be free until we did.'[7]

This, it seems to me, *means a thing*.

Notes

1 James Baldwin, *The Fire Next Time* (London: Penguin, 1964), pp. 42–3.

2 Keith Richards, *Life* (London: Orion, 2010), p. 120.

3 Meg Greene, *Billie Holiday: A Biography* (Westport, CT: Greenwood, 2006), p. 10.

4 Saul Bellow, *The Dangling Man* (London: Penguin, 1973), p. 1.

5 Saul Bellow, 'Art of Fiction No. 37', interviewed by Gordon Lloyd Harper, *Paris Review* 36 (Winter 1966); available at: http://goo.gl/As79sY (last accessed on 2 November 2015).

6 Saul Bellow, *The Adventures of Augie March* (New York: Viking, 1953), p. 1.

7 James Baldwin, 'Sonny's Blues' in *Going to Meet the Man* (New York: Dial Press, 1965), p. 139.

Talking to Strangers

I am sometimes asked which I prefer, writing novels or short stories? It is an impossible question. Usually, I am just glad that poems haven't also been mentioned.

The follow-up question tends to be 'What is the difference between a novel and a short story?' After some thought, I've come up with an answer that I'm almost happy with. But I need to rephrase the question slightly.

'How do you tell the difference between an idea for a novel and one for a short story?'

Well, I think they have different pulses.

If they were animals, one would be a tree sparrow and the other a blue whale. When it presents itself, however, the animal is invisible. In fact, the animal has not yet come into being. All I have to go on is my sense of its probable pulse.

Animals with small, high, rapid pulses are going to have brief and fidgety lives. Animals with stately gonglike pulses can endure for a very long time. By trusting my senses, I hope to be able to tell them apart, despite their non-existence.

This isn't the sort of critical language that I would have been comfortable using until quite recently. When I finished my

English degree, I was thoroughly theorized. Analogies seemed far too vague to work in constructing definitions; now it is their very vagueness that, I think, makes them accurate.

Because the point at which short stories and novels differentiate themselves, in the writer's imagination (call it that), is not one with which literary criticism is familiar. Literary criticism tends to view texts in slow motion or freeze-framed.

Writing, the *act* of writing, not the words that the writing leaves behind, is a flux of instantaneous decisions. Most of these decisions are not consciously made. I have no idea how complex sentences manage to pre-structure themselves in my mind. But it is the ethic of these decisions which ends up being called style.

An inexperienced writer may find writing difficult because they are not yet intimate with their linguistic senses. They may also, for the same reason, blithely find it a doddle. Both are explanations for bad writing. The inexperienced writer has unstylish instincts.

Dissimilarly, a long-time writer may lose faith in their ability to make the right decisions. They no longer trust their instincts. Or they may become sick with the familiarity of their own responses. Their instincts have become mannerist in style.

Late in life, W. H. Auden wrote a squib on this:

To-day two poems begged to be written: I had to refuse them.
Sorry, no longer, my dear! Sorry, my precious, not yet![1]

Critical language finds it hard to cope with the notion that writing is initially a performance. I've used *instincts* here but a better word might come from jazz, *chops*.

Just as improvising musicians practise chords and scales, writers practise sentence-making. They are aware, even when texting or writing emails, or for previous generations when writing letters, of the shape of what they are saying, the clash or chime of sounds, the rhythmic integrity of the phrase. Sometimes these words satisfy, more often they are abandoned in haste. But the basic use of self-conscious language is there, all the time.

And when a story becomes pressing, its pulse loud in the inner ear, those chops come into play. The writer can cope with the intensity of the flux; they don't become confused or panic. They perform.

Even rewriting, I would say, occurs in a milder state of decisional flux. A change to this word *here* necessitates a cascade of alterations up and down the page, throughout the work. These will be seen or felt or known immediately—if the writing is going as it should. The writer will then check back; how does this fit with the pulse?

Because of the accelerated pulse they are dealing with, a short-story writer needs faster instincts than a novelist. There are architectonics to be thought of, but nothing to compare with the huge mind-spans required by most novels. Poems, paradoxically, are both faster and slower still. To be a poet is to be simultaneously subatomic and universal, static and ubiquitous. In this writing, the question of *where* becomes a hindrance. If a novelist loses their sense of located self for any length of time, the novel will collapse. A short-story writer can play hide-and-seek with herself, but she must find and be found for the game to conclude.

This starts to beg the question of time. A pulse occurs within time, time that requires some form of regularity to be perceived. Yet it is a crucial difference between musical and verbal improvisation that the listener's and the musician's time are the same whereas the reader's time and the writer's are not. (I'm ignoring overdubbing because any use of that immediately changes improvisation into composition—and therefore brings it much closer to rewriting.) A page of printed text, however many alterations lie behind each word, exists as a present ongoing descent. It establishes its own time, and the reader tends to trust in this. For the writer, though, the finished page is a palimpsest of improvised decisional moments.

In other words, a writer, while rewriting, has the ability to re-experience the progress of a pulse and to make changes within and against that—changes that are usually imperceptible to the reader. (Improvising musicians have a different relation to time. I don't think they can ever truly replay.)

But the greater the gap in months and years between the initial composition and the emendation, the more likely there are to be joins and the less likely these joins are to be invisible. Henry James was a compulsive reviser or re-visioner. When he prepared an early novel such as *Roderick Hudson* (1875) for his New York Edition, years after first writing it, he found it impossible to re-enter his own pulse. A reader familiar with his mature writing will be able to sense these patches of sudden slowing elaboration.

Part of the process of writing a novel, which may take three or four years, is masquerading, for a necessary line or two, as a previous version of yourself. They are what Poe called 'black patches'. Those lines that get a character from here to there or make their thought followable. Short-story writers are unlikely to have to master this skill. Better altogether to leave the gap and let the reader make the leap.

Note

1 W. H. Auden, 'Shorts II' in *Collected Poems* (Edward Mendelson ed.) (London: Faber & Faber, 1976), p. 643.

STORGY

Which writers influenced you the most?

You catch me at collapse; I have been rethinking what I do, after it stopped being done or being particularly wanted. Before books came the Beatles. The bright lyrics to 'Lucy in the Sky with Diamonds' and the opaque terror of 'Being for the Benefit of Mr Kite' zipping off into the fairground void. The most important writers, for beginning-me, were world-makers and world-changers. So, SF with Chris Foss covers. And *Dune*. *The Glass Bead Blah*. But I've given this answer too many times for it to be true. At the moment, the important writers are D. H. Lawrence, Thomas Bernhard, Franz Kafka, and always always Emily Brontë. Anyone who seems to want to be *live*, and to want their reader to be *live*. Hello, Jack Kerouac, unscrolling the roll version of *On the Road*.

What is your favourite short story?

Is this piece of writing of psychic use? Does it think it can change you? Those seem to me worthwhile questions when faced with a page or a screen that's made up of words. If some-thing's just there for entertainment, fine—I can be entertained.

If it's journalism, fine—I can learn things I didn't know. But take, say, Henry James, *The Beast in the Jungle* (1903). He seems to want to make his readers capable of greater subtlety, capable

What is your favourite short-story collection?

of more interesting humanity, than they ever were. And, because I find my mind's default settings quite objectionable, I like having them altered by writing. Give me instead a James-head, a Brontë-head. It seems strange that writing can do this, as opposed to, yes, drugs, music, surgical intervention and sex, but—despite the other distractions—proper mind-change still seems possible, via words. I've been affected in ways I am still trying to understand by D. H. Lawrence's longer short stories, those collected in *Three Novellas* (1923)—that's 'The Ladybird', 'The Fox' and 'The Captain's

Which current UK writers are exciting you?

Doll', but also 'St Mawr'. So, I would have to choose some kind of bulky and untransportable collection of Lawrence's not-quite-novels that I'd forgo in favour of glue-crumbling orange-spined Penguin editions with Yvonne Gilbert's overreal paintings on the cover. You'll find these in almost any pile of abandoned, unwanted books. The bottom fell out of the David Herbert Market in about May 1979. He's too ambitious; in a way Joyce wasn't. There aren't many current writers who seem to want to climb in through your eyes and rearrange the furniture, perhaps setting fire

What are you working on at the minute?

to the settee. Niall Griffiths is definitely one. Ali Smith is
another. But aren't we all too modest about what we do? Face-
book-friendly. Isn't it better to set-ludicrously-sail-for-wherever
and end up in Pseud's Corner, rather than to stay in your own
little corner, having painted yourself there with your first publication? I've been gathering in what I've been doing. Putting
stories together under the signs of *M* and *N*. The next book is
Life-Like, but was completed a while ago. That's stories about
the middle years. Also, *My Mother's Seven*

Describe your own writing habits?

Which of your short stories are you most proud of?

Spirits Demand Justice, a novel. And ongoing for the moment is
Dead Boy Detectives, a comic. I have been thinking of giving up
on writing novels, but seem to be writing one all the same. I
am writing it by trying to avoid writing it, on a regular basis.
Other things, I write in the way that seems to suit their rhythm.
Say, splurge then ignore then splurge again. Or jigsaw, scatter,
remake. Or plod. There's a lot to be said for plodding, particularly as opposed to plotting.

What advice would you give to aspiring writers?

There's a lot to be said for plodding, as opposed to plotting.
And dwelling as opposed to word processing. As long as you
chuck out everything ploddy once you take flight. And don't
dwell on success. But mostly, if you want to be a writer then

being a writer is probably the worst thing you can be. You'll start out with the likeable characters in the balanced sentences saving the cat, and you'll end up

Best advice you have ever received?

envying poets. Poets seem to be doing the real work. And by poets I mean poets rather than Robert Graves' 'journalists in verse'. However, there are a few things I've written that I think are okay: 'The Hare' and the first section of *Journey into Space* and 'The Monster' and 'Call It "The Bug"' and also the talk on 'Sensibility' and the 'Kafka' introduction. If I felt they had got through to someone, and done for them what the writing I love has done for me, then that would be the best I could hope for. In some ways, trying to do better, it's been approval rather than advice that's helped. Muriel Spark said she liked reading what I wrote. Just a general feeling that you'd managed to amuse someone worth amusing. But I had an art teacher at school, Mr Cox, who sometimes became so passionate speaking about a picture

Top tip for writing a story?

that his speech impediment, a stammer, overtook him. His nickname was Mr C-C-C-Cox. It was mortifying, for a public schoolboy, to stand next to someone who was struggling to express passion—passion about a painting of apples, for fuck's sake. Mr Cox would curl his fingers up in front of his screwed-up face and try to get across to you—smirking, black acrylic blazer, looking forward to lunch break—that you were a smug little cunt and that Cézanne wasn't. Sometimes Mr Cox worked on a painting for years, then destroyed it. At one time, his house burnt down, including most of his work. He wasn't our only

Top tip for editing a story?

art teacher. There was an equally influential one, Mr Lynch. Whereas Mr Cox was a Low Protestant (perhaps even a charismatic Christian), Mr Lynch was a Catholic. Apart from Cézanne, I think they disagreed on most things—and they disagreed utterly on how they saw Cézanne. Mr Cox looked like Frank Auerbach and, I think, might have painted like him if he'd been able to stand impasto. Mr Lynch looked like James Abbott McNeill Whistler but shorter, squatter and with a beard and moustache that—if ever twisted into points—were only twisted into points at the weekend (in Bedford). Mr Cox was all about expressiveness; Mr Lynch was all about control. Mr Cox was grace; Mr Lynch, guilt. Every mark—for Mr Lynch—had to be considered, tonally, in relation to those marks directly adjacent, and to the painting as a whole. No line could flow. It must stitch along, tentatively, like a Euston Road sewing machine trying not to have a nervous breakdown. The art room, with Mr Lynch in it, was the 1950s. His was the passion of suppression—and, if you wound him up the right way, Mr Lynch would rush off into the supplies

Top tip for submitting a story?

cupboard and curse.

QUANTUM *prose* MANIFESTO

As compared with interactive glowing-screen entertainments of all varieties, the novel is too dull to survive—the novel as it mostly stands.

How can any single-authored project compete with movies or video games for which the credits last the duration of two power ballads?

Being more entertaining (fun fun fun) is, for the novel, impossible; being more unique is vocational; being truer is the only public justification.

'Truer' meaning closer to subjective reality; closer to the reality that goes on inside our heads *behind* the retinas.

'Reality' meaning subjectivity as subjectively witnessed by the subject—the subject with a body, the subject with a language.

Novels must fully colonize the invisible and the unseeable.

The single-authored project can bring us closer to one head; one head is more fascinating than a collectively sculpted and generally pleasing impression of headness.

Novels must at least *attempt* to astound, sentence by sentence.

(Notice, I'm raising the bar higher than I think I'll be able to jump.)

Not *Show, Don't Tell* but *Show, Don't Show*.

Fascination, not fun fun fun.

The paragraph really is dead. No one understands what paragraphs are for. We lead lives without these temporary, minor pauses. Yes, we continue to experience major chapter breaks (death, marriage, depression, illness)—and these remain valid. Everything else is syncopated, overlapping, a flickering field.

Novels struggle to portray simultaneity; novels can't cope with true multiplicity; novels mimic slow, fake communities; novels are wonderful at constructing wishful worlds.

The genre public does not want this, the exacting sentence-by-sentence novel—which might just be why it is essential.

The sentence is dead; long live the sentence.

(It is the reader desires the Ivory Tower, not the writer.)

The only justification for the novel is and has always been an immediate engagement with the interior life of others— from Robinson Crusoe to Emma Bovary to Strether to Leopold Bloom to Moses Herzog to Oscar Wao.

All conventional literary novels are now historical novels— either overtly or in disguise.

The most successful non-genre writers become their own genres—and, in the process, die to all interest.

If you are content to be read ritually, that is as mental comfort food, there is no reason for you not to write ritually.

Any contemporary literary novel that is not technologically based, that does not acknowledge in its sentence structure our constant instant communication, is a wishful historical novel.

Science fiction, your time is *now*.

Comfort food is the diet of the Ivory Tower.

Despair at Western culture has always been one of Western culture's most powerful engines; the novel's own self-despair is no exception—see Beckett.

If these are the last rites, there is no reason for them to be any less glorious than the baptism.

Why quantum prose?

Because the astounding sentence has to be both particle and wave.

Because, subjectively, we can be indeterminately in two places at once.

Because, subjectively, we can exist plurally in two or more times, in two or more dimensions, at once.

& How I Came to Think It

On Perversity

When I was at university, I once asked a fellow student (I will call him Hector, although that wasn't his name, and he wasn't a very *good* student) how he went about writing essays.

Hector replied, 'I usually start off with about four or five rhetorical questions—that tends to get things going.'

And so, if Hector were giving this lecture, he would probably begin something like this: *What is identity? What is originality? What is perversion? How do they relate to one another? Are they related at all? Are these relationships, if they exist, of any interest? Is that interest of use? Is that usefulness?* . . . etc., etc.

In attempting to answer Hector's rhetorical questions, I'd like to start by giving you a clear idea of what I'm *not* saying.

This is George Bernard Shaw, writing in the Dedicatory Epistle to *Man and Superman* (1903):

[A] true original style is never achieved for its own sake: a man may pay from a shilling to a guinea, according to his means, to see, hear, or read another man's act of genius; but he will not pay with his whole life and soul to become a mere virtuoso in literature, exhibiting an accomplishment which will not even make money for him, like fiddle playing. Effectiveness of assertion is the alpha and omega of style. He who has nothing to assert has no style and can have none: he who has something to assert will go as far in power of style as its momentousness and his conviction will carry him.[1]

The relationship here between identity and originality is quite plain. A work of art is an 'act of genius'—the direct statement of the true feelings of a strong individual. For Shaw, directness and simplicity are unquestioned virtues. The word 'virtuoso' is used sneeringly. And yet, as he continues, he seems to undermine himself:

> He who has nothing to assert has no style and can have none: he who has something to assert will go as far in power of style as its momentousness and his conviction will carry him. Disprove his assertion after it is made, yet its style remains. Darwin has no more destroyed the style of Job nor of Handel than Martin Luther destroyed the style of Giotto.
>
> . . . *yet his style remains.*[2]

An interesting admission to make. Although it is not presented as an admission.

For Shaw, writing is a healthy activity. Manly. Vigorous. Straightforward. Straight. In Shaw's view, perversity simply does not enter the relationship between identity and originality. Either one has an identity strong enough to write a strikingly original work, or one hasn't. Here, I would say, one can detect traces of second-hand and slightly shop-soiled Nietzsche. (One can also see, I would suggest, though this is slightly less defensible, that Shaw was the kind of man to get up in the morning and do vigorous Swedish exercises.)

A similar strain of literary machismo is detectable in recent American writing. Here is Richard Ford, prize-winning author of *The Sportswriter* (1986) and *Independence Day* (1995), eulogizing Raymond Carver:

> As long as I knew Ray—the next ten years—there was this feeling of so much good and bad that had been left behind in a single lot, so that among my friends, he seemed to be facing life in the most direct and jarring way, the most adult way—a way that made the stories he wrote almost inevitable.[3]

This, I think, is about the most insulting thing one writer could say about another. The *most* insulting would be to accuse them of plagiarism. To say that X wrote a very bad novel is, at the very least, to credit X with having written that novel. To say that Ray's stories were 'almost inevitable' is to relegate them to the level of faeces: he lived (he ate) therefore he wrote (he shat). It is to deny anything the stories might have cost Carver in the writing. It is to negate him as a writer. And it is, ultimately, to negate writing. Even the worst writer in the world (and if you have any suggestions as to who this is or was, I'll be interested to hear them)—even the worst writer should be credited with mere authorship.

Raymond Carver was a better writer than Richard Ford can ever hope to be; and a much more complex and conscious writer than Ford would have us think. We can see this consciousness in the epigraph he chose for his *New and Selected Stories*, also entitled *Where I'm Calling From* (1988):

We can never know what to want,
because, living only one life, we can neither
compare it with our previous lives
nor perfect it in our lives to come.

This is Milan Kundera in *The Unbearable Lightness of Being* (1984). He is discussing, surprise surprise, Nietzsche's theory of Eternal Recurrence. If anything undermines a 'Straight' view of time, of morality, and also of writing, then Eternal Recurrence does.

To elaborate on this idea of 'Straightness'—I've heard it said about British women writers up to, say, Iris Murdoch and Muriel Spark, that they were always held back by something; and this thing was that, before they started to do anything (tell a story, describe a place), they first had to convince you that they were socially *all right*, that they were *genteel*, that they were—essentially—*the kind of person you'd happily let into your house, and leave alone with your china, if not—to begin with—your children.*

It seems to me that a great many—perhaps even the majority—of American male writers suffer from a similar restraint. Before they start to do anything, they first have to convince you—the reader—that they are manly, vigorous, Straightforward, *Straight*. In other words, that they share Shaw's view of the non-Perverse relationship between identity and originality. There is a social element to this. I've often thought that the persona adopted by an American male writer is designed to get them if not accepted then at least *tolerated* by some imaginary American Everyman in some imaginary backwoods honkytonk (or redneck bar). This, of course, is the last place in the world that one could safely appear not-Straight. And so, American male writers are often obsessed with asserting their heterosexual machismo. This can get ridiculous. Here is Martin Amis, writing about the ultimate American wannabe tough guy Norman Mailer:

> For some reason or other, Mailer spent the years between 1950 and 1980 in a tireless quest for a fistfight [. . .]. Having walked his two poodles one night in New York, Mailer returned home 'on cloud nine', 'in ecstasy', with his left eye 'almost out of his head'. He had got into a fight, he told his wife, because a couple of sailors 'accused my dog of being queer'. According to the doctor, it was 'a hell of a beating he took'. But 'Stormin' Norman' was unrepentant. 'Nobody's going to call my dog a queer,' he growled.[4]

But if, in this imaginary honkytonk, the writer gets talking to the imaginary American Everyman sitting on the stool next to him, he is likely to be defensive about what he says he does:

> Yeah, sure, I'm a writer, but I write about manly, outdoor activities—like going fishing or hunting; I write about life on the mean streets of LA and New York; I write about war and heroism; I write about failure and the American dream. Hey and also, I write *damn* hard. The last thing I wrote took me 15 drafts. But that wasn't because I was fancying it up at all. No, I was trying to make the thing as honest and direct and Straightforward and *Straight* as I could.

So, where Virginia Woolf says, 'I'm genteel', Richard Ford says, 'I'm not gay.'

(As an aside, I should perhaps acknowledge how many exceptions to this position there are. When James Baldwin, exceptional in innumerable ways, was asked, 'You're a writer. You were born poor, black and gay. Didn't that make you feel that the odds were stacked against you from the start?' He replied, 'No, I thought I'd hit the jackpot.')

However, in the Bernard Shaw position, which I believe is exemplified by Ford, Mailer and their like, there are two basic misunderstandings.

The first is social. It is the mistaken belief that to be gay is to be Perverse. This is untrue. Nothing is 'Straighter' than a gay person being gay. What is Perverse is for a gay person to pretend—perhaps because society pressures them—that they are Straight.

The second misunderstanding is aesthetic. It is the mistaken belief that the acts of writing, of having an identity, of being original, are non-Perverse.

At this point, I better define what I mean by Perverse. I will start by giving a brief example. Here is a passage from *Middlemarch*. Not, you might think, a particularly Perverse novel. Will Ladislaw has just parted from Dorothea Casaubon:

She sank into the chair and for a few moments sat there like a statue, while images and emotions were hurrying upon her. Joy came first, in spite of the threatening train behind it—joy in the impression that it was really herself whom Will loved and was renouncing, that there was really no other love less permissible, more blameworthy, which honour was hurrying him away from. They were parted all the same, but—Dorothea drew a deep breath and felt her strength return—she could think of him unrestrainedly. At that moment the parting was easy to bear: the sense of loving and being loved excluded sorrow. It was as if some hard icy pressure had melted, and her consciousness had room to expand; her past was come back to her with larger interpretation. *The joy was not less—perhaps it was the more complete just then—because of the irrevocable parting*; for there was no reproach, no contemptuous wonder to imagine in any eye or from any lips. He had acted so as to defy reproach, and make wonder respectful.[5]

The Perversity here is very complex. I won't go into every aspect of it. But here are a few. There is the commonest Perversity: that of human beings not wanting what is good for them, of wanting—instead—what is (on the surface, at least) *bad* for them. Dorothea, one would think, wants to live happily ever after with Will Ladislaw. *No*, in this passage, Dorothea clearly wants to live happily ever after *without* Will Ladislaw. Dorothea is Perverse in terms of action: she does not immediately call Ladislaw back and tell him she loves him. That seems the obvious thing to do. Dorothea is Perverse in terms of the reader: *we* want her to be happy, and *we* think being with Ladislaw will secure her happiness. Dorothea is sexually Perverse. (The imagery of the statue and the melting frigidity is clearly sexual.) Dorothea is really *getting off* on Ladislaw's rectitude, his decency *turns her on*, his renunciation *deeply thrills* her. However, the writing itself is unPerverse. George Eliot is subscribing entirely to the demands of her chosen genre. In a romance, the lovers are constantly forced together in situations where they can't *be* together (as lovers); and then forced apart again.

Here is an example of a different kind of Perversity—literary Perversity. It comes from Malcolm Cowley's memoir *Exile's Return: A Literary Odyssey of the 1920s* (1976):

> The theory of convolutions was evolved in Pittsburgh, at Peabody High School, but it might have appeared in any city during those years before the war. It was generally explained with reference to the game of Odd or Even. You have held an even number of beans or grains of corn in your hand; you have won; therefore you take an even number again. That is the simplest argument by analogy; it is no convolution at all. But if you say to yourself, 'I had an even number before and won; my opponent will expect me to have an even number again; therefore I'll take an odd number,' you have entered the First Convolution. If you say, 'Since I won with an even number before, my opponent will expect me to try to fool him by having an odd number this time; therefore I'll be even,' you are Second Convolution. The process seems capable of indefinite extension; it can be applied, moreover, to any form of art, so long as one is less interested in what one says than in one's ability to outwit an audience.[6]

Let us take this as a model, though we will have to distort it slightly to make it suitable. If we call No Convolution 'Straight' and we call First Convolution 'Perverse'—which satisfyingly makes Straight-Even and Perverse-Odd—then we have the beginnings of a game; a game between writer and reader. What is the writer going to say? How many convolutions will it involve? But let us next admit that the writer doesn't *have* to choose a static position from which to speak; that the writer can speak *as* they move; and—in fact—the direction in which they are moving is one of the most important factors in interpreting what they are saying. Somewhere along this imaginary line between Odd and Even, Perverse and Straight, all writers find their range. A writer such as Shaw attempts to portray himself as unmovingly set upon the furthest verge of the Straight. Yet even with Shaw, a slight oscillation—or movement back and forth—is discernible. I would see this in the statement, 'Disprove his assertion after it is made, yet its style remains.'

To summarize: a writer's identity derives from the range in which they move back and forth, between the two poles of Perversity and Straightness.

However, to complicate things further, a writer may attempt at any point to portray themselves at another—perhaps quite opposite—point. Originality, I would say, is the fascination of this momentary interval. If one is a certain kind of writer, one can play around with these inter-relationships. One can reposition oneself along this imaginary line; taking different aesthetic stances even within a single sentence. One can act the sophisticate or play dumb. One can Perversely attempt straightness or be a straightforward Pervert. Or one can Pervert even more one's hidden Perversity by a further straightening of one's apparent Straightness. One has a choice of choices, all of which give identity the chance to express itself. And if that expression is fascinating, it stands a chance of being discerned as original. And one may do all this in the full realization that while Perversity is, at times, adolescent, Straightness is quite often banal.

★

After reaching about this point, I put this lecture aside for a couple of days, in order to write something else. And, as is usually the case with me, I began to have second thoughts. In fact, I will be honest with you: I began to disagree with a fair proportion of what I'd originally said. Perhaps this was a semi-conscious reaction to having wanted to suppress a sentence that appeared at the end of the Cowley quotation. In fact, reading through, just now, I *did* suppress it. That sentence is: 'We were not conscious of having anything special to say; we merely wanted to live in ourselves and be writers.'

Some of you may be sitting there thinking: *Ah, now he's being postmodern.* Others of you are probably leaning back and thinking: *Oh dear, now he's being too clever for his own good.* But if I'm being postmodern, it's with a great deal of hesitation. I'd avoid such a thing, if I were able. If I'm being too clever, and it's not for my own good, then I'll just have to set my-own-good aside for a while. Plus, I don't believe in pretending to be less clever than one is, just to make one's argument consistent—or one's lecture monolithic.

As I said, I began, when I read over what I'd written so far, to doubt whether I was *as* completely convinced by my own arguments as I pretended to be. Wasn't I, in fact, exaggerating my own Perverseness for effect? Wasn't I secretly attracted to

Shaw's non-Perverse position? Didn't his anti-virtuoso censori-
ousness—like Cowley's self-criticism—call up in me a desire to
recant? (I realize that I'm now employing another series of
Hector-type rhetorical questions.) But then I had a moment of
realization: that this vacillation, this halt, this desire halfway
through writing the lecture to unsay what I'd initially set out
to say, was, in itself, an example of exactly the kind of oscillation between Perversity and Straightness I had set out to
describe.

Thinking ahead to the actual delivery of the lecture, I began
to be slightly afraid of the way in which I would appear—both
to the audience and to myself—at the moment of delivery.
Would I, in the old existentialist jargon, be delivering my discourse in bad faith? Well, I had no guarantee as to whether—
and I'm now referring to the time that a short while ago
became *now*—I would be Straight or Perverse. But, in a way, I
was delighted by this inability to second-guess myself. It
seemed to me that, in admitting my doubts to you, with all
the accusations of pretentiousness that this might bring, and
all the embarrassment I might feel, that I, at one and the same
moment, was be being very Straight and highly Perverse.
Which reconciliation I should probably leave as the last word.

But that would be too easy. Instead, I will attempt to
describe my own writerly identity. I confess, I admire the virtuoso. I can see—even granting that there was such a thing as
a 'mere virtuoso'—exactly why a person would 'pay with [their]
whole life and soul to become a mere virtuoso in literature'.
To paraphrase Shaw, 'Raymond Carver has no more destroyed
the style of Oscar Wilde nor of Nabokov than the late Henry

James destroyed the style of the early.' Which is not to say that I, myself, would pay with my whole life and soul to become a mere virtuoso. But it *is* to say that I'm very glad that there are some writers who *are*. I confess, I love paradox. I love the epigrammatic. I am a contrarian. I have a highly dialectical mind. In conversation, I will often play devil's advocate just for the hell of it. Or, I will pick the weakest possible position, and then try to defend it—or even win from it. But if I feel that I *have* won, I will just as likely switch or reverse my position—and attempt to refute what I was asserting earlier. For this dialectical tendency, I blame, at least in part, my education and, in particular, the Oxford tutorial system. There is a sense in which, because of this, I am interested more in the quality of the argument than in the seriousness of the issues.

And yet, there is, I should say, one issue I take very seriously indeed. It is the attempt that is commonly made, most often by governments, to force everyone, all citizens, to be Straight: to want only what is good for them, to enjoy only what does them no harm.

Ultimately, I oppose Shaw's depiction of writings as manly vigorous straightforward Straight because it is reductive oppressive banal and absolutely no fun whatsoever.

Notes

1 George Bernard Shaw, 'Epistle Dedicatory to Arthur Bingham Walkley', *Man and Superman* (London: Penguin, 1946), p. 35.

2 Ibid.

3 Richard Ford, 'Good Raymond', *New Yorker*, 5 October 1998. Available at: http://goo.gl/S9r8WL (last accessed on 1 December 2015).

4 Martin Amis, 'Norman Mailer: The Avenger and the Bitch' in *The Moronic Inferno and Other Visits to America* (London: Penguin, 1987), p. 70.

5 George Eliot, *Middlemarch: A Study of Provincial Life* (London: Penguin, 1965), p. 683.

6 Malcolm Cowley, *Exile's Return: A Literary Odyssey of the 1920s* (London: Penguin, 1976), p. 21.

W. G. Sebald

Because I cannot hope to turn again
Consequently I rejoice, having to construct something
Upon which to rejoice.

T. S. Eliot, 'Ash Wednesday'

With W. G. Sebald's death his books changed essentially. At the time (11 December 2001) I had read only two of them: *The Rings of Saturn* (1995) and *Vertigo* (1990). I was intending to read the others—those that had been translated into English and published: *The Emigrants* (1992) and *Austerlitz* (2001). This latter I had received in proof from Simon Prosser, my editor at Hamish Hamilton, who a few months before had also become Sebald's editor. I started reading *Austerlitz* almost as soon as it arrived, but stopped after 50 or so pages. Why? The answer to this has, I think, a great deal to do with what has changed about Sebald's books with his death.

I began to make some notes on this subject in a wide wooden shelter overlooking the beach at Southwold. My intention, on setting out on the walk to town that morning had been to go to Southwold's Seamans' Reading Room, and work there on a Sebald essay which had, for some time, been weighing heavily upon my mind. But the weather of the day was so perfect that I couldn't force myself to contemplate going inside. And so I ended up stranded halfway between Sebald's two most important Southwold locations: Gunhill and the Reading Room.

Sitting in the shelter reminded me of an anecdote from Graham Greene's autobiography. It is so choice as to be almost unbelievable, but I present it here as I remember Greene telling it. Once, upon sitting down in a small and very dark shelter overlooking the sea in Brighton (I think Greene may have been there researching the novel that was to become *Brighton Rock* [1938]), Greene found that he was not alone. A voice spoke from the corner of the shelter, out from the gloom: 'I'm Old Moore . . . .' When Greene did not immediately reply, the voice added: 'You know . . . the Almanack.' Now, that is the anecdote, to the best I can recollect it. I know that it's in one of Greene's two autobiographies (*A Sort of Life* [1971] and *Ways of Escape* [1980]) but I do not know which. If I were Sebald, this uncertainty would not be allowed to last—other kinds of uncertainty can endure, but not those of textual or historical reference.

During his lifetime, I had admired Sebald's writing, but it made me feel anxious. After I read both *The Rings of Saturn* and *Vertigo*, I came up with a phrase for what I felt he was doing. (I should apologize for this in advance; it isn't flattering, either to myself or to Sebald.) I called his books 'academic porn'. The reasoning behind this was fairly simple: while writing his non-academic books, Sebald was able to indulge himself in the kind of unfounded speculation that academics can usually only fantasize about in the privacy of their studies. A good example of this comes in the first section of *The Rings of Saturn*. Sebald is writing of Rembrandt's painting *The Anatomy Lesson*, reproduced across two pages, in which a Dr Tulp is shown surrounded by surgeons; the dissection from which this famous image derives took place in Waaggebouw; Sebald writes:

It is somehow odd that Dr Tulp's colleagues are not looking at Kindt's body, that their gaze is directed just past it to focus on the open anatomical atlas in which the appalling physical facts are reduced to a diagram, a schematic plan of the human being, such as envisaged by the enthusiastic amateur anatomist René Descartes, who was also, so it is said, present that January morning in the Waaggebouw.[1]

Sitting in the shelter, making notes, I was harsher on this passage (remembered) than I should have been. I wrote:

In *The Rings of Saturn* [Sebald] indulges himself in a way that would shame even the crummiest biographer; two major historical figures were in a city at the same time, they both shared an interest in anatomy, therefore *it is almost inevitable that they both attended X's lectures*. This is a very low-level parlour game; fascinating and almost as meaningless as Virtual History.

Sebald's tendency, it seemed to me at that time, of allowing himself to get away with the academically discreditable, *or so it is said*, overtook all his work: the introduction of the first person (the exquisitely miserablist narrator), the emphasis on human temporality (of both the narrator and his subjects), the centrality of the haphazard (as both subject-giver and investigational method)—all these distinctive characteristics seemed weaknesses. When challenged that a grocer's son from Stratford couldn't possibly have written Shakespeare's plays, George Bernard Shaw replied that, on the contrary, they were exactly the sort of plays one *would* expect a grocer's son from Stratford to write. The books, I believed, were exactly what you might envisage a German academic's busman's holiday as being. The porny aspect was, I thought, also what made Sebald appeal so strongly to borderline-academic writers such as Susan Sontag (who love-licked him with a famous quote). He was violating some of the same decorums as her. His getting away with it gave these almost-academics licence, a feeling of running-naked-along-the-beach freedom. Imagine that—in Southwold.

After it arrived through the post, I felt no urgency about reading the proof of *Austerlitz*. It might be nice, I thought, to have read it before it came out; to have formed an opinion before the reviewers had formed theirs—not to speak of the public. But *Austerlitz* appeared to me then as merely *another* of Sebald's books. Lawrence Norfolk, with whom I'd discussed Sebald both before and after reading him, had told me that (in his experience), for most people the first book by Sebald they read always remained their favourite. With each further publication, *the* book by Sebald became *a* book by Sebald and then merely *another* book by Sebald—one, now, of a series that would continue until he ceased publishing. In total there would be 12, perhaps, or 14. (The fact that Sebald's books did not come out properly chronologically in England added to the earlier feeling that each was not just *another*.) On his death, *Austerlitz* became if not Sebald's *last* book (we English were playing catch-up again) then his last published book. (There were other prose works to come. The Luftwaffe book, *The Natural History of Destruction* [2004]. Also, a book of poetry, *After Nature* [2003]. Also a rumoured screenplay about Emmanuel Kant.) The fact there was now a definite and already reached limit to Sebald's production was, I thought, of definite benefit to those books that remained. This is the thing that changed in them with Sebald's death: each became instantly more characteristic of itself. Their serial nature corroded—the next few books would not be anothers, they would be uniquenesses. Why is this important? Well, Sebald's work—on one's first encounter with it—is so strange in tone that each further book can only diminish from the reader's sense of that original book's singularity. (This, I think, was Norfolk's point.) There were comparisons to be made: Was *Vertigo* better or worse than *The Emigrants*? With merely one book in print, the question had been more: *What the fucking hell is this? Where can we possibly place it?* Sebald is a librarian's nightmare. He could legitimately be shelved under FICTION, HISTORY, ART HISTORY, AUTOBIOGRAPHY, TRAVEL WRITING, PHILOSOPHY and LITERARY CRITICISM. There was, I was sure, some quality about Sebald's writing which made it amazingly addictive. Perhaps because, unlike so many of the other proses out there, it so resolutely didn't button-hole the reader. But the first book one read was more addictive than those subsequent; the hit was *less* each time.

In *The Rings of Saturn*, Sebald depicts himself as taking a coastal walk—his rough itinerary includes Southwold. As is usual with him, his perambulations lead to thoughts historical.

Here is one such moment of transition (I feel like saying ascension) from the diaristic to the elegiac:

> Footsore and weary as I was after my long walk from Lowestoft, I sat down on a bench on the green called Gunhill and looked out on the tranquil sea, from the depths of which the shadows were now rising. Everyone who had been out for an evening stroll was gone. I felt as if I were in a deserted theatre, and I should not have been surprised if a curtain had suddenly risen before me and on the proscenium I had beheld, say, the 28th of May 1672—that memorable day when the Dutch fleet appeared offshore from out of the drifting mists, with the bright morning light behind it, and opened fire on the English ships in Sole Bay.[2]

There follow three and a half pages describing the Battle of Sole Bay; then comes: 'Just as these things have always been beyond my understanding so too I found it impossible to believe, as I sat on Gunhill in Southwold that evening, that just one year earlier I had been looking across to England from a beach in Holland.'[3] Now, these sentences, or, more accurately, these *kinds* of sentences—parsing the academe—are, for me, the most fascinating in Sebald's writing. (I mean *or so it is said*, and *on the proscenium I had beheld, say, the 28th of May 1672* and *so too I found it impossible to believe.*) They are where the feebleness of his transitions reveals itself as extreme, inventive daring.

Yet the most banal part of me, upon reading this passage, would like an answer to the simple question: *When Sebald sat on that bench, at that hour, did he really have all those facts present in his mind?* I feel a certain envy.

One of the most notable things about Sebald's books (and a contributing factor to their academic porniness) is their total lack of footnotes. This might be presented as an irony of their form: the footnotes, in fact, are the majority of the work, it's just they have been absorbed into the overall text. The two sentences I've quoted above ('Footsore and weary . . . ' and 'Just as these things . . . ') are the original text, what follows is implicitly footnote. Under this interpretation, *The Rings of Saturn* could be reduced to the banal 3,000-word diary of a not-particularly-interesting walking tour. Alternatively, the main argument of the book could be seen to be the meditations—which, in turn, are loosely, collapsingly strung together by overfreighted sentences such as the two. The second one, in particular, spends most of its length saying, 'I was there—remember—I know it's a while ago, and there isn't that much to recall, but I was *there* and *this* is what I was doing.'

However, since his death I have come to characterize Sebald's writing another way; and I would like to approach it by asking a question: *What is the time of Sebald's writing?*

The answer, I think, is that Sebald writes in four completely separate times, often simultaneously. I would define these times as follows:

Real. The time of the initial experience, when Sebald was physically where he describes himself as being.

Diary. The time of written recollection—almost certainly in a different location; a study, library or provincial tea room.

Research. The extended time period during which the suggestions of the initial experience and the elaborations of the written recollection are further elaborated.

Style. This time is not singular but takes up the entire period throughout which Sebald became a writer, went through the first three time periods (*Real, Diary, Research*), wrote, rewrote and finally left alone the sentences of his that he was prepared to publish.

Real time, clearly, may not involve any writing—or even the anticipation that the experience being gone through will one day prove noteworthy. But, Sebald being a writer, some form of inscription does wordlessly take place. Either 'My tables,—meet it is I set it down' or 'Your face forever is remember'd here.'

Diary time is easy to isolate. 'In August 1992, when the dog days were drawing to an end, I set off to walk the county of Suffolk . . . .' Clearly, though, these are not the words that Sebald would have written in his diary the first night of the walking tour. The second half of the sentence reveals the distance that intervenes between him and his remembered self, 'in the hope of dispelling the emptiness that takes hold of me whenever I have completed a long stint of work.' *Style* has intervened and rewritten. Literary overlayings are taking place: Auden, Proust, Chaucer. It might therefore be better to call this *Memoir* time, only I am not sure that Sebald didn't eventually become an inveterate adder-of-distance between himself and his experience. His *Diary* was, I suspect, already half-*Memoir*.

I moved across into Southwold Sailors' Reading Room at about this point in my note-making, as it was getting too cold in the shelter. It was just past 11 a.m. on the 16th of January. There was a great deal more to be said of Sebald's antecedents, but I thought it had already been said, elsewhere, by others, ad nauseam. Sebald, for me, was more interesting—in the times of his writing—than almost all his forbears; Proust, I would exclude.

Research time intervenes at some time, at many times, between the real walk and the finished book. I would say it comes first, at an early stage, well before the first draft. But this would be a guess. I know from Simon Prosser, Sebald's editor, that Sebald was working on another book at the time of his death. It was to take as its main object the silence of Sebald's German elders concerning the years of National Socialism. In particular, Sebald was interested in making use of some home movies he had discovered of SS troops acting out Aryan myths. Simon Prosser suggested to me that Sebald's time of research was almost over and his moment of writing was about to begin. One day, when his manuscripts have become public, probably via Texas, we will all know more about this than we could possibly want. Guessing is more enticing.

Research takes in the reading-up on subjects Sebald remembers having thought about. Going to Gunhill, which has six sea-facing cannons, it seems almost inevitable that thoughts of repulsed invasions would occur to one. But I don't believe that all those facts were present to Sebald at the moment of sitting. (Envy, again.) Thus *Research* added to *Diary* means that it is possible for Sebald to quote half a page of source material without getting a comma wrong. However, Sebald's time becomes at this point confused; or, one might say, elaborated. For his initial *Real* thoughts are partly memories of previous *Research*, which he must now check in further *Research*. Hence *Research* both precedes and post-dates the *Real* moment on Gunhill.

Style is too small and too big a word, but by it I mean intellectual style as well as prose style. *Tone* might perhaps be better, though it would not suggest, as style half does, that it is the style of the man Sebald which led him to be sitting on that bench at that moment. I might here begin to write rhapsodically of Sebald's participation in European intellectual history, and of the maudlin delight he takes in having *Sic transit gloria* meditations in very bad fast-food restaurants. *Style* is the dominant time of Sebald's writing: it is what enables him to write at all. To other writers what is most thrilling about Sebald the time of his *Style*.

When he was alive I felt that there was a certain get-out clause here: that the film-subtitle aspect of Sebald's writing—the fact it is a translation, albeit one in which the writer was a collaborator (to what extent will, I'm sure, become clear in the next few years)—allowed Sebald to say things an English writer writing in English wouldn't dare. Although he is doing something very different; I think there is something comparable here to in the writing of Alain de Botton—particularly in the more fictionally tainted of his books, *Essays in Love* (1993) and *The Romantic Movement: Sex, Shopping and the Novel* (1994). There is something embarrassing about a sentence like this, written in English. 'For those in love with certainty, seduction is no territory in which to stray.'[4]

I was sitting at a wide wooden table. Tacked to the rough surface of the table was a photocopied sheet, outlined in black,

NO CAMERAS. When I lifted my elbows, the surface of the table had left guilty sawdusty white on the black of my coat. A clock with the word REGULATOR upon its glass, in front of the swinging brass pendulum, ticked and very definitely tocked on the far wall.

A pony has just gone past. I've promised to be back by 12 and it is now 20 to.

The moment of Sebald's *Style*, as presented in his writing, is one of great duration.

My epigraph is obvious but unsatisfactory.

Notes

1 W. G. Sebald, *The Rings of Saturn* (Michael Hulse trans.) (London: Vintage, 2002), p. 13.

2 Ibid., p. 76.

3 Ibid., p. 80.

4 Alain de Botton, *Essays in Love* (London: Picador, 2006), p.17.

Against Nature *by Joris-Karl Huysmans*

How do you think about your life? It's not a simple question. *How do you introduce enough distance between yourself, this person who has lived your life, and yourself, this person you are, so as to be able to think of them?* Not think objectively, that is definitely impossible, but with some perspective and therefore, you might hope, some small chance of getting the general outlines at least right. Joris-Karl Huysmans' *Against Nature* (2003) gives instances, or, rather, is an instance, I would say, of two of the most commonly used methods of self-thinking.

Before I get to them, however, I would like briefly to characterize Huysmans' book. *Against Nature* is inseparable from its listless protagonist, the Duc Jean des Esseintes. Like him, *Against Nature* is frail, anaemic, ennervated, perverse. Formally, Huysmans does everything he can possibly do to undermine any expectation that this novel might contain a story. He begins with a prologue that tells us, essentially, all the most interesting things that have happened to des Esseintes—and it also tells us that these things have happened *already*, that we won't be hearing about them in this book except in retrospect. There is enough implied incident in these pages to fill an entire novel, and Huysmans throws it away. By the time the prologue finishes, des Esseintes has exhausted all his desires—and is therefore the perfect subject for a novel with no narrative tension, no quest, with nothing but a voice, an attitude and a desire to disconcert.

Throughout *Against Nature* two tendencies are in opposition, categorization and flow; sometimes flow will come to dominate, sometimes categorization, but never for long—rarely for more than a paragraph. Good examples of both tendencies can be found in almost every chapter, but one of the best is the 'collection of liqueur casks' that des Esseintes calls his 'mouth organ'. This seems quite self-consciously to be an attempt to reconcile the two tendencies in one object. The mouth organ, like much in the novel, is based upon the principle of analogy. 'Indeed, each and every liqueur, in his opinion, corresponded with the sound of a particular instrument. Dry curacao, for instance, was like the clarinet with its piercing, velvety note . . . .'[1] Yet even in this first example, there is a slip towards flow—the taste of curacao is categorized as 'like the clarinet' but to illustrate this the word 'velvety' is used. In other words, taste is like sound is like touch. This confusion of the senses, this fluid crossing of the boundaries separating them, is characteristic of that very poetic condition, synaesthesia. Baudelaire's sonnet 'Correspondances' is the source: 'Les parfums, les colours et les sons se repondent.' ['Scents, colours and sounds all correspond.'][2]

Early on in *Against Nature*, des Esseintes makes close correspondences between books and colours. 'The drawing room, for example, had been partitioned off into a series of niches, which were styled to harmonize vaguely, by means of subtly

analogous colours that were gay or sombre, delicate or bar-
barous, with the character of his favourite works in Latin and
French.'³ Later, books are likened to food, drawing, painting,
the sick and dead body—and the flow of analogy doesn't stop
here, jewels are experienced as food, food as the sick body,
etc. In order to try and categorize this flow, des Esseintes and
Huysmans come up with similar strategies: des Esseintes
divides his life self-consciously into periods; Huysmans divides
des Esseintes' life into chapters. And these are examples of the
first method most people use to understand their lives.

It is impossible to think about your life as an unbroken flow,
from birth, or from when your memories begin, up until the
point you have now reached. In order to understand it in any
way at all, you have to categorize it, either by dividing it up into
periods (infancy, childhood, school, twenties, etc.) or by gathering parts of different periods together under implicit chapter
headings (education, travel, sex, love). Both of these, of course,
involve the distillation of experiences, just as the liqueurs in the
mouth organ have been distilled.

What is fascinating about des Esseintes is how self-
consciously he attempts to categorize the flow of his own
existence—the dandy, by definition, is someone attempting to
turn their life into a work of art. There is a clear collaboration
between des Esseintes and his biographer, Huysmans, but one
of the perverse ways in which the book they share seems to
work is that the life has been lived in order to facilitate the form
of its telling. We know this is not the case, and the illusion
should backfire: the writer, really, surely, is making the subject
convenient for himself. Yet it is clear that des Esseintes just as

much as Huysmans shapes the book by living his life so clearly in periods, which, eventually, will be incorporated into chapters. The interplay between des Esseintes' periods and Huysmans' chapters is what gives the book its distinctive form—it is a syncopation, the one not always lining up with the other: some chapters contain several periods, some only one. This is in many ways the book's only formal tension—otherwise, the novel would resemble a gigantic escalating list. (If one were being really cheeky, one could describe des Esseintes as a prototype Nick Hornby list-boy.) There is almost no plotting as such: the death of the tortoise, which is forgotten then discovered, dead, is one of the few incidents worth mentioning.

It's worth saying that there is nothing at all Natural about viewing a life as divided up into periods. But this tendency has been on the increase throughout human history. The more people there are with some control over their lives, the more self-consciously they will exercise that control. Many people in the past have lacked the chapter-making capacity (or privilege) altogether, and many still do: their life is their life, as it is now so will it continue to be. Popular psychology has popularized the idea of the quantum existence, the life lived in discrete packets of energy—chapters. The message of Oprah is the same message as Rilke's 'Archaic Torso of Apollo' (1908): 'You must change your life.'[4] For unless you see your life as having chapters, you will have no way of changing it, because you will be unable to believe it *can* be changed, because—in turn—you won't be able to perceive the points in the past where it *has* changed.

The other method of self-thinking comes through comparison of the self with what is known of the selves of others.

Against Nature is a book in which and through which and also against which many people have defined themselves. It is, in many ways, a deliberate primer for the personality. Des Esseintes is at once one of the most attractive and repulsive characters in literature. Or perhaps not at *once* but at different periods, and not periods in his life but in our own. The world view of des Esseintes is adolescent: contemptuous of the everyday, easily bored, hypersensitive, sulky. As he cries out at one point, like a teenager refusing to go out with their parents: 'But I just don't enjoy the pleasures other people enjoy!'[5] And the character of des Esseintes, therefore, is far more likely to attract one when one is adolescent, and to repel one more and more the further one gets away from that frustrating and clumsy chapter. What *Against Nature* does is give a very precise series of comparisons-to-be-made. For example, des Esseintes' love of the prints of Jan Luyken:

> He possessed a whole series of studies by this artist in lugubrious fantasy and ferocious cruelty: his *Religious Persecutions*, a collection of appalling plates displaying all the tortures which religious fanaticism has invented, revealing all the agonizing varieties of human suffering—bodies roasted over braziers, heads scalped with swords, trepanned with nails, lacerated with saws, bowels taken out of the belly and wound on to bobbins, finger-nails slowly removed with pincers, eyes put out, eyelids pinned back, limbs dislocated and carefully broken, bones laid bare and scraped for hours with knives.[6]

This, I would guess, apart from the deep-in-adolescence, is a moment of separation between the reading self and that being described. 'No,' the reader is likely to think, 'here we part company—there is no way I could live with such images.' Of course, the black-bedroom-inhabiting, Marilyn Manson–listening, gore-fascinated adolescent is likely to say, 'Cool,' and type JAN LUYKEN into their favourite search engine.

One of the tensions that replaces narrative drama in *Against Nature* is that between novelist and character. It's pretty clear that there is a separation between des Esseintes and Huysmans, and this is clearest in their sense of humour: des Esseintes is amused by cruelty and little else; Huysmans is a sly and brilliant humorist. He follows the Luyken description with this little deadpan gem: 'These prints were mines of interesting information and could be studied for hours on end without a moment's boredom . . . .'[7]

Against Nature is a tempting book, one that, in many sections, attempts to draw the reader into closer proximity with evil. Yet by doing this, and also by granting that authors, books and readers may not all be on the side of the angels, Huysmans reveals himself to be an extremely moral writer. As he notes:

> The truth of the matter is that if it did not involve sacrilege, sadism would have no *raison d'etre*; on the other hand, since sacrilege depends on the existence of religion, it cannot be deliberately and effectively committed except by a believer, for a man would derive no satisfaction whatever from profaning a faith that was unimportant or unknown to him.[8]

Which may explain why *Against Nature* is one of the least perverse and most autobiographically useful novels ever written.

Notes

1 Joris-Karl Huysmans, *Against Nature* (Patrick McGuinness trans.) (London: Penguin Classics, 2003), p. 45.

2 Charles Baudelaire, 'Correspondences' in *Complete Poems* (Walter Martin trans.) (Manchester: Carcanet, 1997), p. 19.

3 Huysmans, *Against Nature*, p. 12.

4 Rainer Maria Rilke, 'Archaic Torso of Apollo' in *Ahead of All Parting: Selected Poetry and Prose of Rainer Maria Rilke* (Stephen Mitchell trans.) (New York: Modern Library, 1995), p. 67.

5 Huysmans, *Against Nature*, p.196.

6 Ibid., pp. 57–8.

7 Ibid., p. 58.

8 Ibid., p. 148.

On Monsters

What is a Monster? In contemporary fiction, a monster will inevitably be post-Marxist, post-Freudian/post-Jungian, post-Cinema, post- or maybe merely mid-genetic manipulation. Which, let's face it, isn't very scary.

'Oh my God, there's a Monster—there's a Monster!' is a lot more scary than 'Oh my God, there's a fictional construct revealing horrific tensions not only within the psyche of its creator but also within the historical dialectic coming! Oh no, because it was created a few years ago it's special effects aren't very convincing—perhaps revealing our own growing fears of inauthenticity!'

Help! It seems to be biting me.

Clearly, what I'm using the Monster to represent here are aberrant eruptions of the unreal or supernatural into Realist fiction. (I'd prefer for the moment deal with the matter in these terms rather than those of genre and mainstream; I'm also going to ally Realism with Rationalism, although their relationship isn't one of straightforward comradeship.)

But there's a very strong argument to be made that Realism is itself the aberration, the Monstrous distortion of human experience. From *Beowulf* to *Gawain and the Green Knight* through

Paradise Lost, Frankenstein, Gulliver's Travels, Jekyll and Hyde and *Dracula*, there have always been major Monsters.

Where do they come from?

In Goya's etching it is 'The Sleep of Reason', which is said to 'Bring Forth Monsters'. But, post-everything-I-listed-at-the-start, it's inescapable that *we* are the Monsters: we are the Wolf Man, we are the Crowd-Beast.

Of course, we are the Monsters, and the problem is that we know so clearly that we are. We have reached what you could call 'the Scooby-Doo impasse': we know the Monster is never the Monster, always the greedy Janitor who wants to take over the Funfair. 'And we'd have gotten away with it, if it hadn't been for you meddling Ids!'

The question, it seems to me, is whether we really—with or without our Monster masks and costumes on—scare ourselves any more?

To be paradoxical, Goya's statement can be reversed, and I think may even be meant to be reversed: The sleep of *Monsters* brings forth *Reason*. Reason is our Monstrous Dream of how the World should be—it's only through Reason that we are able to talk about the World at all.

Or perhaps we can read the reversal another way, the Sleep of Monsters is us pretending that the Monsters we see ourselves as being are asleep. In other words, we understand ourselves so well that our Monster-selves are not only un-scary, they are safely un-conscious.

In this Rational, Reasonable, Realistic world of ours, the Monsters may slumber but they never go completely away. The absence of Monsters would mean the absence of us.

If we want our Monsters to be scary again, we will have to misunderstand them. We will have to misunderstand them vastly—and to do that, we will have to forget all that we've learnt about them. This can't be achieved by an act of will, but it can become political policy—it can be attempted if not achieved by censorship and propaganda.

Since Godzilla, the God-monster, stomped on Manhattan, the 'isolated thing in water', we have been encouraged to believe our Reasonable world is threatened by real Monsters. Our ploughshares have been beaten into swords—and, in the same forge, the Hammer and Sickle has been refashioned into a Cresent. 'Post-al-Quaeda' has to be added to my list of what a monster now can't help but be.

On one side we have the Scary Monsters, on the other it's the Super Creeps. Not an attractive choice, but fiction of all sorts—genre and mainstream—has to accommodate or ignore both.

On Ghost Stories

Otherness is an issue for all writers, but especially for writers of ghost stories.

For us, others provide our others; others step forward to be our others; others—Freud, Marx, Derrida, Spielberg—who are culturally stronger than we are.

To write a ghost story is to deal very directly with otherness. And, partly because of this, our new-created otherness is dealt with very directly—its power is immediately short-circuited.

There are a number, a limited number, of loops through which the electricity is permitted to flow: 'Ah, this ghost is *this* kind of ghost.'

And so our stories are no longer capable of delivering shocks—not unless we compel or, more satisfyingly, persuade our reader to put their finger into the circuit itself.

I am not imagining an age of unrestricted energy flows. Ghost stories have always had to deal with pre-emption—with being understood before they are read.

And the fact that ghost stories, by being undead, are capable of outliving the high points of this or that imposed otherness doesn't improve matters. Another short circuit has merely been superadded to those already installed.

A writer may present their work with the implication *Look, here is something other*, but its other is received as being of a kind; it is immediately converted into other-ness rather than allowed to appear as something truly other. The new-created electricity is provided with a limited wire to flow down—to return upon and negate itself. Forewarned readers know not to stick their fingers in; perhaps because they were so badly shocked early on in life.

The real problem for contemporary writers of ghost stories is that they themselves internalize these short circuits, that they start to pre-know their own othernesses. To do this is simply to provide a labelled switch for the reader: on/off. But I don't believe ghost stories should be so satisfyingly binary. Their subject is haunting; their aim also should be to haunt. They should be able to flow sideways across circuits. They should be able to exist outside wires, as clouds of charged particles, clouds of unknowing.

We are envious of ghost stories from earlier generations because they seem to have been written in blithe disregard of the short circuits that awaited them.

Yet, in my opinion, the great ghost stories are self-consciously post-Marx, post-Freud. They attempt to channel the energy of true others despite the knowledge that the arrayed short circuits await.

Henry James is, for me, the great cloud-writer, the great writer of charged particles. And when his fiercely maintained vagueness floats past a short circuit, it simply blows it—the wires fuse, there is a flash, smoke rises in a second sympathetic cloud.

The question here is whether this power of James is dependent, in its turn, upon his own personal, fiercely maintained vagueness—vagueness with regard to the conditions of manufacture of wires, the libidinal origins of certain energies.

I am not convinced that James, though virginal, was innocent. I think he realized that coming to know true others, and thus creating the possibility of multiple othernesses, is not a matter of focus.

In their being, the true others are no less vague than we are. To encounter them on a limited level of existence or within a distilled quality of existence is to falsify them. The best way to know them is openly to be in their presence while not knowing them.

The language of ghost stories must task itself not to become limited or distilled. That is why it returns to areas rather than points, tones rather than colours, shadows rather than images. But the sites of ghost stories, the places most requiring the passage of clouds, are self-known, definitive. Ghosts haunt the power stations and laboratories of our culture—nurseries, classrooms, palaces, hospitals. Ghosts speak through wires. Ghosts appear in photographs. Ghosts mock the apparatus by which any attempt is made to calibrate or prove them.

Otherness is an issue for writers of ghost stories in a secondary sense—that these stories issue from the attempt to create otherness. But, also, that these stories take issue with too-immediate, too-convenient othernesses. In order to forestall incorporation, ghost stories remain outside the flesh.

As for the writers of these stories, we do not possess ourselves.

Reading

One reviewer of J. K. Rowling's fourth book asked their child what they thought of it. The child said, 'It took a while for the book to disappear, but after that it was great.' This is the best description I have come across of enraptured reading. The second best comes from Wallace Stevens' poem 'The House Was Quiet and the World Was Calm' (1954): 'The words were spoken as if there was no book'.[1] Very strangely, this follows rather than leads up to the more extreme statement that 'The reader became the book'. Which, surely, is the most enraptured of all imaginable readings—when the boundaries of personal identity are felt to have dissolved.

W. H. Auden famously claimed that the purpose of poetry was to 'disenchant'; and at the opposite end of the scale from the disappeared book comes disenchanted reading, the reading of the reader who never forgets the wordiness of the words on the page. Here is a short sentence from Seymour Chatman's *The Later Style of Henry James* (1972), 'There are certain identificational marks worth noting, however, namely that (everything else being equal) an indefinite article or possessive pronoun, especially combined with durative or iterative adverbs, suggests the faculty, while a relative clause or a phrase modifying the noun of perception suggests the thing-perceived.'[2] This, of course, isn't reading *as such*, it is written-up academic stylistics. But the statistical verbal analysis practised by, say, Shakespeare scholars is a kind of reading, deliberately estranged from anything but the grammatical components of the text. It is reading done by a low-grade computer. Beyond this, the activity ceases to be reading and becomes instead photocopying or printing— a straight, uninterpreted repetition.

Most of my reading takes place towards the balanced middle of these extremes, and as I become more and more the professional reader (books of obligation, books of pay) the experience of raptness becomes rarer. It may be hard for most writers—certainly most literary writers—to countenance the idea, but it is a fact that the majority of readers are only peripherally aware of style. They will form an opinion, definitely, of whether a book is good or bad, and part of this may be dependent upon whether it is to their mind well or badly written; it is very unlikely they will be able to describe how this has technically been achieved—not unless it's just a matter of the words keeping as much as possible out of the way of the action. (Perhaps this is the difference between literary and non-literary writers: the literary expect to be admired as stylists, the non-literary to be rewarded for absenting themselves.) As a reader, in terms of style, I feel I have become overconscious of how everything is done. If I want to know what it is to be an amateur again, I have to listen to complex music—pop won't do.

Reading is one of the hardest human experiences upon which to report. And I have deliberately avoided going to academic textbooks, because I've hoped to write of it in as experiential way as I can. There is a scene in the movie of *Fame* (1980) where hapless wannabe Doris Schwartz is at home at the table with the dinner her mother has cooked. During her most recent acting lesson, the teacher has advised all the students to observe themselves as they go about the day-to-day business of living. Doris, remembering this, tries to watch herself as she eats a forkful of mashed potato. Of course, as we watch her doing this, watching herself, it is the most grotesque and stilted mouthful we have ever seen. When trying to observe myself in the moment of reading, I turn into a kind of verbal Doris: although I know that moving my eyes left to right across the page (my fork from plate to mouth) is what I usually do when reading, I am far more aware that what I am doing is nothing like it normally is.

These, as well as I can remember them, are the things I am most conscious of while reading (prose): *the situation* at this point in the book—in a novel, the plot; in biography, the stage of the subject's life; in history, the power relations; in philosophy, the argument, etc.; *the situation beyond the situation*, or the things which have already occurred, the things I expected would occur but didn't and the things I expect will occur; *the general mood* of the book; *the words* being used to depict the situation; the words as they would sound were I to read them out loud; the words as they impress themselves visually upon me (do any of the coming paragraphs contain dialogue? If so, the characters who haven't been speaking are just about to start to); *the book itself*, physically—it's weight, the quality of the paper (perhaps granular, pulpy and hard to read in oblique light); the relative thickness of the book ahead and behind of the open-paged crack in it (Jane Austen plays on this, as with so much else bookish, in *Northanger Abbey* (1817)—'The anxiety, which in this state of their attachment must be the portion of Henry and Catherine, and of all who loved either, as to its final event, can hardly extend, I fear, to the bosom of my reader, who will see in the tell-tale compression of the pages before them, that we are all hastening together to perfect felicity.');[3] *the text design*, and how this contributes to or distracts from the reading— widows and orphans, bunchingupinsomeoldertexts; *the typeface* (I can't force myself to read what I think of as the Fay Weldon typeface, used until recently by Sceptre); *the proofreading*—any typos?; *my body* around the book and most particularly my hands upon it; *my situation*, the physical surroundings, conducive or not, that I find myself in; *the people around me* (sometimes this is equivalent to watching a brilliant production of a great play with a man behind one who sniffs every other minute, wetly); *the necessity of making some kind of aesthetic judgement*, local and general and universal: this choice of word, this shape of phrase, this book; *the author*, and how my reading of this book has formed or altered my impression of them; *my thoughts*, most usually my stray and unwelcome thoughts—of what I have to do later in the day (these are distinct, I'd say, from thoughts called up by the words on the page or the situations described there—memories of similar, unnerving parallel); *my judgements*, usually along the lines of *do I agree—with this metaphor, with this description?*

Poetry is very different. With a poem I usually know exactly where within it I am: it is as if a grid were stencilled on the page, and I can judge exactly where within it my eyes are falling.

I have a clear idea how many lines I have read, how many are still to come (I will flick ahead to check, if the poem runs over more than a page), and I know how far I am into a line. Poetry is less visually disguised than prose, which can maintain a perfect typographical deadpan even while conveying the most devastating news. The typography of a poem is more excitable; it gives itself away, advertises itself in advance. There are, of course, exceptions to this: blank verse offers equally as much opportunity as prose for feeling lost in the page. But these featureless columns are most usually found in modern editions; the originals, with capitalized names, italicized *sententiae*, abbreviations, ampersands, etc., are likely to be far more proselike—far fuller of visual clues. To make an analogy, prose is a forest, poetry is an ornamental garden—if one gets lost in a poem, it is likely to be in a maze rather than a thicket.

Than prose, the reading of poetry is more guilt-inducing. How can one *really* live up to, read up to, read with enough committed intelligence and accessible passion, a Shakespeare sonnet? Each reading is inadequate, and none more so than an immediate rereading after a felt-to-be-inadequate first reading. Some poems lift one swiftly to a level of required intensity—Rilke's 'Duino Elegies' (1923), for example; they make one fail to disappoint oneself. This is a rare abduction into a verbal world, what Keats refers to as 'a little Region to wander in'.[4]

As an experiment, I have decided to reread a poem with which I am familiar, Yeats' 'Leda and the Swan' (1923). I know, or think I know, the opening lines: 'A sudden blow, the great wings beating still / Above the staggering girl, her thighs caressed / By the something something bill / He holds her helpless, breast held to his breast . . . .'[5] About 10 years ago, I learnt the poem by heart, and certain phrases have stuck: 'her thighs caressed' was unforgettable. And I am aware of the overall shape of the poem, both as a sonnet and as a sonnet by Yeats. There is a certain grandeur both to his endstops and his enjambements; he knows what he's doing, he wants you to know he knows. I think of Rilke and his relationship to Rodin and to Rodin's sculptures; how a poem of Rilke's such as 'Archaic Torso of Apollo' is Classical sculpture seen through Rodin's eyes. Yeats, similarly, wishes to give a sense of his work having been hewn from stone—of his work having been work. There is a clear sense of previous, less focussed, drafts: poems simply do not come out this monumental straight off. I remember reading of a doctor ordering Yeats to stop working, because he'd started to cough up blood. This is the glamour of the unceasing craftsman—of Henry James still scribing on his deathbed, right hand moving crablike across the bedsheets; of Kafka, unable to speak, still communicating with pencilled notes. With their boots on. I am aware that 'Leda and the Swan' is a poem about rape, but that this doesn't bother me all that much—that perhaps it should bother me more; a lot more. Yeats puts a great deal of effort into the descriptions of violence and enforced calm, but it remains mythological and then remythologized violence. Perhaps some rapists *have* thought of themselves as swans or animal-incarnated gods; perhaps some rape victims *have*, while it was happening, remembered Leda. Very rarely, certainly recently. What I expect to be feeling, by the end of the poem, is exhilaration; that it hasn't disappointed—it is still as fantastically powerful a verbal construction as I've come to think it. 'Leda and the Swan' is a big fat motorbike of a poem, with plenty of horsepower to shoot one off towards the horizon. Afterwards, I will probably want to read more Yeats—his Greatest Hits: 'Easter, 1916' (1921), 'Among School Children' (1933), 'Byzantium' (1928), 'Sailing to Byzantium' (1928), 'The Fascination of What's Difficult' (1916), 'The Circus Animals' Desertion' (1939). I haven't read a biography of Yeats, though I have of Wilde, Eliot, Pound, Auden, Lowell, and have picked up an amount of information about him second-hand. So I'm not going to be thinking of the circumstances in which Yeats wrote the poem; but, unless they're built into a poem, I rarely do. I might think of Wallace Stevens, dictating lines to his secretary at the insurance company, or of Eliot, in the cinematic shelter overlooking Margate Sands, convalescing. I hope I shall be in among the words, amazed at the controlled power of them; how they seem magnetized, held in tension above the ground. This is what I anticipate. And now I am going to read the poem.

While I am reading a bird begins to sing loudly in the garden behind the house, and a car or perhaps a bus goes past under the railway bridge. I want very much to ignore these sounds, but hear them between the horizontal black and white bars and through the imagined sounding of the poem. My first reaction, on seeing the shape of the words on the pages, is something like 'Ah, here it is!'—a bit like visiting a museum again years after one's first visit, and finding the same great sculpture in the very same spot. This poem is this poem, unmistakably, not another one. The line break, the rupture in the tenth line, is very characteristic. The colon in the first line strikes me, 'A sudden blow:

the great wings beating still'; it is ugly, deliberately so, I think, and I'd forgotten it. The punctuation is radical. I am also impressed by word-combinations I'd forgotten; the thighs are caressed by 'the dark webs'. I'm a little dismayed this hadn't stuck. As I read on, I become more aware of the grandeur of the poem's sound 'And Agamemnon dead.' Dead, as always, is heavily stressed, in my reading-head—I remember that. In the edition I'm reading (Macmillan's *The Poems of W. B. Yeats*) the poem runs across two pages, making a break between lines 11 and 12. This is annoying, and makes me think poems should always be printed on a single page. I am already forgetting, by the end of the sonnet, my response to the start—and I'm aware that I should be doing my best to remember. (I have a piece of paper ready to write my reaction down.) The word 'blood' sticks out most of all: I follow a quick line of thought about Yeats and aristocracy and Lawrence and loins and cut it off before I get to Modernism and Fascism. I feel distracted and not enough in-the-poem; I've failed it. It's almost as if I haven't read the poem at all, just glanced it through: my eyes haven't entered the black of the words, they've just taken in that they are there on the page. Thinking back, I note how the confused grammar of the opening quatrain is followed by the rhetorical balance of the second; the Modernistic syntax of the next two and a half lines; the grand impending rise of the final three and a half. The 'knowledge' to be put on makes me anxious: my own knowledge of the classics is inadequate to appreciate what exactly Yeats is alluding to. The poem seems so small for the presence it has in the literary world, yet it is so strong—a strong poem about overpowering strength, written, I note finally, in 1923.

Leda and the Swan

A sudden blow: the great wings beating still
Above the staggering girl, her thighs caressed
By the dark webs, her nape caught in his bill,
He holds her helpless breast upon his breast.

How can those terrified vague fingers push
The feathered glory from her loosening thighs?
And how can body, laid in that white rush,
But feel the strange heart beating where it lies?

A shudder in the loins engenders there
The broken wall, the burning roof and tower
And Agamemnon dead.

                      Being so caught up,
So mastered by the brute blood of the air,
Did she put on his knowledge with his power
Before the indifferent beak could let her drop?

*

What have I learnt from this? Not a great deal, really, but I have reminded myself of my earlier conviction that reading is a failure to read. Keats was aware of this. In his little Region 'the images are so numerous that many are forgotten and found new in a second Reading: which may be food for a Week's stroll in the Summer?' This, for him, is the point of long poems, for readers 'like this better than what they can read through before Mrs Williams comes down stairs'.[6]

One of the best books about the failure of reading, and also its paradoxical success, is Nicholson Baker's *U & I* (1991). Without rereading any of John Updike's works, Baker analyses what from them has really been left in his memory; very little, it turns out, and that not very accurate. This is partly because Baker, like all of us, does not have a photocopying relationship to the text, and as Derrida has written about Joyce, even the idea of accurate quotation is highly problematic. Perhaps, following Philip Roth's great line from *American Pastoral* (1997), the same goes for books as for people, for reading as for living: 'The fact remains that getting people right is not what living is all about anyway. It's getting them wrong that is living, getting them wrong and wrong and wrong and then, on careful consideration, getting them wrong again.'[7]

The choice of 'Leda and the Swan' for my experiment was perhaps not as random as I first thought it. It is a poem about being overwhelmed, about being rendered powerless—and through that, about gaining power, becoming a wielder of power. The idealized reading experience, the enchanted one, is not dissimilar to this: readers long to be overmastered, their will taken away (I just couldn't put it down)—perhaps there is, too, a sense in which they want to be raped, at the very least mindfucked, by the verbal object they hold in their hands. At the same time, as the book spreads for them, they are in the position of raping or ravishing it—taking all it has to give them and then tossing it, spine broken, aside. This, of course, is partly to recapitulate the gesture of Yeats in making the male active, powerful, violent and the female passive, powerless and abused. It is also to argue that, this being objectionable, there may equally be something objectionable about reading. The rape relationship can easily be reversed: the book penetrates the reader's mind, it vigorously pumps itself into them, leaving its thought-seed behind; the reader, having had these words visited upon them, is likely to become impregnated with ideas half their own which they would not have had without the book. The violence can be seen flowing in both directions.

I'm aware, in all that I've written here, that the fact I am myself a writer perhaps distorts my reading to the extent that it is no longer even vaguely the same activity as for others. The argument of Harold Bloom's *The Anxiety of Influence* (1973) and *Map of Misreadings* (1975), if followed, would have it that I could do nothing other than distort Yeats—probably, though Bloom doesn't really go this far, misread my own misreadings as well as misreading my reading. For Bloom, I read in order to enter or continue an Oedipal struggle with the father-writer—I want to kill the book so that my own books can come to birth. There is, I think, a great deal of truth in this, and it is fairly rare that I feel myself to be reading without anxiety, without aggressively misreading. When I read a great writer, it's with a vengeance.

Notes

1 Wallace Stevens, 'The House Was Quiet and the World Was Calm' in *Collected Poems* (London: Faber & Faber, 1984), p. 358.

2 Seymour Chatman, *The Later Style of Henry James* (New York: Barnes and Noble, 1972), p. 28.

3 Jane Austen, *Northanger Abbey* (London: Penguin Popular Classics, 1994), p. 254.

4 John Keats, Letter to Benjamin Bailey (8 October 1817) in *The Poetical Works and Other Writings of John Keats* (Harry Buxton Forman ed.), VOL. 3 (London: Reeves and Turner, 1883), p. 82.

5 William Butler Yeats, 'Leda and the Swan' in *The Poems of W. B. Yeats* (London: Macmillan, 1983), pp. 214–15.

6 Keats, Letter to Bailey, p. 82.

7 Philip Roth, *American Pastoral* (London: Jonathan Cape, 1997), p. 35.

Writing

Where do you get your Inspiration from?

For the public, all writers whether of poetry or of prose are still Romantics—Shelley-come-latelys—still muse-haunted sensitives, victims of the descending, perhaps-bestowed word. Other art forms have managed to place someone or something between themselves and this version of the creation myth: classical music had Serialism, sculpture Duchamp, painting Warhol. Literature, however, despite the resolutely anti-Romantic efforts of the Dadaists, William Burroughs and the OuLiPo movement, has yet to convince either the public or, I would say, itself that it comes from anywhere other than Inspiration.

Perhaps the biggest reason for the Romantic account of composition still being dominant is that many writers find it, in all sincerity, true to their desk-experience. There are, for them, undoubted advantages to letting those around them continue to believe in it. Being struck by the muse—or, rather, *saying* you have been struck by the muse is a great way of getting people to fuck off and leave you alone; even if all you really want to do is settle down with a cup of tea and the crossword. Tea and the crossword may be an important part of the creative process; walking, hoovering, wanking, getting pissed, too. But these may be harder to explain to the People from Porlock.

Writers lie to themselves consistently about how they work—about how their work works—and I doubt if I can make myself much of an exception. I will try, though.

What have we seen of how writing takes place? Cinema has largely failed to represent it—the recently released *Adaptation* (2002) is the second-best-ever film about writers and how they do what they do; the best, of course, is *The Shining* (1980). Even as worthy an attempt as *Dorothy Parker and the Vicious Circle* (1994) has, basically, to resort to the cinematic cliché of—

INT. STUDY. NIGHT. The clack-clack of typing. Close-up on a wastepaper basket, full of scrunched-up, typed-on sheets. We hear a sigh, a mutter, a curse. Scrunk—as the latest sheet is ripped from the typewriter. We watch as it bounces, tightly scrunched, off the top of the pile, lands on the floor. It is not alone.

This is the best Hollywood has been able to manage. And the Indies haven't done any better.

So, where *do* I get my inspiration from? Sidestep: the history of writing is, in many departments, that of a descent. In *The Moronic Inferno*, Martin Amis traces a descent of subject:

In thumbnail terms, the original protagonists of literature were gods; later, they were demigods; later still, they were kings, generals, fabulous lovers, at once superhuman, human and all too human; eventually they turned into ordinary people. [. . .] Nowadays, our protagonists are a good deal lower down the human scale than their creators: they are anti-heroes, non-heroes, sub-heroes.[1]

Similarly, the location of the source of inspiration has plunged down from God-plain-and-simple to the God-inspired poet to the thing-inspired poet (Nature, Woman, Beauty) to the self-inspired poet all the way to the non-existent poet. Long before Barthes posited the death of the author, Marxist critics were putting forward the argument that '*Little Dorrit* would have been written even had Dickens never existed.'

I don't believe this to be case, in my case; I know that if I hadn't lived in Prague I wouldn't have written three novels about Prague; I know that had I not written those novels, no one else would have. I am not Dickens, you may say, but the Marxist argument should hold equally for every word put down: none of us get a hall-pass from the dialectic. However, I would say that writers *are* capable, for some reason, of having an engaged relationship with the zeitgeist—a two-way relationship. Also, I would defend Shelley's 'unacknowledged legislators' claim: had it not been for the poets of courtly love, the world would not be in thrall to another version of the Romantic. Before 'Cool' came along, love über alles was the greatest viral ideology the world had known (Cool, now, vincit omnia but that's another subject). The disposition of their affections is what is most important to anyone in the world who has been exposed to the idea of poetic love. This was *written*; love was a creation of writers. They took Plato's grotesque image of wheeling four-limbed proto-humanoids, split in two and separated around the world, and they made it the felt truth. There can be no greater legislation than that of hearts.

It is easy, and fun, to give literary critics a good duffing up. Yeats, in 'The Scholars' (1919), defined them as belated misunderstanders:

Bald heads forgetful of their sins,
Old, learned, respectable bald heads
Edit and annotate the lines
That young men, tossing on their beds,
Rhymed out in love's despair
To flatter beauty's ignorant ear.[2]

(That 'tossing' shows Yeats was on the money about wanking long before *Adaptation*.) But I would argue that critics, while the best readers we have of the Written, are, in general, almost useless in regards to *writing*—writing, as Frost put it, which rides on the flux of its own melting.[3] And this despite the fact that they, the critics, come to me, and to themselves, in the form of the written, of the being-written word. Critical writing intersects with towards-literary writing, but for the most part it avoids wildness, lostness, hopelessness. (Derrida is often all three.) Every useful piece of insight and advice I have ever read about sentence-making came from a poet, a short storyist or a novelist.

When the writing is going well (I am avoiding the word 'inspired') it feels as if someone has taken my brain out and filled my head with a very cheap and chemical-heavy soft drink—orangeade or cherryade; I call it this state 'headfizz'. The bubbly liquid being shaken up behind my eyes is brightly coloured, almost day-glo (this brightness is the manifestation of a kind of internal embarrassment: I want to say to myself, 'Fuck off and leave me alone'); I would assume, if at this moment a brain scan were to be taken, the synapses would be seen to be getting themselves in something of a lather. I remember an aside from Les Murray, after a reading at the Troubadour, London, about how he liked to chuck the poem into the back brain, not feel it was being dictated too directly by the flippant forelobes.

I also remember, in the Q&A after another reading, Graham Swift likening his writing process to wiping the dust off an inscription, off a gravestone. Any writer putting forward this argument—that of the pre-existence of the words, their finishedness *before* they arrive at them—is lying. The lie may be necessary, to avoid confronting the Great Terror—the Great Terror being that the blank page is actually that, and that what they are doing is not deciphering but cobbling together. Graham Swift wishes to be like an archaeologist, perhaps even really wishes he was an archaeologist, because he can't live with the truth that he's something else, something worse, not even a grave-robber: a faker.

The greatest single anti-Romantic aesthetic confession I've ever come across is in Edgar Allan Poe's 'The Philosophy of Composition' (1846):

> Most writers—poets in especial—prefer having it
> understood that they compose by a species of fine
> frenzy—an ecstatic intuition—and would positively
> shudder at letting the public take a peep behind the
> scenes, at the elaborate and vacillating crudities of

thought—at the true purposes seized only at the last moment—at the innumerable glimpses of the idea that arrived not at the maturity in full view—at the fully matured fancies discarded in despair as unmanageable—at the cautious selections and rejections—at the painful erasures and interpolations—in a word, at the wheels and pinions—the tackle for scene-shifting—the step-ladders and demon-traps—the cock's feathers, the red paint and the black patches, which, in ninety-nine cases out of the hundred, constitute the properties of the literary *histrio*.[4]

The dirty secret of writing, as Poe makes permanently plain, is that bad is often a necessary step towards good. The world may see the monster but Frankenstein sees only the stitches, the bolt.

When I began to write, I was abashed by lists—I felt myself inadequate because I couldn't, straight out, write a sentence like: 'There are seven reasons why blah blah blah . . . and here they are in descending order of importance.' I believed that the creators of lists wrote them down that way, without a blot. I was deceived; I believed that the surface of the page I was reading had been, somehow, excreted in that perfected form by a real writer; I hadn't read Poe. Perhaps I even went so far as to believe that the words were a discovered inscription, and that I would never make a word-archaeologist; still, I was determined.

What I have learnt since is that, as the old saw sings, writing is rewriting; and not just rewriting of the words but of the writer. Cancellation of a line is also a minor act of self-cancellation.

How do bad writers become good? Alexander Pope knew the answer: 'I believe no one qualification is so likely to make a good writer, as the power of rejecting his own thoughts, and it must be this (if anything) that can give me a chance to be one.'[5]

Each present-time erasure alters in a tiny tiny way what a writer is likely to be willing, in future, to put on paper. (It is often forgotten, particularly by literary critics, that writing is written in the present. However engraved or discovered it may look, it was at one time performed onto the page.) And so all writers write their way out of what I tend to characterize as the primeval sludge and stodge of bad words with which they began, by crossing their bad selves out. A crapness deleted becomes a step forward—all writers, to follow this line of argument, are on their way to being great, some just move faster than others, are quicker learners, hate their crap selves more. Writing, to define it, is a continuous process of self-criticism motivated by aesthetic self-disgust, self-hate. Hate powers. Hate is the motoric force; hate of the embarrassment and humiliation and suicide-inducing idea of being an uninteresting self— of being a self unworthy of being written and incapable of being well written.

Seen this way, writers don't *have* ideas, they *are* ideas; ongoing, ramifying—at the very least, they are the idea that they are or will one day be a writer; at the most, they are the best the language can, in their historical moment, do. (All any writer can hope to be is 'the best living', the best of their period; what they then have to do is hope their period is a great one. I will return to this.)

Writing as the performed self can best be explained by analogy with music, it is writing-as-jazz. The genius of the improvisation is dependent upon the years of hours of practice; the eight bars of God-kissing couldn't exist without the woodshed. Charlie Parker didn't play bum notes. He had good and bad nights, sessions, but never failed to be Parker. To write, really to *write*, is equivalent to having achieved an unmistakable tone on the piano—like Art Tatum, Thelonius Monk—the piano, an instrument that any fool can get 'Chopsticks' out of. And this is the real question-to-be-asked. Not *Where does your inspiration come from?* but *How can you possibly be capable of forcing the language into distinctiveness?* Or, more shortly, *How did you come to own these words?* Compared to language, in other words, to speech plus the dictionary plus the pile-up of all that has been written plus the speeding juggernaut of all that is being written, the piano is a cinch to personalize. Lurking behind the public idea of Inspiration is another idea: although writing is in great part the use of language uniquely, surely such an achievement is beyond a single person. Inspiration is a good explanation, otherwise the writer must either have cheated or have had help. Inspiration is a way of giving credit at the same time as credit is being taken away.

The suspicion behind the question, as with most of the public's whispered asides—*Go on, mate, tell me what it's all really about*—is that there's a trick to it, a scam, a con. One writer I know was so exasperated during a book reading at being asked, again-again-again, the other, more timid form of the Inspiration question, *Where do you get your ideas from?* that they said, 'I

go to www.iamawriterandidonothaveasinglebloodyideahelp-
meplease.com and they give me one.' After the reading, several
in the audience came up to make sure they'd got the address right.

And I'm still, in some ways, managing to avoid answering
the question: *Where does it come from?* Which, for me, is where
the problems really begin—but the problems are also the project. Because although I don't believe in Barthes's unauthored
texts, or that I am the inkjet printer of a particular stage of late
capitalism, I don't want merely to pick my own regression. This
is the easiest way out; a self-Romanticization, leaving the writer
free, like the literary critics, to concentrate on the written and
not on the moment of writing. Romanticism allows the writer
to be absent from their own process: the hands can touch-type
while the eyes are looking out the window at the sunset. I don't
believe, though, that the great writers of the past were ever
faux-naive—not about their workings, their work, their world.
(I don't mean Heaney, Larkin, Carver, Frost, Hemingway,
Lawrence, Hardy, Dickens; I mean Beckett, Celan, Joyce, Rilke,
Proust, James, Browning, Flaubert.) They did what they did at
a point of necessary awareness, and hence difficulty. And this
is where the problems become the project: not that writing
must self-consciously display its self-consciousness. Wink too
often and people of course take it for a tic. But that the Romantic account of composition, at the time of Wordsworth and
Coleridge, was an honestly attempted perception of the means
of word-production.

I would return, in order to explain as accurately as I can the
where, to Poe's Philosophy. Writing falls onto the page haphaz-
ardly, but frequently reads as seamless.

When I am teaching creative-writing classes, I tend to tell the students two things: *You are forgiven* and *You can*. (The inspirational-speaker tone is deliberate.) The second statement is intended to forestall delaying-tactic questions of the 'If I wanted to do X, could I start by doing Y?' sort. There is an anecdote about the philosopher J. L. Austin. He was asked by the child of one of his friends whether time travel was possible. Austin said something along these lines, 'Well, no one's done it so far. But why don't you have a really good go, and see whether you can't.' A lot more will be learnt in the trying-and-failing than in the listening to reasons why not. Which feeds back into the first statement; that in the pursuit of something as ludicrous as time travel, there is no humiliation in any kind of failure. By making the effort, honestly, you are pre-forgiven.

To write is to engage, paradoxically, in a self-critical wildness of mind; the easiest way to deal with this is mentally to separate all the wildness off into the first draft, and to leave the revision and re-revision in the well-manicured hands of the self-critic. But the two states, in my experience, interpenetrate: there is wild criticism, there is critically aware wildness. Another way to cope with the paradox is to pretend to be a writer, exclusively, of one sort or other. Automatic writing is an attempted purity of wildness as, mendaciously it turns out, was Allen Ginsberg's first-thought-best-thought aesthetic. The wild men and women (understandably often American) believe the critic is Censor by any other name. Read Emerson, experience Whitman, discover Blake, convince yourself that your barbaric yawp, your primal scream, will be your highest-holiest sound. Alternatively, become critic entire—as at roughly the same time did Europhile Yvor Winters, Allen Tate, William Empson and, one might argue, wild-fearing, Emerson-Whitman-Blake-denying T. S. Eliot. Write a moderate contemporary version of what consensus reveals to be the best and most intelligent of the past, the Metaphysicals. Never risk a systematic *derèglement* of your senses, and pretend you are happy with a dissociated sensibility: these are lessons learnt from the past which must not be forgotten, even in, especially in the moment of word-worlding, world-wording.

(Apollo, once more; Dionysus, again. Classic; Romantic. Editing; tossing.)

So, if this is writing—critical wildness, aesthetic self-disgust—what is it worth aiming to write?

I am aware that, throughout this essay, I have assumed a fairly untheorized notion of literary greatness; and that's something I do believe in—although it is easier to define than defend. Great writing, like great art, is that which has the capacity to fascinate the future. Not the abstract future, but the individual people of the years to come who pay passionate attention to writing. It is possible that there will be only very few of these people, and that there is almost no reason writing for them. There is no way to second-guess what will fascinate the future, but it seems to me that one of the enduring reasons for reading is to have intimate contact with people from a different historical period; we read the Victorians because we want to read their epoch through them and them through their epoch. Therefore writing that most engages with its own moment, without the caveat of worrying whether it will be comprehensible in 100 years' time, without anticipating and trying to forestall footnotes, will be the most likely to fascinate. Aiming for the literary is not a reliable method of writing what turns out in the end to be literature. The only way that the writing of the past (summarized as 'literary values') can be learnt from is as an encouragement to pursue the oddest hares. Literary history is an object lesson in favourites fallen and weird and unlikely survivals: take Solzhenitsyn, once widely seen as the most important living writer, now a living curio; take Blake, a failure, an Immortal. The cautious, the sensible—these engage us far less than the outrageously unexpected. Yet if our own epoch is seen as one of the dull patches which exist in the past, then our writing, however attempted-great, will go unread. Just as the smooth numbers of the age of Dryden seem aesthetically irrelevant now, so the strident innovation-mongering of the twentieth century will almost certainly come one day soon to seem uninteresting. And while it is possible to imagine a time when Dryden will again be valued above Shakespeare, it is futile to attempt to write so as to be pleasing to it. A thought-experiment I sometimes try is to imagine that we live not in a belated age, as writers since before Homer have felt, but that we are actually primitives. Granted another 2,000 years (a lot to grant, I admit), we will seem as fardistant as the gospels. With the likelihood of some major genetic intervention, what makes humanity is about to change; *Homo sapiens* is about to become *Homo sapiens sapiens sapiens*, *Homo pre-sapiens*. We, to the future, are likely to seem charmingly random—with our chaotic comings-to-birth, our haphazard childhoods, our emotional traumas, we will appear almost feral. To report truly on this awkward present, though probably no more awkward than all those past presents, is one of the hardest things a writer can attempt. We can explain ourselves away in a second (I have an addictive personality; I'm lower middle class; I've got bad genes) or we can participate in the oddness of enacted selfhood. The question may be better reversed, as almost-nonsense:

Where does my inspiration get me from?

Notes

1 Amis, *The Moronic Inferno*, p. 17.

2 William Butler Yeats, 'The Scholars' in *The Poems of W. B. Yeats* (London: Macmillan, 1983), pp. 140–1.

3 'Like a piece of ice on a hot stove the poem must ride on its own melting.' Robert Frost, 'The Figure a Poem Makes' in *The Collected Prose of Robert Frost* (Mark Richardson ed.) (Cambridge, MA: The Belknap Press of Harvard University Press), p. 133.

4 Edgar Allan Poe, 'The Philosophy of Composition' in *Essays and Reviews* (New York: Library of America, 1984), p. 14.

5 Alexander Pope, Preface to *Complete Poetical Works* (Oxford: Oxford University Press, 1978), p. 4.

Film vs Fiction

I'd like to start by reading you something I wrote for television about a year and a half ago. It was a two-minute opinion piece for *The Book Show*, and I was allowed to choose the subject. I chose 'Film vs Books'. (The word 'fiction' doesn't go down very well on TV—although it fares better than the word 'fictions', which immediately loses you the attention of half the audience and the respect of most of the other half.)

I'd like to start with this piece because it *says* most of what I want to say, and so if you space out and start thinking of cigarettes in half an hour's time, you will still be able to sound intelligent discussing the talk afterwards. But also because what I say was put into the kind of simplified concentrated form that television demands—and that, in itself, is a demonstration of one of my points: screens are good at pictures, bad at ideas.

So, here is my opinion piece:

Films won and books lost.

That's the story of the twentieth century—the story of where the stories went.

Moving pictures on brightly coloured screens defeated words on white pages.

Of course films won: they're much more fun to look at.

These days, *looking* is how we understand ourselves. Text is just something we do with mobile phones—to arrange which film to see next.

Or that, at least, is the defeatist view.

Films are good at lots of things—speed, simplicity, spectacle.

But what they are best at is making you forget all the things they aren't doing—aren't doing because they can't.

Films only directly engage two of your senses.

Films imply depth but are one-dimensional.

Films show the outsides of people but life is always experienced from the inside out.

Think of a book—think of *Wuthering Heights*.

Remember how full it is of things you smelt, tasted, touched.

Remember how you didn't encounter that world from seat C12 but were at the centre of it, *essential* to it.

In the end, books are *better than* films at putting you inside someone else's head.

And what goes on here [*points to head*] is more interesting than what goes on here [*draws screen*].

I'd now like to go back and pick my way through this, expanding and illustrating.

Films won and books lost.

I don't think this is a controversial opinion. We live in an almost entirely visual culture. If there are pictures of an event, it is far more likely to become a news story—even if that event is only a cat falling 50 feet out of a tree, and surviving. Political campaigning is constructed around photo opportunities—really, nowadays, video opportunities. If these can be cut down to a half-minute clip on a website like YouTube, then all the better. This is current affairs as Jackass.

I've started by talking about the small screen, about television. But the subject of this talk is 'Film vs Fiction'—and there are important differences between television and cinema. In fact, I'd say, the two media are in lots of ways antipathetic opposites.

Television is about the essential crapness of life; film promises a world of deep glamour and potential cool.

Imagine this scene from a non-existent screenplay, first as videoed for television, then as filmed for cinema:

A man has just had a furious argument with his girlfriend. He slams out of their apartment and into the street, where the rain is falling torrentially. The man walks off into the night.

On the TV screen, this man is doing something essentially crap—he is foolishly getting wet; on the cinema screen, he is doing something deeply glamorous—heroically expressing his emotions via visual metaphor.

Let's take the man a little further.

He walks on through the darkness and the rain. Eventually he sees a light. It is an all-night cafe. He stumbles in and orders a coffee. After a while, he looks around, and finds himself surrounded by other loners and lovers.

On TV, this man is a loser. He has lost his dignity, his comfort and possibly his girlfriend. He is a fitting citizen of the all-night cafe.

On film, he remains unpolluted by the taint of his surroundings. In cinema, the form makes a hero out of the central character—whoever that central character may be. (Think of Freddy Kruger. In the end, because he was the central character, *Nightmare on Elm Street*'s sequels made a hero of him.) Therefore in the film version of this continuation, we know that this is just an interlude: the man will get the girl back, because this is a film. Plus, because there is value added in each cinema scene, the man will gain from his encounter with the round-midnight world. The form reassures us that exciting things will happen.

The distinction I'm making here clearly isn't absolute. Lots of television is cinema *manqué*—created as visual CV by writers, directors and actors who desperately want to work in film. This is aspirational TV—and it never really works. Because TV is at its best only when it is about the essential crapness of life. *Cathy Come Home, Fawlty Towers, The Hitchhiker's Guide to the Galaxy, Hill Street Blues, The Simpsons,* Alan Bennett's *Talking Heads, ER, The Office,* the first series of *Big Brother*—these TV greats are all about the essential crapness of life.

Here, however, I'd like to draw another distinction—that between British television and American television.

I'd like to start by discussing Jim Rockford's answerphone.

Ring-ring.

'This is Jim Rockford. At the tone, leave your name and message—I'll get back to you.'

The first episode of *The Rockford Files* was broadcast in America in 1974.

But even when I watched the repeats on British television in the early 1980s, Jim's answerphone was an object of extreme glamour.

The fact that Jim was a down-at-heel gumshoe who ran his business from a trailer, and was constantly being bitched at by his borderline bum of a father—none of that mattered. He had an answerphone therefore his life was glamorous.

In this, I, along with much of the British audience, was reading the answerphone backwards.

For an American audience, it signified that Jim Rockford was a likeable loser. What? He couldn't even afford a secretary? Only the most desperate potential clients would confess their wants to a machine.

In other words, British audiences often read American television as about the deep glamour when, in fact, it is still about the essential crapness.

For British audiences, Jim Rockford was living the dream. For American audiences, he was a noble Chandleresque knight, respected for his refusal to be corrupted—but, ultimately, if he carried on as he was going, he'd end up a bum like his father.

Looked at this way, you could say that TV is a form particularly suited to British culture, film to American.

I'd like to give another example of this. There are, of course, some TV shows which are made in both British and American versions. For example, a gameshow such as *Wheel of Fortune*.

However, there is a huge difference between the culture underlying these two shows—despite the format being, on the surface, identical.

This isn't merely to do with the fact that prizes on British gameshows used to be so rubbish. Americans had the 64,000-dollar question all the way back in 1955. In the late 70s, we still had Bruce Forsyth offering 'and a cuddly toy'. At the most you were likely to take home a family saloon. The winner of *Mastermind* still nobly gets nothing but a rubbish trophy—and the honour, of course. It took until *Who Wants to be a Millionaire?* in September 1998 for Britain to catch up.

The truth of the matter is that the archetype underlying all American gameshows is Las Vegas, baby, whereas the archetype beneath British versions is the parlour game.

That's why although the greatest *gameshow* format of all time is *Family Fortunes*, because families can't stop being families even when they're on telly—the greatest British gameshow is *Give Us a Clue* with Lionel Blair and Una Stubbs. The synopsis of which, on the UKGameshows website is, 'Charades, err . . . that's it.' It is the greatest because it is the closest to parlour games.

(As Humphrey Littleton once said of Lionel Blair, on *I'm Sorry I Haven't a Clue*, 'Who could ever forget opposing team captain Una Stubbs sitting open-mouthed as he tried to pull off *Twelve Angry Men* in under two minutes?')

But I digress.

A little earlier I gave a list of great television programmes that are based on the essential crapness of life. It would be easy, now, to balance that with a list of great films which are based on the deep glamour of the world. But I'll leave the construction of that list up to you. For the moment, I'll just mention one filmic object, to contrast with Jim Rockford's answerphone, and that is the hat stand in Miss Moneypenny's office. I can't say Miss Moneypenny's hat stand because, as I'm sure Miss Moneypenny would be the first to confess, it is property of Her Majesty's Secret Service.

The point of this cinematic object is that when James Bond walks into the office, stands at the doorway and blithely tosses his trilby towards the hat stand, you *know* that it's going to land perfectly, spin a little and then settle. No matter that it took Sean Connery or Roger Moore 30 or 40 takes to get it right. Because cinema is glamorous, the hat *never* falls to the floor, Bond never has to stoop to pick it up.

In fact, you could make an argument that the physics of cinema and TV are completely different. On TV, the slice of bread lands butter side down. In cinema, the action goes into slow motion and our hero's lightning reflexes allow him to catch the slice before it is halfway to the floor.

From what I've said already, you may be able to guess what I'm likely to say on the subject of 'Film vs Fiction'.

Fiction is superior to Film because it is limited to showing neither the essential crapness of life or the deep glamour. You could argue that, in the epiphany form, Fiction is about the sudden emergence of one from the other. The final paragraph of James Joyce's 'The Dead' (1914), for instance. But usually Fiction is a mixture of the two, crapness in search of glamour, glamour collapsing into crapness.

It should also be clear to you why Film won, why the world has gone visual. There are obvious issues here of adult education and illiteracy rates. A picture appears to need no translation. Why did Bush beat Kerry in the presidential election? Turn off the sound. Look at the pictures. Who looks like a cute baby chimpanzee and who looks like Herman Munster on smack? Who would you prefer to be stuck in a lift with? Who looks least likely to kill you?

So, I began by saying:
Films won and books lost.

That's the story of the twentieth century—the story of where the stories went.

I'd like to spend a little time on the issue of stories. It's no accident that Robert McKee's famous book on screenwriting is called *Story* (1997)—a book based on McKee's famous screenwriting classes. Story is the essence of American cinema—cut to the chase, tell the story.

More and more, this has been interpreted as meaning 'Cut everything which isn't the chase.'

American cinema is the greatest, most intense examination of storytelling since the folk tale died out—or, rather, was incorporated into books, and then assimilated into films.

The best-known example of this is The Hero's Journey—as used by Disney and countless others to three-act-structure their screenplays. The Hero's Journey was extracted from Joseph Campbell's book, *The Hero with a Thousand Faces* (1949), which dissected the stages through which any epic story has to pass.

I have many arguments against this kind of approach to making films. The main one, though, is that by aiming above all for *efficient* and *extreme* storytelling, you will inevitably end up writing the same story as everyone else: the world is always being saved but it's always ultimately personal and always a race against the clock where good buddies try to help and evil villains try to hinder in what always, finally, ends up as a tale of redemption.

Let me give you an example. It is from John Buchan's novel *The Thirty-Nine Steps* (1915). Buchan's hero, Richard Hannay, just as in a movie, has for most of the book been on the run from the police and the secret agents who have framed him for—guess what?—a murder he didn't commit. But at a certain point, towards the climax of the plot, Buchan has Hannay reconcile himself with the police and go on, with their blessing, to foil the secret agents.

Now, no contemporary Hollywood screenwriter would make such a basic error—losing all the tension that you gain by having the hero remain an outlaw until as close to the end of the final reel as possible.

But most Hollywood screenwriters would end up with very similar stories.

And these would be based upon a particularly American idea of justice—coming out of the cowboy myth. This is that true justice can only be achieved by the outlaw. Hence George Bush's foreign policy. That he didn't get a full United Nations mandate for the invasion of Iraq wasn't a failure but a necessity. Otherwise Americans wouldn't have recognized his justice as just. Instead it would have been legalistic, and therefore corrupt.

The consequences of this American drive towards a mono-story are clear to see, both in films and in the world outside. It's also clear that the strongest story that Hollywood can create is by no means universal.

As I said at the start:

Films are good at lots of things—speed, simplicity, spectacle.

But what they are best at is making you forget all the things they aren't doing—aren't doing because they can't.

Films, for example, are very bad at ideas. They find it almost impossible to construct the long kind of unspooling arguments that Western philosophy is based upon.

The most important technique of film, the cut, the edit, has—you could argue—had its own influence on philosophy. Perhaps Wittgenstein's works are a reflection of a jump-cut mentality—argument by juxtaposition and gap rather than by statement and exposition.

I should perhaps clarify what I mean by films being 'bad at ideas'. Films can embody philosophy, but they cannot philosophize. When Slavoj Žižek writes about Hitchcock, he is turning story into philosophy; when Hitchcock made his films, he was turning philosophy—or the residue of philosophy—into story.

This is the common direction, particularly in American cinema. To compensate for being bad at ideas, films concentrate *too much* on story. In doing this, they deny the dreamlike essence of the cinematic experience.

Paradoxically, film is both pure dream and anti-dream. The logic of strong stories is directly against the tumbling illogic of our night visions. Dreams are not efficient—they are all about excess.

Very few directors are able to shoot convincing dreams. Most ring-fence their dream-moments into dream-sequences. A couple of exceptions might be Andrei Tarkovsky in *Nostalghia* (1983) or Terrence Malick in *Days of Heaven* (1978).

But if you take something like *Mission: Impossible III* (2006), which I saw a couple of days ago, then in a sense it is nothing but dream. Or, if it's not dream, then what the hell is it?

I'm getting closer to the end of my opinion piece now:

Films show the outsides of people but life is always experienced from the inside out.

One of the reasons I find fiction superior to film, as a medium for conveying what it's like to be alive as a human being, is that it is much better at doing two things at once. Obviously, films can only show what can be seen. In order to show the unseen, they have to resort to visual metaphor—often excruciatingly crude visual metaphor. My man walking through a rainstorm was just one example.

How does a film do thinking? Well, often it uses its greatest technique, cutting to, cutting away. Whereas a cartoon will have a thought bubble, film will show the object or person being thought about. Or, in a more sophisticated way, will show an object associated with what is being thought about. To achieve this, you need two scenes.

Scene One: A man's father is dying. The man goes outside into a field of rippling wheat and breaks down and cries.

Cut to:

Scene Two: Years later the man is driving across country accompanied by his own son. He suddenly realizes that the car is surrounded by fields of rippling wheat. He stops the car and gets out. The son follows him. 'Why did you stop the car, Daddy?' The man turns round. 'Why are you crying, Daddy?'

A single sentence on a page has no problem in doing two things at once:

'As he walked down the street, she was thinking of Kant's categorical imperative.'

Just think of how much work a film would need to do to achieve the effect of that one sentence.

One example of this would be the end of Proust's *In Search of Lost Time*, where a series of involuntary memories bring the narrator's whole life into his mind.

A film version of this moment, or series of moments, would be completely naff.

This was my conclusion:

In the end, books are better than films at putting you inside someone else's head.

And what goes on here [points to head] *is more interesting than what goes on here* [draws screen].

But of course this is massively oversimplified. And one of the reasons for this is that what goes on here [*points to head*] often has its sources on here [*draws screen*].

Here, I'd like to read a little from my most novel *Ghost Story*.

The main character, Agatha, is starting to think about herself in relation to cinema. She has lost a baby through stillbirth, and is trying, very much by herself, to invent a way of understanding and reacting to this. From outside, you would shorthand this as 'she's grieving'. But Agatha is trying to avoid any shorthand. She is thinking through her emotions:

> As she grew older, Agatha became aware of the way gestures spread through populations—the embarrassment of seeing white Englishmen, in imitation of Americans in films, giving one another the 'high-five'. She felt this, too, in her own most profound physical acts: even at her

most destroyed, weeping beneath the blast of the
shower, she had felt herself to be in imitation of scenes
she had seen, copying what actresses-pretending-to-be-
destroyed had done. This tore her: even putting roses
on the grave had seemed to her secondary, or tertiary
(actors learning from actors). Probably, she thought,
people-before-cinema had based their gestures upon
those of people around them. Perhaps in moments of
argument they had became melodramatic, histrionic,
like the actors in stage-plays they had seen. Agatha
wasn't in any way sure that something essential, Edenic
had been taken away from humanity —but she felt lac-
erated by inauthenticity whenever she tried physically
to express, to herself, what she felt she was feeling. At
some points in the past—these thoughts weren't entirely
new—she had even been desperate enough to consider
taking some sort of class to explore movement and
dance. But that would have been replacing one set of
clichés with another. Hollywood, she had come to feel,
was homicidal; it wanted to kill the human element in
all behaviour. Perhaps she was idealizing a pre-cinematic
world—one where people had kept most emotions
unexpressed, because they had not yet been taught the
codes of flickering face and body. What were the
chances she would ever feel unaffected again? This
wasn't self-consciousness, it was style-consciousness—
and that was why she hated the problem so intensely.
She wanted to get at herself—wanted to feel the breath
of her own life upon her face, even if it was bad breath.[1]

What I was trying to do, in *Ghost Story*, was write in an anti-cinematic way. Most of the action takes place in Agatha's head. One of my models for this was Henry James, who is the master of writing thoughts as events.

As a brief aside, I'd like quickly to examine how film—since its birth—has influenced fiction. Acceleration is the main thing. We now expect our characters to spend a lot less time ponderously pondering and a lot more dynamically doing. In creative writing classes, the common advice is *Show, Don't Tell*. Or, to put it another way, write it as if it were the novelization of the film. The consequence of this is that contemporary fiction writers often employ a visual code established by screenwriters and actors to convey what their characters are thinking and feeling. For many writers, to resort to the words 'She thought' is to have failed. Deep thought is represented, in the code, by putting the head in the hands. Whereas it's quite possible that a person might be thinking deeply while doing the crossword or the ironing. As a result, just as Agatha realizes, people wanting to appear to themselves as thinking deeply are more likely to put their head in their hands than try to solve nine across. Yet fiction, which has been around for perhaps a thousand times as long as cinema, is capable of so much more than mere physical action. 'She thought' is not a failure but fiction's greatest resource. The development of sophisticated subjectivity was the common project of both Victorian and Modernist writers. To unthinkingly obey *Show, Don't Tell* is really to admit to being stupid.

I'd like to end by giving a brief example of how deeply film has penetrated my subconscious—and so, in a way, to admit defeat. But also to show that, by dreaming-through a film, I came up with something beyond that—and so, at the same time, to claim a small victory.

There's a chapter towards the end of *Ghost Story* where Agatha and her husband Paddy, after a long physical estrangement, make love.

Afterwards, Agatha goes down to the kitchen. She finds herself to be extremely hungry—and begins to make a very late breakfast. But she does this in a completely haywire fashion, everything in the wrong order. Paddy comes and joins her—watching as she burns toast, undercooks poached eggs, spills hot fat on herself and, eventually, collapses in tears on the floor. Only then does he intervene.

It was only quite a while after I'd written this that I realized which film-memory of a disaster-breakfast it was based upon.

Can anybody guess?

It's actually the scene from *Kramer versus Kramer* (1978) where Ted Kramer (Dustin Hoffman), who has previously left most of the child-raising business to Joanne Kramer (Meryl Streep), cooks breakfast for the first time for his son Billy (Justin Henry). Joanne has left them, and now they must cope alone. In a grotesquely moving sequence, Ted attempts to jolly things along while making French toast. 'This is fun, isn't it?' he says, in an increasingly crazed manner—eventually freaking the boy out totally.

The payoff for this scene comes at the end of the film, where a thoroughly domesticated Ted, who has recently lost custody of Billy to Joanne, is able to move like an automaton through the choreography of perfect French-toast-making.

When I first realized where my disastrous breakfast scene came from I was ashamed and horrified. But then I began to see the many ways in which fiction had manipulated film. I won't go into them now, but if you want a weep, rent the movie. If you want to weep and think, buy my book.

Note

1 Toby Litt, *Ghost Story* (London: Hamish Hamilton, 2004), pp. 111–12.

Fame vs Genius

First off, given the choice, I would swap a healthy literary culture for a single great writer.

A great writer is, I think, more likely to emerge from an unhealthy literary culture.

A healthy literary culture sounds like something Joseph Goebbels would approve of.

The relation between the literary and the healthy is tenuous, to say the least. The parallels between writing and illness, writing and madness (mental ill health) are far more convincing.

But to address the question: *Is literary celebrity good for literary culture?*

To defer the question: It depends what you want writers to be—what you think their function is.

Writers are not, in my opinion, to be protected from society as it is—poets, perhaps there is a case for protecting poets; not novelists, though. Journalists need to be right where the biggest mess is; novelists must be aware that the mess is accumulating —they must be directly affected by the mess—they must fear and use the mess.

The greatest writers engage in dialogue with their society—meaning, their society does pay *some* attention to them: Dante, Shakespeare, Tolstoy, Joyce. They are celebrities in a way that minor writers—Hopkins, Kafka, Dickinson—are not. It was partly through lack of personal celebrity that these writers remained minor.

Our culture, at the moment, is negotiating its way towards a new understanding of celebrity as more than merely *being very widely known*.

My partner, who teaches English to undergraduates at Westminster University, keeps a close track on their language. In the past couple of years, she has noticed an alteration in the way they use one particular word: *prolific*. When an 18-year-old calls someone 'prolific' it's likely that they're expressing a value judgement; they're saying that someone is important, not just that they are productive. I will occasionally get introduced as 'one of the most prolific writers of his generation'. Depending on who is introducing me, this may mean different things. To an older moderator, it may just be a statement of fact: I 'produce works in abundance'; I have published 10 books since 1996. To a younger moderator, it may mean that I am one of the most significant writers of my generation—because I have occupied a lot of media space. In this sense, prolific becomes its own transposition: *profilic*. I have a lot of profile. And this is one way of looking at celebrity. A Warholian way. The occupying of the media space is itself the work—the thing to be admired. To be prolific is, as a name, as an image, to proliferate through web pages, blogs, tweets. And this comes to mean something. We're not quite sure what, but it has something to do with power. Not power in the traditional political sense. The traditional political sense, however, has less and less purchase on the dream-lives of the people.

Let me be clear about this: I am not famous. I am not even well known. I am, at most, well known in literary society. I get about 40,000 results on Google; Zadie Smith gets 10 times that; Salman Rushdie gets half that again. Martin Amis gets a million and a half results. Tony Blair gets 2.1 million. Lady Gaga gets 19 million. Michael Jackson gets 36.5 million.

What do I mean by fame? How does it link to the dream-lives of the people?

This is the opening paragraph of Don DeLillo's early novel *Great Jones Street*, published in 1973. To my mind, it's the best thing he's ever written:

Fame requires every kind of excess. I mean true fame, a devouring neon, not the somber renown of waning statesmen or chinless kings. I mean long journeys across gray space. I mean danger, the edge of every void, the circumstance of one man imparting an erotic terror to the dreams of the republic. Understand the man who must inhabit these extreme regions, monstrous and vulval, damp with memories of violation. Even if half-mad he is absorbed into the public's total madness; even if fully rational, a bureaucrat in hell, a secret genius of survival, he is sure to be destroyed by the public's contempt for survivors. Fame, this special kind, feeds itself on outrage, on what the counselors of lesser men would consider bad publicity—hysteria in limousines, knife fights

in the audience, bizarre litigation, treachery, pandemo-
nium and drugs. Perhaps the only natural law attaching
to true fame is that the famous man is compelled, eventually, to commit suicide.[1]

This clearly derives from J. G. Ballard, and specifically from
Ballard's *The Atrocity Exhibition* (1970):

Using assembly kits constructed from photographs of
(a) unidentified bodies of accident victims, (b) Cadillac
exhaust assemblies, (c) the mouth-parts of Jacqueline
Kennedy, volunteers were asked to devise the optimum
auto crash victim. The notional pudenda of crash victims exercised a particular fascination. Choice of subjects was as follows: 75 percent J. F. Kennedy, 15 percent
James Dean, 9 percent Jayne Mansfield, 1 percent
Albert Camus.[2]

To apperceive our culture, writers need to be involved with
this. They probably need to get up close and personal with it.

On a practical level, writers can gradually be destroyed if
they become too famous. Or too rich as a result of being
famous.

Kazuo Ishiguro, after the success granted by *The Remains
of the Day* (1989) winning the Booker Prize, reckoned he had
to spend an entire year publicizing each subsequent novel.
Hotel rooms have very little new in them for the writer. You
end up like the rock star writing an album about being on tour
and then touring that album. This is the press junket as focussed
destruction of what caused that artist to be interesting in the
first place.

Salman Rushdie, before the fatwa, was a half-decent writer. Only a small percentage of readers got to the end of *Midnight's Children* (1981), but Rushdie wrote some interesting sentences—in thrall to Saul Bellow, Günter Grass, Gabriel Garcia Marquez. And, in India, his work was of genuine historic importance. After the fatwa, however, he became one of the most famous men on the planet, a phenomenon, and the writer of genuinely unreadably bad books: *The Ground Beneath Her Feet* (1999), *Fury* (2001). It's not his fault; self-preservation prevented the life-stability necessary for novel-writing.

One of the things writers most need is contact with the ordinary, unmediated speech of their society. In other words, they need to be able to sit unnoticed on the bus. It's essential for them to be able to overhear what people say to one another. It's a basic requirement that they deal with unscheduled events—that their lives aren't too planned.

These are generalizations. Beckett and Joyce needed their exile, because the everyday speech of Dublin—the backbiting and affable gabble—was unbearable to them. They needed to escape it to be able to hear it, to process it.

It helps if a writer isn't being asked every other day to summarize a great novel in 50 words, to give their top five favourite films of all time, to debate the merits of literary celebrity, or simply to talk continuously about the marvellous mystery of what they personally do.

Writers need empty time, not emptied time.

Beckett said: 'Success and failure on the public level never mattered much to me, in fact I feel much more at home with the latter, having breathed deep of its vivifying air all my writing life up to the last couple of years.'[3]

But it is impossible to be Beckett, much as I'd like to be. He existed at a particular time in European history—the existentially examined, agonizingly anguished post-war. We are not in an entirely different society.

The danger, when writers feel they have no audience, is that they become bitter, and thereafter find all they can write are disguised allegories of their own predicament—of being ignored, unappreciated. This is what often happens to unpublished writers. It was happening to me, before I got published. No audience is a greater danger to writers than personal fame, which brings with it many bad readers but also some good, engaged, sustaining readers.

Notes

1 Don DeLillo, *Great Jones Street* (London: Picador, 1973), p. 1.

2 J. G. Ballard, *The Atrocity Exhibition*, REVD EDN (V. Vale and Andrea Juno eds) (San Francisco: RE/Search, 1990), p. 98.

3 Samuel Beckett, Letter to Alan Schneider, cited in Deidre Bair, *Samuel Beckett: A Biography* (New York: Touchstone, 1978), p. 461.

Against Historical Fiction

Historical fiction depends for its existence upon a pair of bad faiths—a reciprocal pair of bad faiths—the bad faith of the writer and the bad faith of the reader.

By 'bad' I don't really mean 'bad'—not in the sense of malevolent, evil. I'm using the term in something like the way Jean-Paul Sartre did; which means that although I may think historical fiction is deeply bogus, I don't think it's essentially reprehensible. To give historical fiction a serious kicking is a bit like berating cuddly old Stephen Fry for not having pursued an obscure and second-rate academic career writing on A. E. Housman. Historical fiction exists, gives pleasure to many, and will continue to do so whatever I say. It wouldn't be worth the effort, trying to persuade devotees to stop reading it. But I would like to spend some time examining how it is consumed and how it was produced.

It's not hard to demonstrate that historical fiction is written in bad faith. All you have to do is, for a moment, forget about bad faith and think about the purest good faith.

First, imagine an entirely naive reader who picks up a novel by Philippa Gregory because they want to learn the truth about

Anne Boleyn. Let's call this reader Alex. Alex completely trusts the writer not to mislead her (or him—Alex could be either) in any way about the past.

Philippa Gregory goes to a literary festival near where Alex lives and, because Alex feels s/he learnt so much about Anne Boleyn from Philippa Gregory's book, s/he goes along to say thank you. Alex stands in line with all the other Philippa Gregory fans—and when s/he gets to speak to her, and have his or her copy of *The Other Boleyn Girl* (2001) signed, Alex says something like this: 'Dear Philippa, thank you for telling me the truth about the past. I believe Anne Boleyn was exactly as you described her. Having read your novel, I feel no need to read any other books about Anne Boleyn or her minx of a sister.'

On hearing this, how does Philippa Gregory feel? What does she say? Does she feel, 'Ah, I've done my job'? Or does she feel, 'Look, here is my ideal reader'? And does she say, 'You're quite right—there's no need to read any other books about Anne Boleyn—mine is the only true one because I am the only person who really understands the past'?

No, clearly she does not.

The relationship between the writer of historical fiction and the reader of it is much more complicated, much more implicated, than this. I'll come back to this later, and try to describe the relationship in detail.

But, if my first example of the innate bad faith of historical fiction didn't convince you, maybe my second will.

How would you feel if you knew that the history teacher teaching your child about the Tudor Period—call them Terry—how would you feel if Terry had read nothing about that period but historical fiction?

You would, I think, feel that Terry wasn't qualified to be a history teacher—because what Terry knew couldn't in any way be described as history. Yet if all Terry's reading material had, in fact, been written in good faith, why would you have any doubts about Terry's competence?

I'd go further—if I found out that my child's history teacher preferred reading historical novels to history books, I would instantly lose a great deal of trust in them. If, on the other hand, they confessed to reading—only the once, on holiday—a single Philippa Gregory novel (just to see what they were like), but with a constant queasy feeling of self-disgust, I would immediately trust them more *as a history teacher*.

So, I think, if you're honest, would you.

And the reason for this? The reason is that I believe most history books are written in good faith—which is to say, they are written in the honest hope of saying something useful and truthful about the past.

If this truth turns out to be less picturesque, dramatic, romantic or readable than the evidence previously suggested, or than the less reliable sources put forward, then the history book will still assert this dull truth. The same can't be said of historical fiction. In fact, it is inevitably drawn to the more speculative areas of the past—hidden love lives, disguised conspiracies.

A history textbook will not establish itself on the territory of pseudo-subjects—such as, to take one example, the secret sexual relationship between Queen Elizabeth I and the Earl of Essex.

So, how does the contract between the historical fiction writer and the historical-fiction reader work? And why am I describing it as being, at both ends, in bad faith?

Here, I'll have to try to define bad faith. As it takes Sartre about 30 dense pages of *Being and Nothingness* (1943) to do this, you'll understand that a certain amount of simplification will be required.

Here's part of the definition from the glossary at the back of the book, supplied by the translator. Bad faith is 'A lie to oneself within the unity of a single consciousness. Through bad faith a person seeks to escape the responsible freedom of Being-for-itself. *Bad faith rests on a vacillation between transcendence and facticity which refuses to recognize either one for what it really is or to synthesize them.*'[1]

Now, you'll see that I'm not talking about 'the unity of a single consciousness'—I'm talking about a duality of two consciousnesses, writer and reader. But I think, in each case, the second part of the definition holds true.

This is clear even in the term 'historical fiction'. The first word is the element of facticity, the *what was* of the world; the second element is the transcendence, the *what might have been* of the world. To yoke the two words together is to create an oxymoron. (Historical fiction is neither historical nor fictional.)

Those who would defend historical fiction inevitably start to do as Sartre says, to 'vacillate between transcendence and facticity'.

Transcendence, in my argument, can be taken to mean anything that begins to rise above the available historical facts. So, when a defender of historical fiction says, 'It's all just a bit of a romp—why can't you take it for what it is?' *that's* the transcendence. The romp, the energy of narrative arising out of a supposed historical basis, is a transcendent value.

Similarly, when a defender says, 'There are imaginative leaps that the historical novelist can make which the plain historian wouldn't dare, but which may come closer to the truth than facts could ever tell'—*that's* the transcendence.

But the real proof of my argument comes when the defenders of historical fiction switch, or rather vacillate, from transcendence to facticity. At this point, they say something like, 'A lot of historical novelists put a great deal of time and effort into making sure that they get the details of their historical period right.' And *that's* the facticity. Or they say, 'Even if you don't agree historical fiction is a reliable source of information about the past, you'll surely admit that a person who reads *The Other Boleyn Girl* knows more about Anne Boleyn after finishing the novel than they did before starting it.' *That's* the facticity.

And I would answer, extremely austerely, by saying that, No, I believe that the reader would *know* less about Anne Boleyn for having read the novel. Because they would have entirely corrupted their criteria of *knowing* anything about the past. In starting to read the novel, they would have accepted a woozy melding of fact with fiction—of accurate fripperies of dress and inaccurate motivations of the heart. And so they would have no basis for saying what they did or did not know to be true. What the reader will do is *feel* they know more about the past. They may even feel they know more about *how the past felt*, or *how the past felt itself to be as a passing present*. This kind of knowledge is as bogus as any writer saying, 'This is what I think Queen Elizabeth felt she felt about the Earl of Essex.'

These two sentences from Sartre's *Being and Nothingness* are, for me, the killer. They precisely anatomize the mental slippages required in order to produce and consume historical fiction.

For the writer, 'Bad faith apprehends evidence but it is resigned in advance to not being fulfilled by this evidence, to not being persuaded and transformed into good faith. It makes itself humble and modest; it is not ignorant, it says, that faith is decision and that after each intuition, it much decide and *will what is*.'[2]

For the reader, '[. . .] bad faith in its primitive project and in its coming into the world decides on the exact nature of its requirements. It stands forth in the firm resolution *not to demand too much*, to count itself satisfied when it is barely persuaded, to force itself in decisions to adhere to uncertain truths.'[3]

To conclude, I'd like to try to state the terms of the contract-in-bad-faith between the writer and the reader of historical fiction. Remember, this isn't a contract that Alex, our naive reader at the literary festival, would subscribe to. Alex is after the past in good faith. Neither is it a contract that any decent historian would go anywhere near. They, too, are after the past in good faith—even to the extent of spending most of their time questioning and analysing the amount of bad faith this may involve.

The writer of historical fiction says to the reader: *It wasn't like this, but this is how I'm going to say it was.*

The reader of historical fiction says to the writer: *You say it wasn't like this, but we're going to read it as if it was.*

In other words, they mutually establish the ground upon which they are going to meet—a bracketed ground in which their pleasure will derive entirely from a vacillation between facticity and transcendence, between what may very well have been true and what can be proven to be bogus, between—in other words—the historical and the fictional.

Notes

1 Jean-Paul Sartre, *Being and Nothingness* (Hazel E. Barnes trans.) (London: Routledge, 2001), p. 629; emphasis added.

2 Ibid., p. 68; emphasis added.

3 Ibid.

'Here Is London, Giddy London'
Some Drawing Lessons from Hogarth

The 'drawing lessons' of my title are the things that a contemporary novelist—one not too dissimilar to myself—might learn from William Hogarth. The 'giddy London' part comes from a Morrissey song—anyone able to name it? It's 'Hairdresser on Fire' from *Bona Drag* (1990). The full line goes, 'Here is London, giddy London, is it home of the free—or what?' 'Hairdresser on Fire' is not a song that I particularly like, but 'giddy' is exactly how London makes me feel—and never more so than when I'm expected to generalize on the subject. The last time I did, I wound up in *Private Eye's* Pseuds' Corner—for only the second time, I might add; which is pitiful given the number of attempts I've made to be noticed.[1] But, then, I was writing a think-piece for *Libération*—so, if I hadn't got into Pseuds' Corner, I really wouldn't have been doing my job.

I feel a little giddy now, partly because I've missed the earlier papers, for which I apologize, (I was trapped in a creative-writing class), and partly because I am aware that I am trespassing on your territory. I don't claim to be an eighteenth-century scholar, so embarrassing me with questions of date and detail wouldn't be difficult. I've come to the Hogarth show as a non-committed admirer—and also, just as I go everywhere, as a merciless cannibalizer. Whatever there is to be got from this art, I want to get, so that I can use it in future, or so that I can better understand what I've already done. Hogarth, for me, is the supreme artist of 'giddy London'. That's what I go to him for—for confusion, for the sordid, for snapshots of Yeats' 'dying generations', for things I've been trying to do in my own writing, recently, with greater or lesser success.

And so I'm going to start by stating the really bleeding obvious: Hogarth's pictures—not all of them, but certainly his most characteristic, and usually his best—(in my opinion, anyway)— *Hogarth's pictures have a lot of different people in them doing a lot of different things, all at once.*

They are *crowded* pictures, in that they contain a lot of detail—particularly human detail; detail of physical appearance, social behaviour—and they are also crowded in that they very often show crowds.

I'd even go as far as to say that crowds are Hogarth's archetypical subject. His street scenes made his reputation, but his domestic interiors, too, often feel overcrowded. Even his bedrooms feel like public spaces—which, in historical fact, they probably were; a lot more than ours are, anyway. Pause for nervous laughter. You only have to look at the fourth plate of *Marriage-à-la-Mode* (1743–45) to see how crowded a boudoir can be. When was the last time you had 10 people in *your* bedroom? (Pause for more nervous laughter.) (You don't have to answer that. Though I'll be interested if you do.)

Even when the couples of Hogarth's *Before* and *After* scenes are alone in the bedchamber, they are still behaving as part of the *beau monde*. The women recoil as if their fall from virtue was being witnessed by spectators. And, in fact, the figures in the paintings-within-the-paintings *do* look on and comment. Hogarth's lovers are also crowded out by moralizing objects—which they jostle, and which fall over and smash.

Added to this, Hogarth's *Before* and *After* scenes suggest that, once done, the men have somewhere else to be, and soon. There is never any sense of the lovers' mutual isolation in time and space, as in John Donne's 'The Good-Morrow' (1633):

For love, all love of other sights controules,

And makes one little room, an every where.[2]

Freud insisted that when two people go to bed, four people are always present. I would go further than this. Because many of Hogarth's female lovers—elsewhere, not in the *Before* and *After* pictures—are prostitutes, they bring with them an implicit crowd of ex-lovers. His males are serial seducers, and their pasts, too, are infectiously present.

For Hogarth, even the single isolated subject can imply the crowd—none more so than *The Shrimp Girl* (1740–45). No other picture I know of places an individual so clearly in the midst of an unseen but sensed crowd. Her gaze is public; her beauty is her publicity—and it certainly succeeded in attracting Hogarth. We, too, view her as if picked out of the crowd, whose whirl is felt to be around us. *The Shrimp Girl* seems to draw her healthy energy from the crowd around her; in fact, her health is almost feverish. (I'm going to return to the subject of health later on, and more than once.)

In portraits of actors, too, a crowd is expectedly implied: they are men who exist most of all before the eyes of the thousand. Hence, David Garrick as 'Richard III'.

At this point, I should probably define my terms more exactly. I've used the word 'crowd' slightly more loosely than perhaps I should have. If I were being strict, I would divide the concept of 'crowd' into two parts: one would remain as 'crowd', meaning a gathered mass of people collectively engaged in being a crowd; the other would be altered to 'multitude'—for want of a better word—meaning an amorphous mass of people individually engaged in whatever they happen to be doing at the time. A crowd watches a hanging at Tyburn; a multitude populates Southwark Fair—although most of them are likely to be looking for entertainment of one sort or another.

However, I've deliberately kept my terms fuzzy, because a multitude needs only a galvanizing event—a shout, a punch—to turn into a crowd, and a crowd, as soon as it is bored or disengaged, becomes a multitude. (The 50,000-strong crowd gathered to watch a football match become a multitude at half time.) I think it's often questionable as to whether what we see in Hogarth's pictures is a focussed crowd or an interplexing multitude. I prefer to speak of crowds because the people in Hogarth's pictures seem, to me at least, to be conscious of being in a crowded world—and most of them revel in it. The multitude is more likely to be made up of people who can't stand the crush. The citizens of Gin Lane don't seem to want to hide themselves away.

Of course, there are exceptions to the crowdedness of Hogarth's pictures. He did, on commission, paint small groups and portraits. But, as a general rule, for most of his most inter-esting work, it holds true. And I'd even suggest that Hogarth seems to have felt in some way *compelled* to add face after face after face to his drawings and paintings. In *Heads of Six of Hog-arth's Servants* (*c*.1750–55), he disregards their bodies entirely, floating their heads one beside the other in a Brown Windsor soup of a background.

In *The Laughing Audience* (1733), perspective is adhered to, but a large number of physiognomies are included, stacked up like a pile of rotting fruit. Hogarth likes to create walls of faces, allowing himself to collapse, flatten and violate pictorial space in order to do so. Only rarely does he show a quarter or a half of a face, however; his crowds tend to arrange themselves for the benefit of his eye, disporting themselves so as to be satis-factorily viewable. The orange-seller with her basket, reaching up to tug the gentleman's sleeve in the upper gallery of *The Laughing Audience* shows only her forehead and plump cheek. But she is clearly less a character and more a mere pictorial device, linking the two halves of the painting.

Characters & Caricturas of 1743 is one of the purest expres-sions of Hogarth's head-shrinking/head-counting compulsion. Here, the myriad faces exist *only* in pictorial space—covering one another up, but only so as to leave room for more revealing profiles to be crammed in. There is a clear hierarchy of prefer-ence for facial features. Hogarth was fascinated by noses, mouths, eyes; ears, he seems to have been largely indifferent to. Or perhaps he simply doesn't show them because they were so often, in his time, covered over by wigs. The important thing, though, was to put as many people onto the page as he could.

And this is one of the points where my attempts to construct statements is likely to crumble into a pile of questions.
Because, what is the status of the face in a Hogarthian crowd?
Are these carefully observed individuals, taken from reality? Or
are they carefully observed individuals, chosen to as to represent a recognizable social type? Or are they closely observed
social types, tricked out so as to appear individual? Or are they
closely observed types, depicted so as to be instantly recognizable (to the contemporary viewer) as *types*?

The answer, I think, hedging, is a confusion of all these
things. Because, at the time Hogarth was painting, the idea of
typical character was perhaps at its strongest. Dickens' characters
draw much of their pungency from seeming to derive from
eighteenth-century patterns—their modernity does not give
them recognizability; it is because their types have been around
for a while that we know them.

Despite the overt intention of *Character & Caricaturas*, I still
think the nature of Hogarth's faces is indeterminate. Even if
they are straight characters, taken from life, on what principle
were these individuals chosen? Not because they were uninteresting and anonymous, but because they fully represented
themselves—and in doing so, showed a crowd individuating
and transcending itself.

Which brings me, for the first time, up against the main
thing I'd like to talk about. How does Hogarth relate to writing
practice now?

The contemporary novel is not great on character. One reason for this is psychoanalysis. Another, the advance in dental
techniques. Improved personal hygiene also has something to

do with it. And less idiosyncratic educations (basic national norms leading up to the National Curriculum and away from the village schoolmaster being able to bullshit away for years without fear of correction). All of these things have led to people being less strongly individuated.

But I think I need to say a little more about psychoanalysis. Subjectively viewed characters act out of conscious or unconscious motives; objectively viewed ones behave, or misbehave. In other words, we see people more clearly when we don't attempt to understand them *from inside*. The less sophisticated a theory of personality we have, the stronger the characters we will—as a culture—create.

Characters used to emerge into popular culture from novels. Dickens' characters frequently became bywords. But, in recent years, the main two characters to transcend the page are Bridget Jones and Harry Potter—although, strictly speaking, Bridget Jones began as a newspaper column, not a book, and was a character outside a novel before she became a character inside one. Harry Potter, as a character, lacks character—necessarily so; he is a cipher that every child can fill.

Film and, even more so, television is the domain, now, of the instantly recognizable character. *Borat*, to take one recent example. Or the grotesques of *Little Britain*—Vicky Pollard, Daffyd, Lou and Andy. Or *The Fast Show*'s Swiss Tony. Harry Enfield's Loadsamoney. These are our typical characters.

I'd like, now, to return to the bleeding obvious statement I made at the beginning; that *Hogarth's pictures have a lot of different people in them doing a lot of different things, all at once.*

And that is what cities are like. They have a lot of different people in them doing a lot of different things, all at once. That's what's so great and terrible about them.

To put this another way, more academically, Hogarth's pictures are concerned with both multiplicity and simultaneity. And these, I believe, are the greatest difficulties facing any contemporary writer attempting to write about London—or, more directly, to write London.

'How do you write the crowd?' This was a question I dealt with directly in *Hospital*.

The question, however, is a little more subtle that I've just presented it: *How do you write the crowd not as the crowd?*

More accurately still: *How do you write the crowd so as both to represent its simultaneity and to take account of its multiplicity?*

Here, I could insert my usual digression about *Finnegans Wake* and about how Joyce managed to solve the problems of simultaneity and multiplicity, and also to write the crowd. But I find that the words *Finnegans Wake* have the magical effect of making almost everyone in an audience feel profoundly anxious, either because they haven't read it and feel they should, or they have read it and feel they should be rereading it that very moment. Instead, I'd like to stick with Hogarth. First, by way of exemplum and then by way of contrast. Because Hogarth's pictures, like *Finnegans Wake*, brilliantly solve both the problems of simultaneity and multiplicity. But he is presented, in his turn, with opposite problems—non-simultaneity (or temporal expansion) and non-multiplicity (or individuality). These are the inevitable problems of his given form, the pictorial image. It cannot avoid simultaneity in the sense that each picture exists before us totally and in one moment. And, as I said earlier, it courts multiplicity, although it does so in a way that constantly engages with individuality.

As his rootedness in the values of the eighteenth century would lead you to expect, Hogarth's—in the end—is a would-be neoclassical art of attempted balance. He wants to extend as far as he can in both directions, towards simultaneity and towards temporal expansion, towards multiplicity and towards individuality.

I'd like to look now at simultaneity versus temporal expansion. Hogarth frequently creates images whose main if not sole purpose is to go beyond the limits of the merely pictorial—to escape the seemingly inevitable bounds of the form. For example, his pictures are of course totally silent; unless it falls off the wall, not one of them will ever make a noise; yet *The Enraged Music Master* (1741) does everything it possibly can to create a visual cacophony. In this, it is a crowded precursor to Munch's *The Scream* (1893)—although the cry of Munch's figure is just as much psychological and inward-directed as it is an attempt to make the canvas appear to sound out.

Or, to take a more subtle example of Hogarth's attempts to defy formal limitations, each pictorial image, while representative of a moment, and able—through detail—to show what has happened in the past, cannot travel forwards into the future. But Hogarth does all he can to overcome this. The child falling head first onto stone steps in *Gin Lane* (1751) is not yet dead, but we do not doubt that it will die. More subtly, Hogarth's pictures frequently contain emblems of futurity—emblems which, while they cannot tell us what *will definitely* happen, can give us a pretty clear idea what is *almost certain* to happen.

(As an aside, it's worth noting that there are no reversals of fortune in Hogarth; all his downwardly mobile characters— Rakes, Harlots and Apprentices alike—continue unstoppably in that direction. Hogarth's wastrels go to waste, not to Alcoholics Anonymous.)

Among the most frequently appearing of these emblems of futurity (so frequent as to be, otherwise, slightly puzzling— unless they are just taken to be a record of historical fact)—in fact, Hogarth's most characteristic emblem is the black patch covering a syphilitic spot. This, especially when appearing on infectious children, is a particularly clearly written doom: 'For I the Lord thy God *am* a jealous God, visiting the iniquity of the fathers upon the children unto the third and fourth generation of them that hate me.'[3] The disabled child being held up to kiss its mother in the sixth scene of *Marriage-à-la-Mode* is the most extreme example of this. Hogarth was clearly more interested in syphilis as illustrated fate than as medical diagnosis. The progress of the disease was inevitable, though the pace might be unpredictable. Tom Rakewell is destined for lunacy and an early grave; his black spot is as fatal as any handed out by the pirates of *Treasure Island*. For Hogarth, syphilis is less a disease than a means of overcoming the limitations of pictorial form. It extends moments simultaneously both forwards and backwards in time. And Hogarth, I'd say, is more concerned with this time travel than with showing the wages of sin.

Of course, the main way in which Hogarth tried to go beyond the limited simultaneity of the single image was to create series. He is perhaps England's greatest narrative artist—and certainly the most novelistic of them all.

In *The Rake's Progress* (1732–33) and *The Harlot's Progress* (1732), in *Marriage-à-la-Mode*, but even more so in *Industry and Idleness* (1747), Hogarth manages to extend the pictorial image in time—to stop it being instantaneous and to smear it over the years. By presenting parallel lives, *Industry and Idleness* gives us, almost as a visual pun, a return to simultaneity; while the industrious apprentice piously attends church, the idle other—at one and the same moment—frolics sinfully in the graveyard.

And there is yet another way in which Hogarth's images overcome their simultaneity. He can show us, in an instant, 50 different figures and physiognomies. But it will take us a lot longer than that instant to apprehend each of them in their glorious or disreputable or gloriously disreputable individuality. Each picture is a perfect capitalistic sales device, an advertisement for itself. We need time, at home, to take in all the details presented to us in the shop window. If you were to be stuck in a dentist's waiting room for an hour, you would better have a Hogarth print than, say, an Andy Warhol, or even a scaled-down reproduction Rothko. From either of these, you could go off into reveries about cultural production or the reification of vision, but the Hogarth would entertain you—would keep your mind a little more off the approaching drill. It would repay your attention; the closer you got to it and the more time you spent exploring it, the more you would see is there to be seen. Hogarth's prints are among the most perfect *products* imaginable. They go some way to explaining what people did before TV was invented: they looked at complicated things in detail.

How do we look at a Hogarth? When you stand in front of one, you have to move from side to side—as if you were in a crowd, looking at something that had drawn a crowd, a fist fight, say, or a very good street performer. You, so to speak, rubberneck them. You peer round your own head to get at them.

One of the things my art teacher taught me was that, on visiting any gallery, assessing any art, it's worth seeing what it looks like when squinted at. Hogarth's crowds, seen this way, dissipate. We see sky above, a muddy muddle in the middle and dark objects to either side, probably buildings. The image, however, doesn't really exist. Look at a Cezanne squintingly, and the image becomes almost radically clarified—to the point of becoming nearly photorealistic. (I'm serious. Try it.) But Hogarth's are meant to be seen clearly, close up, in a good light. A magnifying glass wouldn't go amiss, and wouldn't be an affectation. To really appreciate them, we need to own them. And, because they were mass-produced, we can.

And this, finally, is another way in which Hogarth overcomes the simultaneity of the pictorial image. If we look at it over a period of years, returning to it in different moods and with failing eyesight, it becomes a radically extended thing. Ownership changes its appearance, and Hogarth's pictures are meant to be owned.

(In another aside, I would say this argument doesn't hold as well for his paintings. But I find his paintings hugely inferior to his etchings: the sense of space in them is fudged. Usually, I don't wish to return to them repeatedly but to get away from them as fast as possible.)

That will do for simultaneity. As for individuality, there seems far less to say. At least, less to say that hasn't already been said on the subject of character. Hogarth's portraits are, like all portraits, attempts to encapsulate the individuality of their sitters. In this, they are not as interesting or as distinctive as his crowd scenes. The further he moves towards concentrating upon the individual Christian soul, the more boring he becomes. In his portraits, he is just doing what every other portraitist does; in his crowd scenes, he is unique.

So, what can the contemporary novelist learn from Hogarth? What are the drawing lessons to be drawn from him? I think it must be something more than just 'Artistic forms are flexible, and there to be extended.' A novelist can easily enough write: 'The crowd of around 200 advanced down the Strand . . . .' But that is to reduce and betray the multiplicity of those comprising the crowd. It depicts them as mere simultaneity; bodies present, here, now. To be more accurate in terms of number is simply to be ridiculous. 'A crowd of exactly 212 advanced down the Strand . . . .' And to deal with each crowd member individually is also to be ridiculous. 'A crowd comprising, in alphabetical order, Naseem Aziz, Frankie Bergonzi, Christopher Columbus . . . etc., advanced down the Strand . . . .'

But it was this last ridiculous option that I went for in trying to write the crowded simultaneity and multiplicity of *Hospital*. Almost everyone who appears gets a name and some kind of description. It being a large and busy building—26 floors above ground and 6 beneath—there are a lot of characters; about 125 in all. Once you get into the book, you should, at any time, I hope, be aware of what is happening on 4 different floors to 10 or more different characters. There are also lots of crowds of various sorts—crowds milling, crowds marauding.

Here's one short section:

At ten o'clock exactly, Hospital, most of Hospital, was either asleep already or settling itself down to sleep. Many offices, busy during the day, were now empty or occupied by solitary figures trying to finish paperwork. Consulting rooms and the corridors outside them, waiting rooms with their rows of uneasy chairs—their televisions were off, their drinks machines and water-coolers unbothered. On the administrative floors, computers in gray and faun stood reflecting one another dimly in undusty screens. Here and there, a cleaner followed a questing vacuum-cleaner or a porter pushed a sodden mop. By now, Geriatrics patients were expected to have turned their bed-lights out, despite insomnia, night-terrors and pain of infinite variety. The newborn babies in Neo-Natal, lying in the suspended plastic trays of their trolleys, swaddled in soft blankets, were remarkably placid—a few only needed to be rocked by their mothers. On the Children's Wards, Sisters had mostly established a calm of pre-slumber—broken sometimes by sobs or giggles. It was quiet, too, down in Pathology, where the day's corpses—zipped in bags—lay within their long metal compartments. But elsewhere the twenty-four hour sounds continued: ululations from birthing pools, snickings and slurpings and Classical music in operating theatres. Noisiest of all, just gearing up for its busiest time, was A&E on the ground floor.

This was what some Emergency Medic, years and years ago, had nicknamed 'the Flood'. Chucking out time from the pubs always brought with it an influx of cases, trivial and fatal. But the hour before closing was already an alcohol-lubricated rush of viciousness, clumsiness, stupidity and tragedy. Here came scuffed knees, twisted ankles, dog bites, sprained wrists, broken fingers, flattened noses, reddened mouths, glassed faces, dislodged retinas, broken arms, knifewounds, ruptured spleens, gaping throats, broken necks, gunshot wounds. Here came, one after the other, chancers thrown out by bouncers and looking for an opportunity to sue for a couple of scratches, Munchausens, contrite fathers, apologetic taxi drivers, naughty nurses and cheeky devils from the hen-night-gone-wrong, dinner jacketed pale-faces from the stag-party-turned-nightmare, street preachers with their average visions of the apocalypse, the lost and upset wanting directions from someone in uniform or to use a phone to say they've had their phone nicked and they'll be home late or that they're not fucking coming home ever fucking again, sobbing wannabe blood-donors, homeless looking for somewhere to get warm and have their kissy sores rebandaged. Here came the weeping girlfriends, weeping ex-girlfriends, weeping ex-girlfriend's best friends, and weeping ex-girlfriend's ex-best friend's exes. Here, too, motorbike accidents by the score, failed and soon-to-be-successful suicide attempts, overdoses of both sorts, schizophrenics in need of more medication or silence or light or another head, old people with chest pains and breathing difficulties, policemen and women with facial abrasions (and abrasions on their knuckles, as well— scuffed toecaps, too), carpark footballers with groin strains, diabetic dwarves, men whose foldable bikes had folded while they were riding them, women who had walked into doors or fallen downstairs or been beaten semi-unconscious by someone they preferred not to name, kids—girls and boys—gone into toxic shock after inserting their first tampon, candidates for the rape kit. Here came fallen-off-garden-wall burglars, fish-fryers with worse than usual fat burns, chubby young women going into labour who don't even know they are pregnant, bloody-faced Asian boys surrounded by dozens of mates accusing the staff of racism for not seeing their friend fast enough, gone-wrong and got-stuck rectal insertions of all sorts (carrots, kiwi-fruit, light bulbs, staplers, mobile phones set to vibrate in plastic bags, even the occasional dildo). Here came all human life and death—the quiet night in gone amusingly or horrifyingly wrong, the no-babysitter children who managed to get into the garden shed, to get into the drinks cabinet, to get into the knife-drawer. Here came the dying and the almost-dead and the dead.[4]

This was my attempt at writing London, although I did not specify London. My *Hospital* is a scaled-down city, a place which witnesses that old chestnut 'all human life and death'. A place where there are *a lot of different people doing a lot of different things, all at once.*

In *Finnegans Wake*, Joyce's solution to the problem of the fictional crowd is simply to make everybody everybody else—everybody else, that is, of the same sex and family position. In describing Humphrey Chimpden Earwicker, he describes Goliath, Napoleon, James Joyce, Charles Stuart Parnell, and all possible men. Anna Livia Plurabelle is all women. Shaun and Shem are all sons. Issy is all daughters. This, you might say, is cheating. But it's the best anyone has done, in prose.

Hogarth, using a different form, probably does it better. Everybody, in his pictures, is somebody—of the crowd but individuated. Constantly, however, Hogarth is pushing towards a more novelistic vision. Perhaps all artists envy the strengths of the art forms which are not their own. And this envy brings close scrutiny, from which lessons are to be drawn.

Notes

1   I mainly think about London, consciously, when it becomes an annoyance to me—an obstruction: London is often what prevents me getting to London; it's the sweaty horror of the Northern Line in August, it's the misted-up top deck of a Number 3 bus in January, it's the tourists jamming the pavements at Piccadilly Circus. But, as I travel, I do so in the belief that there's somewhere truly worth arriving: London.

2   John Donne, 'The Good-Morrow' in *Poetical Works* (Oxford: Oxford University Press, 1985), p. 7.

3   Deuteronomy 5:9.

4   Toby Litt, *Hospital: A Dream-Vision* (London: Hamish Hamilton, 2007), pp. 60–2.

Writing Twenty-First-Century London

A Preface. Let me begin by saying, when I have finished addressing an academic audience I always feel a failure—an intellectual failure.

I know I'm not *necessarily* going to disappoint them/you, but definitely I will disappoint myself.

What I argue, by not running along the established lines of academic discourse, may come to you as light relief or an exciting report from the battlefront; but, to me, it almost always—in retrospect—seems not to have engaged with the question. (Again and again, I have failed to grasp the nettle—and only a monstrously bad academic would ever refer to attempting 'to grasp the nettle'.)

This feeling of failure isn't because I feel academic discourses are necessarily any closer to truth or reality or accuracy of expression or nettles than those I will use.

It's more that I am perpetually dissatisfied with my own approaches to truth, reality, accuracy of expression and grasping.

This must be one of the reasons I continue to write. If I felt I had achieved something approximating to what I perceive, I would have less motivation to assemble more words into sentences. (Except to satisfy the cravings of my own sentence-habit; I have a serious sentence-habit.)

Writers of fiction, put simply, are nowadays pretty stupid when compared to Proust, Joyce, Woolf, Beckett. I'm ashamed of what we're failing to do, in their wake. It—the production of complex ideas—is part of our task; we're failing at it.

Complex ideas. This is not the level—this is no longer the level—upon which writers of fiction are expected to discourse. What we are here to do is tell amusing stories. To refuse the pleasures of narrative is to refuse the opportunity of an audience is to refuse a *raison d'être* and possibly to refuse any reason for anyone ever to publish what you write.

While we are telling our amusing stories, no one really likes it if ideas slow us down or make things less entertaining. And so, the longer fiction writers go on, the more stupid we become—the stupider we're allowed to get away with being.

I don't know of many contemporary novelists who even come up to the intellectual standard of, say, Colin Wilson (author of *The Outsider* [1956])—a writer it's a reflex to sneer at. Second-hand Nietzsche; but engaged with Nietzsche, at least. Not living or pretending to live in some unphilosophical space; some mutually agreed common-sense universe.

A. S. Byatt, writing approvingly of David Mitchell, said, 'He has an absolutely classic authorial voice, very like clear glass, and doesn't advertise his own cleverness.'[1]

In other words, the cleverness that is there (and Byatt is one of the cleverest people I've ever met, and Mitchell is no idiot)—

the cleverness in the author must be subsumed into the narrative, where it can do no harm; the cleverness must spend most of its time disguising the cleverness. Seemingly we're back to elevating windowpane prose to the highest fictional achievement. In the *Guardian*'s recent survey of rules for writers, David Hare encapsulated this as: 'Style is the art of getting yourself out of the way.'[2] This derives from Elmore Leonard's cardinal rule: 'If it sounds like writing, I rewrite it.' (Publication of Leonard's *10 Rules of Writing* [2010] was the peg on which this feature was hung.) But perhaps here—in referring in such a deadpan way to glass—Byatt is being slightly mischievous. Glass is a subject with which she has a great fascination. The last time I met her was at the launch of Isobel Armstrong's *Victorian Glassworlds: Glass Culture and the Imagination, 1830–1880* (2008). A book which historicizes the glassiness, the pellucidity, of glass.

It is always necessary to emphasize, over and over, that each age has its own idea of clarity. And that one of the hardest things to see is the clearly clear medium through which we ourselves are gazing. It is easier to concentrate on the flaws in our own apparatus of vision. But, even when we focus on these, we still do so in the belief that our kind of clarity is better than the clarity of previous generations. A secular clarity, for example, must be better than the incense-beclouded vision of the religious believer; Galileo saw more clearly than the Vatican. We are smugly on Galileo's side.

Add to this, that we are an age that values clarity extremely highly. This was another thing to emerge from the survey that was the *Guardian*'s compilation of writers' rules for writers.

Writers must strain to write clearly, towards our consensus on clarity.

We are also an age that very easily mistakes simplicity of form or expression for clarity of thought. To see things clearly isn't necessarily to see things accurately. Some forms of existence—perhaps most forms of existence—are cloudy, blurry, smeared, begrimed.

Which brings me to London.

Preface over.

First, I'm going to give you an overview of what I see as some of the basic problems of writing London, a multimillion occupant city.

And then—together—we're going to attempt to write the Great Twenty-First-Century London Novel. Or we're going to begin planning it, at least. Here, I'd like you to play a full part— to make suggestions—so be ready.

I'll begin by saying, London-writing in itself—in its London-ness—isn't a vexation that causes me anxiety. I am more concerned with the problematics of writing about large numbers of diverse people. This, I have approached in a number of books. There's been, up to and including *King Death* (2010), a constant dialectic of the Many vs the Few in what I write.

To take only the more recent books: *Finding Myself* has about 11 main characters; *Ghost Story* has 2; *Hospital* has around 140; *I play the drums* has 4; *Journey into Space* has over 20 main characters, and centres around a spaceship crew of a steady 100, but writes about them over a period of 200 years; *King Death* has 2; *Life-Like*—which I'm working on at the moment—has around 25 main characters.

A couple of years ago, after a visit to China, I became preoccupied with the thought that the novel form is very bad at two main things: multiplicity and simultaneity.

It *can* do both, and do both at the same time, but only with a strain; it can do both if it puts a lot of other things aside or on hold.

There are a couple of grammatical solutions to dealing with simultaneous multiplicity and simultaneity: in other words, a lot of different people who are all doing different things, all at once.

The first way is simply to tell the reader, 'They (the lots of people) were doing lots of different things . . . .' In a novel, the sentence wouldn't arrive as crassly as this one. It might say, 'The crowd—young and old, rich and beggarly alike—milled around the gallows, an atmosphere of expectation bordering on bloodlust running through it.'

The second way is to write the sentence that might, in a novel, follow on from the previous sentence. This would show individuals about their individual business: 'He was doing this thing and she was doing that thing and he, way over there, was doing this other thing . . . .'

In our imaginary historical crowd scene, this would read, 'A buxom apple-seller moved through the crowd plying her rosy wares. Two former cellmates of the condemned man discussed loudly whether or not, at the final moment, he would cry out to his maker. A small boy, perched on his father's shoulders, asked whether he would have to wait much longer to see the naughty man die?'

The sophisticated writer would even bring a couple of her multiplicitious characters into simultaneous conjunction. 'As the apple-seller swung past, the uglier of the two former cell-mates reached out to try and steal one of the juicy Cox's—and received a slap in the face for his trouble.'

It's all coming to life, isn't it?

The novelist then finishes their work by re-emphasizing the crowdedness: 'But the apple-seller's aim as she struck out was not of the best—and several of those crushed in close proximity to her complained of having been caught by a sideswipe.'

Blah.

If the novelist just sticks with the first approach ('They were doing lots of different things . . . ') what they will end up writing is *A Novel of Crowds*. 'The crowd did this thing, then this thing.'

If the novelist uses the second approach ('He did this thing and she did that thing . . . ') they will write *A Crowded Novel*.

A combination the two would be *The Crowded Novel of Crowds*.

And this, in dealing with multiplicity and simultaneity, is about the best any novelist can do.

It's what I did, or tried to do, in *Hospital*.

This novel, which takes place in an H-shaped tower of 26 floors above ground and 6 below, contains a lot of named characters and the reader knows what is happening to most of them, moment by moment, as the actions progress and as time passes from eight at night to four in the morning.

Because the novel is bad at multiplicity and simultaneity, because the language itself is bad at them, the novel is bad at cities. What better definition of a city is there than 'a place of multiplicity and simultaneity'?

I won't discuss short stories here. Short stories don't tend to bother themselves with multiplicity, not of characters, anyway. They far prefer singularity—singularity of event, singularity of character. And, when they come across it, short stories work by *implying* simultaneity. Short stories imply just about everything.

By definition, a city novel—a Twenty-First-Century London Novel—doesn't exist except by becoming a mad attempting-to-portray-simultaneous-multiplicity-and-simultaneity. How else do you capture that feeling of cityness—that it's something around you, that it's vast, that it's more complex than you can possibly understand, that it's totally unclear.

Here, I'd like to talk about other art forms—and to admit that most of them do cities far better than the novel does, because other art forms are better at multiplicity and simultaneity.

Although Stravinsky's *Rite of Spring* (1913) is supposed to be depicting a rural, pagan ritual sacrifice, I've always heard the most intense sections of it as pulsatingly mechanistic, as unmistakably metropolitan.

Steve Reich's *Drumming* (1970–71) gives a sense of million-footed Manhattan, of incessantly repeating of cyclical processes —elevators going up and down, escalators journeying.

There's hardly a song in American jazz that doesn't first of all portray the city's moods, day and night, crowded and empty, dry and torrential—from Louis Armstrong's 'West End Blues' to Duke Ellington's 'Take the "A" Train' to Sonny Rollins' 'The Bridge' to Miles Davis's 'On the Corner / New York Girl / Thinkin' of One Thing And Doin' Another / Vote for Miles'. Rural jazz has been attempted; but *jazziness* is a quality of cities and city people—as F. Scott Fitzgerald knew. Gatsby may live out at West Egg but, when he parties, he imports the lights and sounds of the city.

Pop songs, too, encapsulate cities incredibly well. When I hear Joy Division's 'Shadowplay', I feel 'This is Manchester in 1979.' I don't feel it's missing anything. Ian Curtis' lyrics aren't the greatest, but they say exactly what needs to be said: 'To the centre of the city where all roads meet, waiting for you . . . .'

There is no work of fiction, long or short, which makes me feel this way—of achieved city-capturing.

Perhaps I have missed the right novels; perhaps you can point them out to me, afterwards.

Even songs which I resist, which I think aren't very good, manage to achieve more sense-of-the-city than novels. I hate it when, on 'Bullet the Blue Sky', Bono sings: 'And through the walls we hear the city moan / groan / moan / groan / Outside is America / America / And we run, and we run / And we run into the arms of America', but this song, too, gets the job of doing New York done.

Certain drum'n'bass tracks from the mid-90s bring me high-speed wet-Tarmac looming-dark London better than any paragraph of prose.

I don't think this triumph of music over writing is inevitable. It's a failure on the part of the writers. A failure on my own part. We haven't written acutely enough.

Now, the visual arts. At their most successful, painters seem to be partial, too—depicting a little bit of the city which may stand for the whole. Employing synecdoche, New York.

An iconic city-image such as Edward Hopper's *Nighthawks* (1942) works by exclusion and implication. It shows only four people, yet it still depicts a city-mood. In this way, Hopper is a short-story painter, not a novel painter.

It's hard not to take this approach. The intensity of visual detail in a city is extreme, though perhaps no less so than the complexity of an oak tree.

One artist who does attempt to depict almost everything he perceives, every one of the hundreds of windows in each skyscraper, is Stephen Wiltshire—this ambition, though, is linked to his autism. And he is not, as you'd expect, particularly interested in the people who punctuate the architecture.

The clearest attempt to do the multiplicity and simultaneity of London that I've come across, in the visual arts, is William Hogarth; particularly his prints—which were themselves, of course, multiple.

An even greater master of the many-at-once is Pieter Breughel the Elder. Here we really do get individuated crowds in a way that the expository form of prose can't cope with. We see them in a second; we can never read more than one sentence at a time—one sentence per second.

Breughel's *Little Tower of Babel* (1563) is perhaps the single most successful image of a city.

Photography has been more devoted to capturing the city than painting has. Probably because it seems just as easy to point a camera at 500 people or at the skyline of Hong Kong as at a bowl of fruit. Yet it's only recently, with the digital manipulations and vast prints of Andreas Gursky, that we are starting to get a real sense on the gallery wall of how hyperreal a city can be. Up until this point, in relation to our visual field, most cityscapes have been miniaturizations.

Finally we come to cinema—an urban form which, from the start, has effortlessly captured the city and assimilated the crowd. Yet it's also fought shy of them. Cinema is deeply anxious about human multitudes. When they are shown, it's usually as antlike commuters or as rioting blurs. It takes totalitarian cinema to show the masses acting choreographically—Leni Riefenstahl's *Triumph of the Will* (1935) or Czechoslovak images of the mass Spartakiad gymnastics at Strahov Stadium.

Recent advances in digital animation have allowed directors to have a thousand people on screen without having to transport them all out to a vast set and make sure they are provided with costumes, make-up, lunch and toilet facilities. What *Birth of a Nation* (1914) and *Ben Hur* (1959) and *Cleopatra* (1963) did with a crowd of cheap Hollywood extras, *Lord of the Rings* (2001–03) or *Avatar* (2009) do with a crowd of 800 relatively cheap outsourced digital renderers based in New Zealand. It's in the 1970s and 80s that Hollywood avoided crowds on the grounds of cost.

But relating the individual to the group to the crowd is problematic for cinema.

I think this must be, in part, to do with Hollywood's preference for conflict over communality (in screenplays)—and, because of this, its almost total aversion to showing successful collectives. The hero is always picked out from the stupid crowd, the suicidally bickering group. The hero is exceptional, is excepted.

However, I've strayed too far. I hope I've said enough to give some idea of how other art forms have found solutions to depicting cities that are unavailable to prose. It's now time for us, together, to begin writing The Great Twenty-First-Century London Novel.

What should it contain? Like Whitman, multitudes; and, to be comprehensive, it should clearly go from top to bottom of society, from the powerful to the disenfranchised—so let's begin with someone at the top.

(We are, I should remind you, writing fiction here. So please don't suggest the Queen or Jack Straw.)

[Suggestion from the audience: Let's begin with a Member of Parliament, and to top this off let's make her a Cabinet frontbencher.]

OK, let's go to the bottom of society.

[Suggestion: A homeless person, living in cardboard, on or around the Strand.]

Now, let's think of some way we can get from the holder of power to the disenfranchised—or some way that the powerless can get at or get to the powerful.

[Suggestion: Drugs? Prostitution? A crime? The murder of a tramp on an obscure backstreet that leads to consequences for the very seat of justice?]

Already you see how pretty soon one ends up rewriting Tom Wolfe's *The Bonfire of the Vanities* (1987), just with a London background. Here we have the top of society (the Master of the Universe) represented by Sherman McCoy, a WASP Bond Trader, and the bottom by Henry Lamb, a black kid from the Bronx.

Is there any point rewriting *The Bonfire of the Vanities*? Not as far as I can see. It is, itself, a self-conscious rewrite of the nineteenth-century Zolaesque, well-researched novel.

And as soon as one starts trying to do this top-meets-bottom kind of thing in London, one heads for TV-series territory. *State of Play* (2003) goes from the politician down to the teenage drug dealer.

Crime is, perhaps, too obvious a way of slicing through the city. Though it's what I did in *Corpsing* and have done again in *King Death*.

Instead, let's scrap our first attempt at the panoramic-but-linked-up novel and aim instead for 800 pages of intense but subtle human interrelation. We'll get in all of London's diversity that way—courtrooms, kitchens, bedrooms, overpasses.

So, now, just please suggest five properly diverse characters for us to begin with:

[Suggestion: Danya, the girlfriend of a Russian Oligarch, born in the Ukraine to a Polish father and an Ethiopian mother

Kingsley, a Nigerian financier

Eduardo, a Mexican kitchen porter

Pavla, Czech nanny

Zainab, an Iraqi surgeon]

Immediately we come up against the question: In what language or languages is the Great Twenty-First-Century London Novel going to be written?

Are we—the novelist—going to spend the next 10 years learning different languages in order to write the multilingual novel? No. As far as I know, nobody has. There are very few truly bilingual novels (although *War and Peace* occasionally flirts with French).

So let's admit we're not going to be *that* diverse. What we'll have is all the dialogue in English, though an English that attempts to mimic the speech-patterns of Russian, Urdu, Czech, Mandarin, etc.

Isn't this, immediately, to admit something bogus into the heart of the diverse novel? Isn't it to argue implicitly that folks are the same all the world over? Because the Yemeni soul can be expressed through the English language? But that's wrong, surely? We find our particular existence, our particular essence, through language, don't we?

OK, let's scrap our second attempt and begin on a third. This time we're having one main main English-speaking character who we will follow through encounters with the diversity of London, and will attempt to depict and understand them, but will not pretend to understand their subjectivity or true otherness. We shall choose someone to represent and encapsulate the city as it really is now. What kind of person?

And what if they could be someone real?

[Suggestion: How about the Great Lily Allen Novel?]

But haven't we given up on the city as subject here? Isn't this just the person as subject with the city as background?

OK, fourth go. We concentrate instead on a group of knowable friends—they will probably be middle class, university educated. We ourselves are middle class and university educated, like most of the people who attempt to write the Great Twenty-First-Century London Novel or think the Great Twenty-First-Century London Novel is worth attempting to write. Our group of friends come across various members of the underclass, but spend much of their time avoiding intimate contact with anyone radically unlike themselves. As E. M. Forster wrote in *Howard's End*, 'We are not concerned with the very poor. They are unthinkable, and only to be approached by the statistician or the poet.'[3]

But this is no longer a novel about London, it's a novel about *a part of London*; and this has been done hundreds of time before. We could give examples from the 1940s Earl's Court of Patrick Hamilton's *Hangover Square* (1941) to the contemporary Shadwell of Tony White's *Foxy T* (2003). Perhaps this is the best solution; it's not ours. We still want to write the Great Twenty-First-Century London Novel.

Last go, we forget truly existing contemporary London altogether—or pretend we do. Instead, we create an other-London, an under-London, a parallel-London. Here, we are free to range everywhere because everywhere is invented. Something of the imaginative liberty of Charles Dickens immediately becomes available to us. We know the argot of our subclasses backwards, because we invented it. We know what the powerful do when they are alone in their offices, because we put them there, we did their interior decoration. And so we will write something like Michael de Larrabeiti's *The Borrible Trilogy* (2003) or China Miéville's *Perdido Street Station* (2000) or Will Self's *How the Dead Live* (2000). But all three of these writers have already done this, and pretty well. It will be hard to do something that isn't awfully derivative.

And here, on top of all this, are another couple of difficulties: virtuality and something beyond multiplicity.

Virtuality is more and more of a fact of London life. We are present, simultaneously, in technological otherworlds. We are in communication with people far-distant. If it avoids this, the contemporary novel is avoiding being truly contemporary. It becomes, in fact, a historical novel in disguise. Teaching creative writing at Birkbeck, I've had my first student tell me that she is writing a novel set in the 1990s *mainly* because she doesn't want any of the characters to have easy access to the Internet or to mobile phones. If those things are around, she says, they will stop the action she intends taking place. It depends, I'm pretty sure, on people losing touch with one another. I can see that, faced with characters who are perpetually in touch, what we're going to have more and more of is the pseudo-contemporary novel—the novel in which characters are, for some reason, cut off from one another, technologically.

The alternative (preferable to my mind) is that we will focus on different kinds of failure of communication; we will explore different kinds of journey—not from Calypso to Penelope, through the wilderness, but from illness to health, from sanity to madness . . .

The technologically honest contemporary novel also has to admit that ring-fencing London, as a subject, makes little sense any more. Any Twenty-First-Century Novel explodes into the global the moment someone goes online, calls via satellite.

The next superadded difficulty is what's beyond multiplicity. Because multiplicity is still a pretty conservative approach; what about true and total incommensurability? What about generic assumptions, beneath fictional surfaces, which are entirely at odds, but which need to be included within a single work if it is to represent London: the medical and the cartoonish, the microbiological and the statistical, the poetic and the psychoanalytic. How can you put a fictional city together when one part of it is Lego and another is blancmange, when one part is molten steel and another is pigeon feathers?

And so, for the moment, faced with these difficulties, we will abandon the attempt to write the Great Twenty-First-Century London Novel.

But thank you for trying.

Notes

1 A. S. Byatt, cited in David Mitchell, *The Thousand Autumns of Jacob de Zoet* (London: Sceptre, 2010), jacket text.

2 David Hare, 'Ten Rules for Writing Fiction', *Guardian*, 20 February 2010; available at: http://goo.gl/QBc1ru (last accessed on 7 November 2015).

3 E. M. Forster, *Howard's End* (London: Penguin, 1984), p. 58.

The Mays

Writers face an increasingly certain future. The inessentials of what we do, the things by which we used to be known—getting a publishing deal, having a book come out, being reviewed in the papers—all these things are evanescing. What will soon be left to writers is what we always had, words for company. Words with no livelihood attached, no career; no industry. Words with other words to left and right, above, below. Whatever else happens, within the world of publishing, within the global world, writers will go back to words—go back to words for fun, politics, consolation, self-making. Writers will dwell in and flower through and seek redemption via the arrangement, rearrangement, deletion of words. Once, this last sentence might have concluded *words on paper* or *words on the page*. These are two of the evanescent things. The words will exist on a flat, readable surface of some sort—until they migrate inside the eye itself, or back onto the breath. Mostly, for writers, the words will exist within thoughtforms: sentences, rhythms, stories, arrangements that somehow seem stronger or truer than other arrangements, very occasionally in poems. Some writers will write best by not overthinking it, others by a long Flaubertian passion or

Bloomian agon or Joycean pun-upon-pun; some writers will be rewarded by the fame which makes them too busy to write, others will find a few readers and lose them, find a few more and lose them also. What is certain is that the greatest writers will be those who continue to believe most passionately in words. Not those who prettify them or are afraid to fuck around with them. But those who believe passionately arranged words (passionately fast, passionately slowly—passion is passion) are capable of anything. Capable of more, certainly, than cinema, games, drugs, sport. Words are capable of making magics—making things happen that shouldn't really be able to happen. Magics inside people's bodies. Magics in whatever part of them that would like to move towards being a soul, even if they know such a thing is impossible. Even if they know any form of magic is impossible, fake.

It's possible that some of the writers in *The Mays* anthology have come to writing for motives that aren't entirely pure. And I'd say that's a good thing. At their age, I wasn't far from wanting what Freud said drove all artists on: 'honour, power, riches, fame, and the love of women'. Or at the very least, I wanted to have a book come out with my name on it, and for people to know I'd had a book come out with my name on it. In a sense, at this emerging stage, having mixed motives gives you a lot more to write about, makes you a lot more interesting as a writer, than just setting up shop in some vague holy magic temple of soul-creation. This doesn't necessarily mean, however, that where you and your shop end up—years later—won't be exactly that. Or something equally unexpected.

I've been asked a few times my advice for young writers. On this occasion, I'll say this: *In order to write something great, you will need the intelligence to begin and the stupidity to finish.*

Organisms

'On Tolstoy and Gogol via Ricardo Lísias', commissioned by Ted Hodgkinson for granta.com to accompany the Granta Best of Young Brazilian Novelists list, November 2012.

'Headfuck Fiction via Carlos Labbé', commissioned by Ollie Brock for granta.com to accompany the Granta Best of Young Spanish-Language Novelists list, November 2010.

'B. S. Johnson', introduction to a new edition of *Albert Angelo* (Picador), commissioned by Kris Doyle, published in February 2013.

'Kafka', essay in *Morphologies: Short Story Writers on Short Story Writers* (Comma Press), edited by Ra Page, published in February 2014.

'Ballard' was the afterword to *J. G. Ballard* (Continuum), edited by Jeanette Baxter, published in 2008.

'Spark' was delivered as the Annual Muriel Spark Lecture on 9 November 2006, at the Augustine United Church, George IV Bridge, Edinburgh, under the title 'Muriel Spark and Greatness' at the invitation of Eric Dickson, secretary of the Muriel Spark Society.

'Literature and Technology', first delivered at the 34th AEDEAN (Asociación española de estudios anglos-americanos) International Conference, Universidad de Alméria, Spain, on 12 November 2010; subsequently appeared in truncated form on granta.com as 'The Reader and Technology' and in the anthology *Technology: A Reader for Writers* (Oxford University Press), published in 2014.

'Sensibility', 'Souls' and 'Swing' were given as lectures to the MA in Creative Writing students at Birkbeck College on 4 May 2010 and 8 May 2012. 'Sensibility' was subsequently published in *Body of Work: 40 Years of Creative Writing at UEA* (Full Circle Editions), edited by Giles Foden, published in 2011.

'Talking To Strangers' was the introduction to an anthology of short stories in conjunction with Decode Media, edited by Paul Cunliffe, published in January 2007.

'STORGY' was an interview with the Storgy website, questions from Tomek Dzido, June 2014.

'QUANTUM prose MANIFESTO' was written in 2011 to be published in an anthology to accompany an exhibition at the Tate Modern.

'On Perversity' was given as part of a British Council seminar on 'Identity' which took place in Oradea, Romania (13–15 April, 2000). The original title was 'Sexual/Textual Identity: Originality and Perversion'.

'*Against Nature* by Joris-Karl Huysmans' was commissioned by Helen Conford for penguin.co.uk in May 2003 to accompany a reissue of *Against Nature* by Penguin Classics.

'On Monsters' was written to be read out at a panel event on science fiction, with John O'Connell and Justina Robb, at the Institue of Contemporary Arts on 15 May 2003.

'On Ghost Stories' was written for the 3rd edition of the Assises Internationales du Roman (International Forum on the Novel) at Villa Gillet in Lyon, France, 25–31 May 2009, at the invitation of Adélaïde Fabre and Guy Walter.

'Reading' was published in *Poetry Review* (93[2], Summer 2003: 56–61). 'Writing' was published in *Poetry Review* (93[3], Autumn 2003: 42–50). Both were commissioned by Robert Potts.

'Film vs Fiction' was given as the Sussex Creative Writing Asham Lecture in the Medical School Lecture Theatre, Sussex Campus, on 13 May 2006, at the invitation of Richard Crane.

'Fame vs Genius' was my initial contribution to a debate titled 'Is Literary Celebrity Good for Literary Culture?' Also debating were Claire Harman and Claire Squires. This took place at 503 Russell Square on 3 December 2009.

'Against Historical Fiction' was first read out as part of 'The Irish Pages Debate—On Historical Fiction', an event at the inaugural Belfast Book Festival, 27 February 2009, and subsequently published in *Irish Pages*, edited by Chris Agee.

'"Here is London, Giddy London": Some Drawing Lessons from Hogarth' was delivered at the conference 'Seduced by the City: From Hogarth's London to Today', which took place in the Clore Auditorium, Tate Britain, London, on 9 March 2007.

'Writing Twenty-First-Century London' was a lecture delivered at the University of Westminster on 11 March 2010, at the invitation of Monica Germana.

'The Mays' was the introduction to *The Mays XX* anthology of writing by students from the universities of Oxford and Cambridge, edited by Andrew Griffin, published by Varsity Publications in June 2012.

Acknowledgements

The author and the publisher would like to acknowledge the receipt of kind permission to use in this volume quotations from the following sources:

Mystery and Manners: Occasional Prose by Flannery O'Connor on pp. 74–5, published by Farrar, Straus and Giroux, reproduced by permission of the Macmillan Publishers Ltd; *The English Auden: Poems, Essays and Dramatic Writings, 1927–1939* by W. H. Auden on p. 88, published by Faber and Faber, reproduced by permission of the Faber and Faber Ltd; *The Fire Next Time* by James Baldwin on pp. 134–5, published by Penguin Books, reproduced by permission of the Penguin Publishing Group; *The Dangling Man* by Saul Bellow on pp. 145–6, published by Penguin Books, reproduced by permission of the Penguin Publishing Group; *The Adventures of Augie March* by Saul Bellow on p. 147, published by the Viking Press, reproduced by permission of the Penguin Publishing Group; *The Moronic Inferno and Other Visits to America* by Martin Amis on p. 169, published by Penguin Books, reproduced by permission of the Penguin Publishing Group; *Exile's Return: A Literary Odyssey of the 1920s* by Malcolm Cowley on p. 172, published by Penguin Books, reproduced by permission of the Penguin Publishing Group; 'Ash Wednesday' by T. S. Eliot on p. 178, published in *The Complete Poems and Plays of T. S. Eliot* by Faber and Faber, reproduced by permission of the Faber and Faber Ltd; *The Rings of Saturn* by W. G. Sebald, translated by Michael Hulse, on pp. 180–3, published by Jonathan Cape, reproduced by permission of the Random House Group Ltd; *Against Nature* by Joris-Karl Huysmans, translated by Robert Baldick, on pp. 190–4, published by Penguin Classics, reproduced by permission of the Penguin Publishing Group; *Great Jones Street* by Don DeLillo on pp. 247–8, published by Picador, reproduced by permission of the Macmillan Publishers Ltd; *Being and Nothingness* by Jean-Paul Sartre, translated by Hazel E. Barnes, on pp. 254–6, published by Routledge, reproduced by permission of the Taylor and Francis Group.

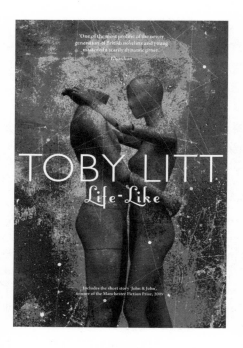

TOBY LITT

Life-Like

274 pp | 6 x 9 inches | 978 0 8574 2 207 1 | $27.50, £19.50

SHORTLISTED FOR THE EDGE HILL SHORT STORY PRIZE, 2014

'Litt has a streak of playfulness in him. . . . His narratives freely
venture into unexpected forms, from cartoons to a screenplay to a
Twitter feed. But the subject is the age-old one of connection.'

Wall Street Journal